TRIALS OF THE WORD

The imaged Word, it is, that holds
Hushed willows anchored in its glow.
HART CRANE, "VOYAGES VI"

TRIALS OF THE WORD
Essays in American Literature and the Humanistic Tradition
R. W. B. LEWIS

New Haven and London   *Yale University Press*   *1965*

FOR GLADYS BALDWIN BARR AND STRINGFELLOW BARR

My dear Oak and Winkie:

            Not all these poets and novelists
are among your favorites, but I want to dedicate the book
to you because of my enduring affection for you both, and
because for many years you have led me along fascinating
paths of literature and history. I am especially grateful
to you, Winkie, for introducing me to the great traditions
of Western humanism. And I am especially grateful to you,
Oak, because when I was an undergraduate you gave me the
best advice a fledgling critic could receive—advice I
try to pass on to my own students. What you said was:
"Be a little tentative."

            Your devoted nephew.

PREFACE

Most of these essays were written in the last five or six years, and most of them—the long concluding essay is the exception—were written at the suggestion of an editor or the chairman of some literary symposium. I hope I may be forgiven for taking as my title a phrase I have used before, though in a less conspicuous place (as the title of a subsection in another book). Like the benighted fellow in Frost's poem, I like having thought of it so well, I cannot resist saying it again. But it is, I think, apt for my intentions here. For these are in fact trials—that is, attempts or essays, efforts to come to terms with certain phenomena made up of words, to explore certain phases of the language of literature. They are also tests of certain hypotheses about the nature of poetry and fiction (the essays on Whitman and Conrad, for example) and about the relation between the available forms of literature and the observable forms of life (as in the discussions of Hawthorne and James and of Edith Wharton). But they do not derive, so far as I can retrospectively make out, from any very stringent theory about literature itself; and, in any case, I prefer to move toward theory by exemplifying it rather than by elaborating it as it were in cold blood.

But just as one has temperamental preferences, so one has congenital and recurring interests; one is drawn all helplessly, time and again, to the same center of imaginative attraction. What attracts me, more often than not, is the tug of the transcendent: or, rather, the fertile tug-of-war between the transcendent and the concrete. I am drawn to testing the energy of the Word within the word—to watching any imaginative attempt to body forth "the imaged Word," in Hart Crane's phrase—in order to see how or to what extent the reality of the natural and phenomenal and human world may, through the resources of the literary arts, appear (in Crane's fine figure) to be anchored in and receive its illumination from the Word-made-image.

To put it differently, I tend to focus upon those phases of a work of literature in which what have to be called religious considerations are overtly or secretively paramount. But this volume is by no means a contribution to that field of study known as "religion and literature"; nor is the religious element explored, any more than the religious viewpoint at work, by any means unequivocally Christian. My present notions about all this are set forth as plainly as possible in the essay called "Hold on Hard to the Huckleberry Bushes," which is as close as the volume comes (and not very close at that) to a theoretical statement. The problem is one of cultural history and its relation to the perennial human consciousness; and two quotations come to mind in aid of explanation, as providing a dialectic—thesis and antithesis—which I am happy to embrace. The first is from Edmund Wilson at his terse and hard-spoken best: "The word *God* is now archaic, and it ought to be dropped by those who do not need it for moral support" (from "Religion," in *A Piece of My Mind,* 1956). The second is from Melville, offering Mr. Wilson a cautionary answer a century in advance: "Take God out of the dictionary, and you would have Him in the street." And there indeed, or so these essays will sometimes suggest, is where the banished Word has to be looked for in the modern epoch: in the streets, and in the exacerbated experiences of the men and women who walk them. It is to be looked for, that is, in the poetic and fictional representations of those places and persons and experiences; and it is to be found above all in the artistic evocation, the summoning into being by drama and metaphor, of a lurking elusive force that had otherwise been known to us only by negation, in the void and in the blasphemy. These are perhaps hard sayings, even dark sayings; but the discussion of *The Wings of the Dove,* among several others, may bring them closer to the light. But to be concerned with modern literature is, I believe, to be deeply concerned with the devious ways in which the irrepressible religious consciousness finds expression in the midst of its resolutely secular and frequently very ordinary materials.

These essays proceed, as well, from the assumption that American literature is a sizable and intermittently handsome body of writing, and that the case for its importance—much less for its existence—need no longer be argued. No doubt it has its own distinctive features and vocabulary, its own obsessions and quirky angles of vision; it manifests its own kind of masterpiece and minorpiece and contains writings that triumph or fail in a specifically American manner and idiom. I await, without impatience, the day when our universities will have departments of American, as they now have departments of English and of French. Nonetheless, the greatest writings by American authors continue to be definable in relation to the whole body of Western literature —to the whole long humanistic tradition. In part, this is simply a matter of common sense. But in part it is due to the unrivaled hospitality of the American imagination to the literatures of other nations. For all its occasional parochialism and its periodic bursts of cultural nativism, American literature at its most original and adventurous is also the most international, the most cosmopolitan, the most *Western* of the literatures of the Western world. This may be merely the inevitable obverse of parochialism; it is, anyhow, a quality rather to be taken into account than to be bragged about. If, for example, T. S. Eliot's *The Waste Land* in the previous generation and Saul Bellow's *Herzog* in our own are unmistakably American products, it is exactly because both the poem and the novel reveal such an extravagant appetite for the whole range of Western literature, philosophy, and theology, and for seizing again upon the archetypal human dilemmas embodied therein. The analogy with the external historical process is obvious. Much has been said, in echo of Henry James, about the complex fate of being an American, though I should suppose it was a fate complex enough merely to be a human being under the modern circumstances; but it may be the peculiar and the rather terrible fate of the modern American that he feels himself required by history to assume the burden of representative Western man. This has been the disconcerting tendency our literature has reflected, resisted, and abetted—as, in the final essay, I mean to imply.

By way of footnote, I might add that the traditional aspect of this volume would have been a bit more visible if I had included one or two other essays which had been in my original table of contents: essays, in particular, on Virgil's *Aeneid* and Shakespeare's *Pericles*. I was persuaded by my editors—I think rightly—to omit those essays in the interest of symmetry and of chronological focus. They await the accumulation of further trials and other words.

R.W.B.L.

New Haven, Conn.
March 8, 1965

"Walt Whitman: Always Going Out and Coming In" was the introduction to the Whitman section in *Major Writers of America*, edited by Perry Miller (New York, Harcourt, Brace & World, Inc., 1962). The essay on Melville's tales and poems was the introduction to *Herman Melville: a Reader* (New York, Dell Publishing Co., 1963); and that on *The Confidence-Man* was the Afterword to the New American Library Signet edition of the novel (New York, 1964). "Hawthorne and James: The Matter of the Heart" first appeared in *Centenary Essays* (Columbus, Ohio, Ohio State University Press, 1964). "Hold on Hard to the Huckleberry Bushes" was published in *The Sewanee Review*, Vol. LXVII, No. 3 (Summer, 1959). The essay on *The Wings of the Dove*, delivered at the Modern Language Association meeting in December, 1956, was published by *Modern Fiction Studies* (Spring, 1957). "Edith Wharton and *The House of Mirth*" served as introduction to the Houghton Mifflin Riverside edition of Mrs. Wharton's novel (Boston, 1963). "Malraux and His Critics" appeared in *Malraux: a Collection of Critical Essays*, edited by the author (Englewood Cliffs, N.J., Prentice-Hall, 1964). "The Sense of Fair Play" and "Days of Wrath and Laughter" are published here for the first time. I am most grateful to the publishers and editors concerned for permission to reprint.

The lines from "Skunk Hour" on page 187 are from *Life Studies*, © 1956, 1959 by Robert Lowell; reprinted by permission of Farrar, Straus, and Giroux and Faber and Faber. The other lines on pages 187–88 are from *Lord Weary's Castle*, Copyright © 1944, 1946 by Robert Lowell; reprinted by permission of Harcourt, Brace & World, Inc., and Faber and Faber.

CONTENTS

TRIALS OF THE WORD

WALT WHITMAN: ALWAYS GOING OUT AND COMING IN

Walt Whitman is the most blurred, even contradictory figure in the classical or mid-nineteenth-century period of American Literature. Recent scholarship and criticism have been clearing things up a good deal; but both the poet and his work remain something of a jumble. For a number of decades, Whitman was the most misrepresented of our major poets; and the misrepresentation began with Whitman himself, in the last twenty-five years of his life. It was during those years, from 1867 onward, that Whitman —initially a very self-exposed and self-absorbed poet—became willfully self-concealing, while at the same time he asserted in various ways an entity, a being, a persona radically other than the being that lay at the heart of his best poetry.

The chief mode of such concealment and assertion was not creative; it was editorial. Whitman wrote little poetry of lasting value after "Passage to India" (1871); what he did do in those later years was constantly to reshuffle the contents of his expanding book: to disperse the poems out of their original and effective order, to arrange them in new and fundamentally misleading groups, to suppress some of the more telling and suggestive of the items, and to revise or delete a series of key passages. The result of this process was a serious shift of emphasis whereby the authentic Whitman was gradually dismembered and replaced by a synthetic entity that was more posture than poet, more mere representative than sovereign person. It, or he, was the representative—in nearly the conventional political sense— of a rather shallowly and narrowly conceived democratic culture:

From *Major Writers of America*, Volume I, edited by Perry Miller, © 1962 by Harcourt, Brace & World, Inc., and reprinted with their permission.

a hearty voice at the center of a bustling and progressive republic, a voice that saluted the pioneers, echoed the sound of America singing, itself sang songs of joy that foretold the future union of the nation and the world and the cosmos, chanted the square deific, and wept over the country's captain lying cold and dead on the deck of the ship of state. Other and truer aspects of Whitman continued to exert an appeal, especially in certain lively corners of Europe. But in the English-speaking world, it was primarily the bombastic, or, as his disciples sometimes said, the "cosmic" Whitman that was better known; and it was this Whitman that was either revered or—in most literary circles after the advent of T. S. Eliot—dismissed or simply disregarded.

So much needs to be said: for our first task is to disentangle Whitman, to separate the real from the unpersuasive, to separate the poet from the posture. To do that, we have, first of all, to put Whitman's poems back into their original and chronological order. It might be argued that we have no right to tamper with the poet's own editorial judgment; that *Leaves of Grass* is, after all, Whitman's book and that we are bound to take it in the order and the form he eventually decided on. The answer to this proposition is that there is no satisfactory way around the critical necessity of discriminating among Whitman's successive revisions of his own work, of appealing from the Whitman of 1867 and 1871 and later to the earlier Whitman of 1855 and 1856 and 1860. The dates just named are all dates of various editions of *Leaves of Grass;* and the latter three, the ones we appeal to, are those of the editions in which most (not all) of the real Whitman is to be found. This Whitman is a great and unique figure who is also the recognizable ancestor of many significant poetic developments since his creative prime—from *symboliste* poetry to imagism to more recent neoromantic and, less interestingly, "beat" writing; a chief, though by no means the only, American begetter of Wallace Stevens and Hart Crane, to some extent of Ezra Pound (as he once reluctantly confessed), and to an obscure but genuine degree of T. S. Eliot.

The importance of chronology, in Whitman's case, cannot be exaggerated. Without it, we can have no clear sense of Whitman's development as a consciousness and as a craftsman: an affair of far graver concern with Whitman than with many other poets of his stature. For, as I shall propose, the development of his consciousness and his craft, from moment to moment and year to year, is the very root of his poetic subject matter. It is what his best poems are mainly about, or what they re-enact: the thrust and withdrawal, the heightening and declining, the flowing and ebbing of his psychic and creative energy. Whitman's poetry has to do with the drama of the psyche or "self" in its mobile and complex relation *to* itself, to the world of nature and human objects, and to the creative act. What is attempted here, consequently, is a sort of chart of Whitman's development—in the belief that such a chart is not simply a required preliminary for getting at Whitman, but, rather, that it is the proper way to identify the poetic achievement, and to evaluate it. And in a case like Whitman's, the chart of the development is not finally separable from the graph of the life, or biography; the biographical material, therefore, has likewise been distributed among the successive commentaries on the editions of Whitman's single lifelong book.

I: 1855

When *Leaves of Grass* was published on July 4, 1855, Walt Whitman, now thirty-six years old, was living in Brooklyn, with his parents and brothers, earning an occasional dollar by carpentering. Both his family and his carpentry served as sources of allusion and metaphor in the poetry; but neither—that is, neither his heredity nor his temporary employment—help much to explain how a relatively indolent odd-jobber and sometime journalist named Walter Whitman developed into Walt Whitman the poet. His mother, whom he salutes in "There Was a Child Went Forth" for having "conceiv'd him in her womb and birth'd him" (the birthday being the last day in May 1819; the place, rural Long Island), was of Dutch and Quaker descent, not especially cultivated, and remembered by her son, in the same poem of 1855, as quiet and mild and clean. His father was a farmer of deteriorating fortunes, temper, and health: "manly, mean, anger'd, unjust" in his son's account; and it is a psychological curiosity that the father died within a week of the son's first public appearance, or birth, as a poet. Other members of the family were sources of that compassionate intimacy with the wretched and the depraved reflected, for example, in "Song of Myself":

> *The lunatic is carried at last to the asylum a confirm'd case . . .*
> *The prostitute draggles her shawl, her bonnet bobs on her tipsy*
>   *and pimpled neck . . .*
> *Voices of the diseas'd and despairing and of thieves and dwarfs.*

Two of Whitman's brothers were diseased, one of them dying eventually in an insane asylum and the other (who was also a drunkard) married to a woman who became a prostitute. Yet another brother was a congenital idiot; and one of Whitman's sisters suffered from severe nervous melancholy. From these surroundings emerged the figure who, in the carpentering imagery of "Song of Myself," felt "sure as the most certain sure, plumb in the uprights, well entretied, braced in the beams"; a figure who not only felt like that but could write like that.

So remarkable and indeed so sudden has the appearance of Whitman the poet seemed, and out of so unlikely and artistically inhospitable a background, that literary historians have been driven to making spectacular guesses about the miraculous cause of it: an intense love affair, for instance, with a Creole lady of high degree; an intense love affair with an unidentified young man; a mystical seizure; the explosive impact of Emerson or of Carlyle or of George Sand. The literary influences can be documented, though they can scarcely be measured; with the other guesses, evidence is inadequate either to support or altogether to discount them. But perhaps the problem itself has not been quite properly shaped. Whitman's poetic emergence was remarkable enough; but it was not in fact particularly sudden. Nor was the career, seen retrospectively, as haphazard and aimless as one might suppose. Looked at from a sufficient distance, Whitman's life shows the same pattern of thrust and withdrawal, advance and retreat, that pulsates so regularly in the very metrics as well as the emotional attitudes of his verses; and to much the same effect. Up to about 1850, when he was thirty-one, Whitman—like the child in the autobiographical poem already quoted—was always going forth, always brushing up against the numberless persons and things of his world, and always *becoming* the elements he touched, as they became part of him. After 1850, he withdrew for a while into the privacies not only of his family but, more importantly, of his own imagination, in touch now with what he called the "Me myself"—his genius, or muse. It was this latter union between man and muse that, by 1855, produced the most extraordinary first volume of poems this country has so far seen.

One of the things Whitman did not become was a scholar, or even a college graduate. His school days, all spent in the Brooklyn to which his family moved in 1823, ended when he was eleven.

Thereafter he was apprenticed as a typesetter for a Long Island newspaper; and characteristically, the boy not only worked at the job, he *became* a typesetter, and typesetting became a part of his imagination. The look of a printed page and the rhetoric of punctuation were integral elements in his poetry—the printing of which he actually set with his own hands or carefully supervised. Between 1831 and 1836, Whitman occasionally wrote articles as well as set type for the paper; and he continued to compose fugitive little pieces from time to time during the five years following, from 1836 to 1841, while he was teaching in a variety of schools in a variety of Long Island villages. Writing, too, became part of him; and Whitman became a writer—at least by intention, announcing very firmly in a newspaper article of 1840, that he "would compose a wonderful and ponderous book . . . [treating] the nature and peculiarities of men, the diversities of their characters. . . . Yes: I *would* write a book! And who shall say that it might not be a very pretty book?"

In 1841, Whitman moved into New York City, where he was absorbed especially by what he called "the fascinating chaos" of lower Broadway, and by the life of saloons and theaters, of operas and art museums.[1] Operatic techniques and museum lore went into his later verses; but what Whitman became at this stage was that elegant stroller, or *boulevardier,* known as a dandy. This role persisted during the five years passed as reporter for a number of New York newspapers; and even after he returned to Brooklyn in 1846 and became editor of the *Eagle,* he came back by ferry to stroll Manhattan on most afternoons. But he was a dandy much caught up in public and political affairs. Among the personae he took on was that of the political activist, an ardent Freesoiler in fact, arguing the exclusion of Negro slavery from the territories with such editorial vehemence that the newspaper's owner fired him in February 1848. Within a matter of

1. Of special importance to Whitman were the Brooklyn Art Union, established by a group of Brooklyn painters about 1850, and the Egyptian Museum at 629 Broadway, in Manhattan. Whitman wrote an article about the former for the *New York Evening Post* in February, 1851; he was personally acquainted with several of the younger painters involved, and he was particularly observant of their techniques for handling light and color. Through visits to the Egyptian Museum, meanwhile, and through considerable study under the supervision of his friend, the Museum's proprietor, Dr. Abbot, Whitman became remarkably well versed in Egyptology—allusions drawn from which are frequent and suggestive in *Leaves of Grass.*

days, however, Whitman left for what turned out to be a three-month stay in New Orleans, where he served as assistant editor to that city's *Crescent*. It was there that rumor once assigned him the affair with the Creole lady, that soul-turning initiation into love that is said to have made a poet of him. The legend is almost certainly baseless; but something did happen to Whitman nonetheless. During the long weeks of travel, passing over the vast stretches of land and along the great rivers and the lakes (all that "geography and natural life" he catalogues so lavishly in the 1855 Preface), Whitman had his first encounter with the national landscape, and became (it may be hazarded) another of the personalities announced in *Leaves of Grass:* an American.

Back in Brooklyn, Whitman accepted the post of editor-in-chief on the liberal *Freeman* and stayed with it till he resigned in political outrage the following year. He had clearly "become" a journalist, an uncommonly able and effective one; his best poetry sprang in good part from a journalistic imagination—"I witness the corpse with its dabbled hair, I note where the pistol has fallen." At the same time, the forthgoing impulse was nearly—for the moment—exhausted. After expressing his sense of both national and personal betrayal by the Fugitive Slave Law in 1850, Whitman withdrew from the political arena; withdrew from active or regular journalism, and from the life of the city. He moved back to his family and commenced a leisurely existence in which, according to his brother George, "he would lie abed late, and after getting up would write a few hours if he took the notion"—or work at "house-building" for a bit, with his father and brothers, if he took that notion. Now he became a workman; and it was in the role of working-class artisan that he presented himself both in the verses of the 1855 *Leaves of Grass* and in the portrait which appeared as substitute for the author's name in the front of the volume.

For Whitman, I am suggesting, the act of becoming a poet was not a sudden or an unpredictable one. He had always been in process of becoming a poet, and the figures he successively became, from his school days onward, were not false starts or diversions, but moments in the major process. Typesetter, reporter, dandy, stroller in the city, political activist, surveyor of the national scenery, skilled editor, representative American workman: none of these was ever fully replaced by any other, nor were all at last replaced by the poet. They were absorbed into the poet; and if they do not explain the appearance of genius (nothing can explain that), they explain to some real degree the kind of writing—observant, ambulatory, varied, politically aware, job-conscious—in which *this* particular genius expressed itself.

Signs and symptoms of the poet proper, however, can also be isolated over a good many years. The determination to write a "wonderful" book, in 1840, has already been mentioned; but that was presumably to be a philosophical disquisition in prose. In the early 1840s, the writer-in-general became a writer of fiction, and Whitman contributed a number of moralistic short stories to different New York periodicals, all signed by "Walter Whitman" and none worth remembering. Not much later than that, certainly not later than 1847, Whitman's aspiration turned toward poetry. He began to carry a pocket-size notebook about with him; in this he would jot down topics for poems as they occurred, experimental lines, and trial workings of new metrical techniques. The process was stepped up from 1850 onward. In June 1850, the New York *Tribune* published two free-verse poems by Whitman, the second—later called "Europe: The 72d and 73d Year of These States," on the uprisings of 1848—to be included as the eighth item in the 1855 *Leaves of Grass*. It was probably in 1852 that he composed, though he did not publish, a fairly long poem called "Pictures," which had everything characteristic of his genuine poetry except its maritime movement. And in 1854, the repeal of the Missouri Compromise, and the arrest in Boston of a runaway slave named Anthony Burns, drew from Whitman a forty-line satiric exclamation that would comprise the ninth poem in the first edition—later called "A Boston Ballad."

These creative forays were increasingly stimulated by Whitman's reading, which was not only wide but, as evidence shows, surprisingly careful. He had reviewed works by Carlyle, George Sand, Emerson, Goethe, and others for the Brooklyn *Eagle*. He had known Greek and Roman literature, in translation, for years. "I have wonder'd since," he remarked in *A Backward Glance* (1888), "why I was not overwhelm'd by these mighty masters. Likely because I read them . . . in the full presence of Nature, under the sun . . . [with] the sea rolling in." (The comment suggests much of the quality of Whitman's poetry, wherein a natural atmosphere and sea rhythms help provide fresh versions of ancient and traditional archetypes.) It should be stressed that Whitman's literary education at this time, though it was by no means skimpy, was fairly conventional. It included the major English poets, Shakespeare and Milton especially, but it did not include Oriental writing or the literature of the mystical tradition or that of German idealism—except as those sources reached him faintly through his occasional readings in the essays of Emerson. This is probably to be reckoned fortunate: Whitman's mystical instinct, during his best creative years, was held effectively in check by a passion for the concrete, a commitment to the actual; and discussion of his "mysticism" is well advised to follow his example. Whitman became acquainted, too, with such American writers as Longfellow and Bryant, both of whom he came later to know personally. In addition, he took to making extensive notes and summaries of a long list of periodical essays, mostly dealing with art and artists.

"Art and Artists," in fact, was the title of an essay which Whitman himself read to the Brooklyn Art Union in 1851. And it was here that he first developed his large notion of the artist as hero—of the artist, indeed, as savior or redeemer of the community to which he offers his whole being as champion (sacrificial, if necessary) of freedom and humanity and spiritual health. "Read well the death of Socrates," he said portentously, "and of greater than Socrates." The image of the modern poet as godlike—even Christlike ("greater than Socrates")—was to run through and beneath Whitman's poetry from "Song of Myself" to "Passage to India"; and often, as here, it drew added intensity from Whitman's disillusion with other possible sources for that miraculous national transformation scene he seems to have waited for during most of his life. It was an extravagant notion; but it was one that anticipated several not much less extravagant images, in the twentieth century, of the artist as hero. It was this image, anyhow, that Whitman sought to bring into play in the whole body of the 1855 *Leaves of Grass* and particularly in "Song of Myself."

The first edition contained a long Preface introducing the poet-hero, who is then imaginatively created in the poems that follow. There were twelve of the latter, unnumbered and untitled and of varying length, with unconventional but effective typography—for example:

> *The atmosphere is not a perfume . . . . it has no taste of the*
>   *distillation . . . . it is odorless,*
> *It is for my mouth forever. . . . I am in love with it.*

The first and by far the longest entry was, of course, the poem that in 1881 was labeled "Song of Myself." It is in part genuine though highly original autobiography; in part, it is a form of wish projection. We may think of it, among many other things, as a free-flowing recapitulation of the two processes I have been describing —the process by which a man of many roles becomes a poet, and the process by which the poet becomes a sort of god. There are as many significant aspects to "Song of Myself" as there are critical discussions and analyses of it; if the comment here is mainly limited to the enlargement of its central figure—that is, to the question of its structure—it is because the structure tends to confirm one's sense of Whitman's characteristic movement both in life and in poetry. For if, again, this strange, sometimes baffling, stream-of-consciousness poem does have a discernible structure, an "action" with a beginning, middle, and end, it is almost certainly one that involves the two events or processes just named.

More than one astute reader, while acknowledging a typical pulse or rhythm in the poem, a tidal ebb and flow, has nonetheless denied to it any sustained and completed design. But it may be ventured, perhaps, that "Song of Myself" has not so much a single structure as a number of provisional structures—partly because Whitman, like Melville, believed in a deliberate absence of finish in a work of art; more importantly because of what we may call Whitman's democratic aesthetic. Just as the political activist was absorbed into the poet at some time after 1850, so, and at the same moment, a practical concern with the workings of a democratic society was carried over into the aesthetic realm and applied to the workings of poetry, to the writing and the reading of it. The shape of "Song of Myself" depended, in Whitman's view, on the creative participation of each reader—"I round and finish little," he remarked in *A Backward Glance,* "the reader will always have his or her part to do, just as much as I have had mine." In a real sense, the poem was intended to have as many structures as there were readers; and the reason was that Whitman aimed not simply to create a poet and then a god, but to assist at the creation of the poetic and godlike in every reader.

Like Emerson, Whitman was here giving a democratic twist to the European Romantic notion of the poet as mankind's loftiest figure. For both Emerson and Whitman the poet's superiority lay exactly in his representativeness. "The poet is representative," Emerson had said, in his essay "The Poet." "He stands among partial men for the complete man, and apprises us not of his wealth, but of the common wealth." This is what Whitman meant when he spoke of "the great poet" as "the equable man"; and it is what he asserted in the opening lines of "Song of Myself":

> *I celebrate myself and sing myself*
> *And what I assume you shall assume.*

As one or two commentators—notably Roy Harvey Pearce[2]—have rightly suggested, "Song of Myself" is the first recognizable American epic; but, if so, it is an epic of this peculiar and modern sort. It does not celebrate a hero and an action of ancient days; it creates (and its action *is* creative) a hero of future days—trusting thereby to summon the heroism implicit in each individual.

Considered in these terms, as the epic consequence of a democratic aesthetic, "Song of Myself" shows a variable number of structural parts. This reader discovers but does not insist upon the following. The invocation leads, in Sections 1 and 2, into a transition from the artificial to the natural—from perfume in houses to the atmosphere of the woods; uncontaminated nature is the first scene of the drama. Next comes the recollection of the union—mystical in kind, sexual in idiom—between the two dimensions of the poet's being: the limited, conditioned Whitman and the "Me, myself," his creative genius, what Emerson might have called the Over-Soul. This was the union that was consummated somehow and sometime in the early 1850s, and out of which there issued the poem in which the union was itself re-enacted.

There follows a long portion, continuing at least through Section 17, where—as a result of union—the *man* becomes a *poet,* and by the very act of creation. What is created is a world, an abundant world of persons and places and things—all sprung into existence by the action of seeing and naming:

> *The little one sleeps in its cradle,*
> *I lift the gauze and look a long time . . .*
> *The suicide sprawls on the bloody floor of the bedroom,*
> *I witness the corpse with its dabbled hair . . .*
> *Where are you off to, lady? for I see you.*

2. *The Continuity of American Poetry* (Princeton, N.J., 1961), especially pp. 59–82.

The democratic aesthetic is most palpably at work here. What we take at first to be sheer disorder, what some early reviewers regarded as simple slovenliness and lack of form, is in fact something rather different. It is the representation of moral and spiritual and aesthetic equality; of a world carefully devoid of rank or hierarchy. In "Song of Myself," this principle of moral equivalence is not so much stated as "suggested" (one of Whitman's favorite words), and suggested by "indirection" (another favorite word)—by the artfully casual juxtaposition of normally unrelated and unrelatable elements, a controlled flow of associations.[3] Thus:

> *The prostitute draggles her shawl, her bonnet bobs on her tipsy*
> *and pimpled neck . . .*
> *The President holding a cabinet council is surrounded by the*
> *great Secretaries,*
> *On the piazza walk three matrons stately and friendly with*
> *twined arms,*
> *The crew of the fish-smack pack repeated layers of halibut in*
> *the hold,*
> *The Missourian crosses the plains toting his wares and his*
> *cattle*

and so on. In the 1855 Preface, Whitman was willing to make the case explicit: "Each precise object or condition or combination or process exhibits a beauty." And he there illustrated the idea in a succession of still more surprising incongruities: "the multiplication table . . . . old age . . . . the carpenter's trade . . . . the grand-opera."

When, therefore, toward the end of this phase of the poem, the speaker begins to claim for himself the gradually achieved role of poet, it is as the poet of every mode of equality that he particularly wishes to be acknowledged. The announcement runs through Section 25:

> *I play not marches for accepted victors only, I play marches*
> *for conquer'd and slain persons . . .*
> *I am the poet of the Body, and I am the poet of the Soul. . . .*
> *I am the poet of the woman the same as the man . . .*
> *I am not the poet of goodness only, I do not decline to be the*
> *poet of wickedness also.*

3. Cf. the essay on Whitman by David Daiches in *The Young Rebel in American Literature,* ed. Carl Bode (New York, 1960).

The *poet* now makes ready for the second great adventure, the long journey, as we may say, toward *godhood*. By way of preparation, he undergoes a second ecstatic experience in Sections 26 and following: an experience of an almost overpoweringly sensuous kind, with the sense of touch so keen as to endanger his health or his sanity: "You villain touch! . . . . you are too much for me." The poet survives, and in Section 33 he is "afoot with [his] vision." In the visionary flight across the universe that is then recounted, the poet enlarges into a divine being by *becoming* each and every element within the totality that he experiences; while the universe in turn is drawn together into a single and harmonious whole since each element in it is invested in common with a portion of the poet's emergent divinity. It is no longer the prostitute who draggles her shawl, the President who holds a cabinet council, the Missourian who crosses the plain: it is "I" who does all that:

> *I anchor my ship for a little while only . . .*
> *I go hunting polar furs and the seal . . .*
> *I am the man, I suffer'd, I was there . . .*
> *I am the hounded slave, I wince at the bite of dogs.*

And the "I" is itself no longer the individual man-poet; it is the very force or *élan vital* of all humanity.

The journey lasts through Section 33; and in its later moments, as will be noticed, the traveler associates especially with the defeated, the wretched, the wicked, the slaughtered. Whitman's poetic pores were oddly open, as were Melville's, to the grand or archetypal patterns common to the human imagination—so psychologists such as Carl Jung tell us—in all times and places; and the journey of "Song of Myself" requires, at this point, the familiar descent into darkness and hell—until (Section 33) "corpses rise, gashes heal, fastenings roll from me," and an enormous resurrection is accomplished. But what gets reborn, what "troop[s] forth" from the grave is not the poet simply; it is the poet "replenish'd with supreme power," the poet become a divine figure. Just as, by the poetic act of creating a world, the man had previously grown into a poet; so now, by experiencing and, so to speak, melting into the world's totality to its furthest width and darkest depth, the poet expands into a divinity. He has approximated at last that "greater than Socrates" invoked by Whitman in 1851; he has become that saving force which

Whitman had proposed was to be the true role of the American poet. It is the divinity who speaks through Sections 39 to 51, proclaiming his divine inheritance ("Taking to myself the exact dimensions of Jehovah," etc.), performing as healer and comforter ("Let the physician and the priest go home"), exhorting every man to his supreme and unique effort. For it is a divinity who insists at every turn that he speaks but for the divine potential of all men. And, having done so, in Section 52 he departs.

Wallace Stevens, the most sophisticated among Whitman's direct poetic descendants, once specified his ancestor's recurrent and dual subject matter in the course of a resonant salute to him in "Like Decorations in a Nigger Cemetery":

> *Walt Whitman walking along a ruddy shore*
> *. . . singing and chanting the things that are part of him*
> *The worlds that were and will be, death and day.*

"Death and day," with its corollary "life and night," is as apt a phrase as one can think of for the extremes between which Whitman's poetry habitually alternates. "Song of Myself" is Whitman's masterpiece, and perhaps America's, in the poetry of "day"—"the song of me rising from bed and meeting the sun"—while "To Think of Time" or "Burial Poem," as Whitman once called it, belongs initially to the poetry of "death," and "the Sleepers" to the poetry of "night." But although both the latter, in their very different ways, explore in depth the dark undergrounds of experience, both return—as "Song of Myself" does—with the conviction of a sort of absolute life. "I swear I think there is nothing but immortality": so ends the meditation in "To Think of Time." And such is the determining sense everywhere in the 1855 edition; we shall shortly have occasion to contrast it with the sense of things in the edition of 1860. It may be helpful, meanwhile, to glance at the 1855 poem "There Was a Child Went Forth," to see how Whitman's characteristic psychological movement was reflected in his poetic technique—how the shifting play of his consciousness was reflected in the shifting play of his craft.

"There Was a Child Went Forth" is Whitman's most unequivocal account of the thrust toward being. It is a poem about growth, about burgeoning and sprouting; and it grows itself, quite literally, in size and thickness. The difference in the sheer physical or typographical look of the first and last stanzas is an immediate clue to the poem's thematic development. Yet what the poet enacts, on the technical side, is not an altogether uninterrupted increase in substance and vitality. The process is rather one of alternation, of enlarging and retracting, of stretching and shrinking—in which, however, the impulse toward growth is *always* dominant. The quantitatively shrunken fourth stanza, for example, is flanked by the longer eight-line stanza that precedes it and the longest or eighteen-line stanza that follows it and completes the poem's swelling motion: giving us a process in fact of stretching-shrinking-stretching. The same process is present more artfully still within the first stanza, with its rhythmic shift from short line to longer line to still longer and back to shorter once again; but where the line that contains the quantitative shrink is nonetheless a line accentuated by the word "stretching"—"Or for many years or stretching cycles of years." The psychic stretching is thus quietly affirmed at the instant of technical shrinking; and it is the stretching impulse that triumphs and defines the poem.

The same effect is accomplished metrically. "There Was a Child Went Forth" is what is now called free verse; and no doubt the word "free" in this context would have had, had Whitman known the whole term, a political aura, and become a part of his democratic aesthetic. Whitman was the first American poet to break free from the convention of iambic pentameter as the principal and most decorous meter for poetry in English; in so doing he added to the declaration of literary independence—from England, chiefly—that had been triumphantly proclaimed for his generation in Emerson's "The American Scholar" and was the predictable artistic consequence of the political fact. Whitman's was a major gesture of technical liberation, for which every American poet after him has reason to be grateful; every such poet, as William Carlos Williams (a manifest heir of Whitman) has said, must show cause why iambic pentameter is proper for him. But it was not an act of purely negative liberation; it was emancipation with a purpose. It freed Whitman to attempt a closer approximation of metrics and the kind of experience he naturally aimed to express; and it made possible an eventual and occasional return to older and more orderly metrics—to possess them, to use them freshly, to turn them to the poet's established poetic intentions. The long uneven alternations I have

n's permission—adorned the back cover of the
greet you at the beginning of a great career."
he new poems, consequently, was one of achieved
fertility. This is the poetry of day and the poetry
ow. The feeling, indeed, is so large and intense as
sense of profound awe: a sense, almost, of terror.
ses from Whitman's convinced and total association
cundity ("Spontaneous Me") with that of nature
s Compost"), an association itself enough to intox-
arises, too, from Whitman's startling view that the
mplishment—of the man-poet and of nature—issues
ing superficially ugly or shameful or diseased or
taneous Me" mingles two kinds of poems: those that
the artistic act and those that are involved with the
. The act of love, the expression of sexual energy,
taphorical or physical, whether heterosexual or homo-
ries with it a sweeping sensation of shame ("the young
or'd, red, ashamed, angry"). But the experience fulfills
iumph and pride, just as Whitman had deliberately
the erotic dimension of the new volume in triumph
; it leads to a great "oath of procreation," procreation
sort; it ends in a full consciousness of wholesome abun-
much the same way, nature, in "This Compost," re-
life each spring out of the rotting earth: "Every spear
rises out of what was once a catching disease." The
of nature—creating life out of death, health out of
, beauty out of foulness, "sweet things out of such cor-
'—provided Whitman with an example, an analogy to
creative experience, so immense as to terrify him.
terror, needless to say, did not disempower but elec-
him. The most far-ranging and beautiful of the new poems,
sing Brooklyn Ferry," shows Whitman writing under the
rce of his assurance—of his assured identification with the
vital of all things. The interplay of the self and the large
it thrusts forward into is on a scale not unlike that of "Song
yself"; the flow of the consciousness merges with the flow of
ty. Every item encountered is a "dumb beautiful minister"
Vhitman's responsive spirit; all the items in the universe are
ries strung like beads on my smallest sights and hearings."
complex of natural and human and created objects now
ms a sort of glowing totality that is always in movement, al-

been describing could hardly have been conveyed by recurring five- and four-stress lines. Whitman instinctively depended, not on the regular alternating current of the iambic, but on an irregular alternation of *rising* and of *falling* rhythms—which corresponded happily to the rise and fall of the felt life, to the flowing and ebbing—and the rising rhythm, once again, is always in command:

There was a child went forth.

And in the poem's conclusion—when a world and a child have been brought fully to interdependent life—the rhythm settles back in a line that neither rises nor falls; a line that rests in a sort of permanent stillness; a subdued iambic of almost perfectly even stress—a convention repossessed in the last long slow series of monosyllables broken only and rightly by the key words "became," "always," and "every":

> *These became part of that child who went forth every day, and*
> *who now goes, and will always go forth every day.*

It is not possible to invoke the imagery of stretching and shrinking without being reminded of sexual analogies, and thereby of the sexual element so prevalent in Whitman's poetry. That element was notably, even blatantly more central to the 1856 edition—it was about several poems in this edition that Thoreau, otherwise much taken with Whitman, said that "It is as if the beasts spoke"—and it operated most tellingly in 1860. Still, it was evident enough in 1855 to startle sensibilities. "Song of Myself" exhibits a degree of sexual bravado mixed with a trace of sexual nostalgia. But the sexual aspect is more apparent in the poem that inhabits the world where Freud and Jung would look for signs of the sexual impulse—the world of dreams. "The Sleepers"—or "Sleep-Chasings," according to its 1860 title—is not only a poem of night and death—"I wander all night in my visions . . . the white features of corpses"—it is a poem of profound psychic disturbance, as the speaker makes clear at once in a superb line that gained force from the 1855 typography: "Wandering and confused . . . . lost to myself . . . . ill-assorted . . . . contradictory." A portion of sexual shame contributes to the uncertainty and deepens the sense of terror—the terror, as Richard Chase has usefully hazarded, of the ego, or conscious self, confronting the id, or the unconscious, and being threatened by extinction.[4] But, in the manner typical of the first *Leaves of Grass,* the poem moves to the discovery of solace amid fear, of pattern amid the random. Descending through the planes of night, "The Sleepers" encounters in its own heart of darkness sources of maternal comfort and spiritual revelation. Guilt is transcended and harmony restored. The adjectives of the opening stanza—"wandering and confused, lost to myself, ill-assorted, contradictory"—are matched and overcome by the adjectives of the poem's close: "sane," "relieved," "resumed," "free," "supple," "awake." There has occurred what Jung would call the "reintegration of the personality"; the ill-assorted psyche has become whole again after passing through what Jung would also call the "night journey." In "The Sleepers," Whitman displayed once more his remarkable talent for arriving by intuition at the great archetypes. And the night journey concludes in that confident recovery of day, that perfect reconciliation with night, that is the distinctive mark of the edition of 1855.

II: 1856

The second edition of *Leaves of Grass* appeared in June 1856, less than a year after the first. There had been several more printings of the latter; and, indeed, during the intervening months Whitman was mainly occupied with the new printings and with reading—and writing—reviews of his work. He still lived with his family in Brooklyn, but he had virtually given up any practical employment. He had "no business," as his mother told Bronson Alcott, "but going out and coming in to eat, drink, write and sleep."[5] The same visitor from Concord quoted Whitman himself as saying that he only "lived to make pomes." Over the months he had made twenty new ones, and included them all in the considerably expanded second edition.

Conventional norms of printing crept back a little into this edition. All the poems, old and new, were now numbered and given titles, the new poems always including the word "poem" —a word that obviously had a magical power for Whitman at the time. Among the poems added were: "Poem of Wonder at

4. *Walt Whitman Reconsidered* (New York, 1955), pp. 54–57.
5. Roger Asselineau, *The Evolution of Walt Whitman* (New York, 1960), pp. 92–93.

the Resurrecti
Compost"; "Bu
down Poem"—
appearance of tl
tional, as the ec
abandoned in fav
thereby its vivid in
silence, of utteran
psychic and artistic
I suffered . . . . I was
and contraction into
the earlier mode of pr
ingly tiresome; and W
necessary combination
the most vigorous of ta

For the rest, the new
and emotion of the first
evil, both general and pe
to be evil/ . . . Had guil
speak/ . . . the wolf, the s
unmistakable and highly su
III.iv.87 ff.—Whitman dre
or his critics have normally
doubt of his own abilities—'
blank and suspicious"—a no
the 1860 edition. But by and
one of unimpeded creative ferti
ing energy. It registers the enorn
vocation and of its miracle-mak
to the experience of having pul
the headiest of the reviews of the l
including Whitman's forgetful old
had a reasonably good sale; and
America and England, some were
perceptive, and one or two were dov
of Whitman as almost that "greater
hoping to become. Much the most stir
was the famous letter from Emersor
Grass "the most extraordinary piece
America has yet contributed," with "
incomparably well in it." One senten

20   *Walt Wh*

without Emerso
1856 edition: "
The tone of t
and boundless
of unending fl
to produce a
That sense ari
of his own fe
at large ("Th
icate one. It
creative acc
from somet
dead. "Spon
result from
physical ac
whether me
sexual, car
man all co
itself in t
expanded
and pride
in every
dance. I
produces
of grass
conduct
sickness
ruption
his ow
The
trified
"Cros
full fo
élan
worl
of M
reali
to
"gl
Th
for

ways frolicking on. "Crossing Brooklyn Ferry" presents a vision
of an entirety moving forward: a vision that is mystical in its sense
of oneness but that is rendered in the most palpable and concrete
language—the actual picture of the harbor is astonishingly alive
and visible. And the poem goes beyond its jubilant cry of the soul
—"Flow on river!"—to reach a peace that really does surpass
any normal understanding. Whitman was to write poetry no less
consummate; but he was never again to attain so final a peak of
creative and visionary intoxication.

III: 1860

Whitman, as we have heard his mother saying, was always "going
out and coming in." She meant quite literally that her son would
go out of the house in the morning, often to travel on the ferry
to Manhattan and to absorb the spectacle of life, and would come
back into the household to eat and sleep, perhaps to write. But
she unwittingly gave a nice maternal formula to the larger, recurring pattern in Whitman's career—the foray into the world and
the retreat back into himself and into a creative communion with
his genius. The poetry he came in to write—through the 1856
edition just examined—reflected that pattern in content and
rhythm, and in a way to celebrate the commanding power of the
outward and forward movement. The early poetry bore witness
as well, to be sure, of the darker mode of withdrawal, the descent
into the abysses of doubt, self-distrust, and the death-conscious-
ness; but it was invariably overcome in a burst of visionary renewal. The poetry of 1855 and 1856 is the poetry of day, of flood
tide.

The 1860 *Leaves of Grass,* however, gives voice to genuine
desolation. In it, betimes, the self appears as shrunken, indeed as
fragmented; the psyche as dying; the creative vigor as dissipated.
The most striking of the new poems belong to the poetry not of
day but of death. A suggestive and immediate verbal sign of the
new atmosphere may be found in the difference of title between
so characteristic a poem of 1855 as "There Was a Child Went
Forth" and perhaps the key 1860 poem, "As I Ebb'd with the
Ocean of Life." Yet the case must be put delicately and by appeal
to paradox. For, in a sense, the new death poetry represents in
fact Whitman's most remarkable triumph over his strongest feelings of personal and artistic defeat. There has been a scholarly

debate over the precise degree of melancholy in the 1860 edition, one scholar emphasizing the note of dejection and another the occasional note of cheerfulness; but that debate is really beside the point. What we have is poetry that expresses the sense of loss so sharply and vividly that substantive loss is converted into artistic gain.

During the almost four years since June 1856, Whitman had once again gone out and come back in; but this time the withdrawal was compelled by suffering and self-distrust. Whitman's foray into the open world, beginning in the fall of 1856, took the form, first, of a brief new interest in the political scene and, second, of a return to journalism, as editor-in-chief of the Brooklyn *Daily Times* from May 1857 until June 1859. In the morning, he busied himself writing editorials and articles for the newspaper; in the afternoon, he traveled into New York, to saunter along lower Broadway and to sit watchful and silent near or amid the literati who gathered in Pfaff's popular Swiss restaurant in the same neighborhood. In the evening, he continued to write—prolifically: seventy poems, more or less, in the first year after the 1856 edition and probably a few more in the months immediately following. Then there occurred a hiatus: a blank in our knowledge of Whitman's life, and apparently a blank in his creative activity. We cannot say just when the hiatus began—sometime in 1858, one judges. It ended, anyhow, at some time before the publication in the December 1859 issue of the New York *Saturday Press* of a poem called "A Child's Reminiscence," its familiar title being "Out of the Cradle Endlessly Rocking."

On the political side, Whitman's disenchantment was even swifter than usual. The choices offered the American public in the election of 1856—Buchanan, Frémont, and Fillmore—seemed to him false, debased, and meaningless; and he called—in an unpublished pamphlet—for a president who might play the part of "Redeemer." His disappointment with the actual, in short, led as before to an appeal for some "greater than Socrates" to arise in America; and, also as before, Whitman soon turned from the political figure to the *poet,* in fact to himself, to perform the sacred function, asserting in his journal that *Leaves of Grass* was to be "the New Bible." (Not until 1866 would the two aspirations fuse in a poem—"When Lilacs Last in the Dooryard Bloom'd"—that found a new idiom of almost biblical sonority to celebrate death in the person of a Redeemer President, Abraham Lincoln.) Meanwhile, however, Whitman's private and inner life was causing him far more grief and dismay than the public life he had been observing. A chief cause for Whitman's season of despair, according to most Whitman biographers, was a homosexual love affair during the silent months: an affair that undoubtedly took place, that was the source at once of profound joy and profound guilt, and that, when it ended, left Whitman with a desolating sense of loss. Such poems as "A Hand-Mirror" and "Hours Continuing Long, Sore and Heavy-Hearted" testify with painful clarity both to the guilt and to the subsequent misery of loneliness. At the same time, poems such as "As I Ebb'd with the Ocean of Life" and "So Long!" strike a different and perhaps deeper note of loss: a note, that is, of poetic decline, of the loss not so much of a human loved one but of creative energy—accompanied by a loss of confidence in everything that energy had previously brought into being. There had been a hint of this in "Crossing Brooklyn Ferry" in 1856— "The best I had done seem'd to me blank and suspicious"—but there self-doubt had been washed away in a flood of assurance. Now it had become central and almost resistant to hope. It may be that the fear of artistic sterility was caused by the moral guilt; but it seems no less likely that the artistic apprehension was itself at the root of the despair variously echoed in 1860. If so, the apprehension was probably due to a certain climacteric in Whitman's psychic career—what is called *la crise de quarantaine,* the psychological crisis some men pass through when they reach the age of forty. Whitman was forty in May 1859; and it was in the month after his birthday that he wrote two aggressive and, one cannot but feel, disturbed articles for the Brooklyn *Daily Times*—on prostitution and the right to unmarried sexual love—that resulted in his dismissal from the paper. Characteristically dismissed, Whitman characteristically withdrew. But no doubt the safest guess is that a conjunction of these factors—*la quarantaine,* the temporary but fearful exhaustion of talent after so long a period of fertility, the unhappy love affair—begot the new poems that gave "death and night" their prominence in the 1860 edition.

The edition of 1860 contained 154 poems: which is to say that 122 had been composed since 1856, and of these, as has been said, seventy by the summer of 1857. Most of the other fifty, it can be hazarded, were written late in 1859 and in the first six months of 1860. It can also be hazarded that among those latter fifty poems were nearly all the best of the new ones—those grouped under the title "Calamus," the name Whitman gave to his poetry of masculine love. These include "Scented Herbage," "Hours Continuing," "Whoever You Are," "City of Orgies," "A Glimpse," "I Saw in Louisiana," "Out of the Cradle," "As I Ebb'd" (published in the April 1860 issue of the *Atlantic Monthly* as "Bardic Symbols"), and "So Long!"

"A Hand-Mirror" records a feeling of self-loathing almost unequaled in English or American poetry. And it is representative of the entire volume in its emphatic reversal of an earlier work and an earlier course of feeling. In "This Compost," in 1856, Whitman was seized with a wonder verging on terror at the capacity of nature and of man to produce the beautiful out of the foul or shameful; here, in 1860, he is smitten with the dreadful conviction of having, in his own being, produced the foul and the shameful out of the potentially beautiful. "Hours Continuing Long, Sore and Heavy-Hearted" is a statement of pain so severe, so unmitigated, that Whitman deleted the poem from all subsequent editions of *Leaves of Grass*. These poems of pain are uncommonly painful to read; and yet, in the other major new poems of 1860, we find Whitman executing what might be called the grand Romantic strategy—the strategy of converting private devastation into artistic achievement; of composing poetry of high distinction out of a feeling of personal, spiritual, and almost metaphysical *ex*tinction. Keats's "Ode on a Grecian Urn" offers an example of the same, at one chronological extreme; as, at another, does Hart Crane's "The Broken Tower."

That strategy is, indeed, what the 1860 edition may be said to be about; for more than the other versions of *Leaves of Grass,* that of 1860 has a sort of plot buried in it.[6] The plot—in a very reduced summary—consists in the discovery that "death" is the source and beginning of "poetry"; with "death" here understood to involve several kinds and sensations of loss, of suffering, of disempowering guilt, of psychic fragmentation; and "poetry" as the awakening of the power to catch and to order reality in language. What had so fundamentally changed since 1855 and 1856 was Whitman's concept of reality. In 1855, as we have seen, the thought of death led to a flat denial of it: "I swear I think there is

6. See the Facsimile Edition of the 1860 text, edited with an introduction by Roy Harvey Pearce (Ithaca, N.Y., 1961).

nothing but immortality." But in "Scented Herbage" of 1860 he arrives at an opposite conclusion: "For now," as he says, "it is convey'd to me that you [death] are . . . the real reality." If Whitman's poetic faculty had formerly been quickened by his sense of the absolute life, it now finds its inspiration in the adventure of death. In "So Long!" Whitman confesses to the death of his talent: "It appears to me that I am dying. . . . My songs cease, I abandon them." Yet in "Scented Herbage" poetry is identified as the very herbage and flower of death, as Baudelaire had a few years earlier identified poetry as the flower of evil; his new poems, for Whitman, are "growing up above me above death." By 1860 Whitman had reached the perception of Wallace Stevens—in "Sunday Morning" (1923)—that "death is the mother of beauty."

Stevens' phrase might serve as motto for the 1860 edition; as it might also serve for another of the several titles for the poem that was first called "A Child's Reminiscence," then "A Word Out of the Sea," and finally (in 1871) "Out of the Cradle Endlessly Rocking." Whatever else occurs in this in every sense brilliant poem, there unmistakably occurs the discovery of poetic power, the magical power of the word, through the experience —here presented as vicarious—of the departure and loss, perhaps the death, of the loved one. It is one of the most handsomely *made* of Whitman's poems; the craft is relaxed, firm, and sure. Only an artist in virtuoso control of his technical resources would attempt a poem with such effortless alternation of narrative (or recitatif) and impassioned aria, such dazzling metrical shifts, such hypnotic exactitude of language, not to mention a narrative "point of view" of almost Jamesian complexity: the man of forty recalling the child of, say, twelve observing the calamitous love affair of two other beings, and the same man of forty projecting, one assumes, his own recent and adult bereavement into the experience of an empathic child. Whitman, by 1860, was very impressively the poet in that word's original meaning of "maker," in addition to being still the poet as inspired singer; and "Out of the Cradle Endlessly Rocking"—for all its supple play of shadows and glancing light—will bear the utmost weight of analysis. But it has perhaps been sufficiently probed elsewhere,[7] and I will instead take a longer look at "As I Ebb'd with the Ocean of Life."

7. For example, in the four essays by Stephen E. Whicher, Paul Fussell, Jr., Richard Chase, and Roy Harvey Pearce contained in *The Presence of Walt Whitman*, ed. R. W. B. Lewis (New York, 1962).

We will not be far wrong, and in any case it will illuminate the pattern of Whitman's career, if we take this poem as an almost systematic inversion of the 1855 poem "There Was a Child Went Forth," as well as an inversion of a key moment—Sections 4 and 5—in the 1855 "Song of Myself." As against that younger Whitman of morning and of spring, of the early lilacs and the red morning-glories, here is the Whitman of the decline of the day and of the year—a poet now found "musing late in the autumn day" (the phrase should be read slowly, as though the chief words were, in the older fashion, divided by dots). All the sprouts and blossoms and fruit of "There Was a Child Went Forth" are here replaced, in the poetically stunning second stanza by:

> *Chaff, straw, splinters of wood, weeds, and the sea-gluten,*
> *Scum, scales from shining rocks, leaves of salt-lettuce, left*
> *by the tide;*

to which are added, later, "A few sands and dead leaves," "a trail of drift and debris," and finally:

> *loose windrows, little corpses,*
> *Froth, snowy white, and bubbles,*
> *(See, from my dead lips the ooze exuding at last . . . .)*

The poem's rhythm, instead of pulsating outward in constantly larger spirals (though it seems to try to do that occasionally), tends to fall back on itself, to fall away, almost to disintegrate; no poem of Whitman's shows a more cunning fusion of technique and content. It is here, quite properly, the falling rather than the rising rhythm that catches the ear. As against:

> *There was a child went forth,*

we now hear:

> *Where the fierce old mother endlessly cries for her castaways*

—a dying fall that conveys the shrinking away, the psychological slide toward death, the slope into oblivion that the poem is otherwise concerned with.

The major turn in the action appears in the grammatical shift from the past tense of Section 1 ("As I ebb'd," etc.) to the present tense of Section 2 ("As I wend," etc.). It is a shift from the known to the unknown, a shift indeed not so much from one moment of time to another as from the temporal to the timeless, and a shift not so much accomplished as desired. For what produces in the poet his feeling of near-death is just his conviction that neither he nor his poetry has ever known or ever touched upon the true and timeless realm of reality. The essential reality from which he now feels he has forever been cut off is rendered as "the real Me." To get the full force of the despondent confession of failure, one should place the lines about "the real Me" next to those in Sections 4 and 5 in "Song of Myself" where Whitman had exultantly recalled the exact opposite. There he had celebrated a perfect union between the actual Me and the real Me: between the here-and-now Whitman and that timeless being, that Over-Soul or genius that he addressed as the Me myself. *That,* I suggest, was Whitman's real love affair; that was the union that was consummated in 1855 and that ended—so Whitman temporarily felt—in disunion three or four years later; "the real Me" was the loved one that departed. And now, divorced and disjoined from the real Me, the actual Me threatens to come apart, to collapse into a trail of drift and debris, with ooze exuding from dead lips. (So, by analogy, a Puritan might have felt when cut off, through sin, from the God that created him.)

Still, as Richard Chase has insisted, this poem is saved from any suggestion of whimpering self-pity by the astonishing and courageous tone of self-mockery—in the image of the real Me ridiculing the collapsing Me:

> *before all my arrogant poems the real Me stands yet untouch'd, untold, altogether unreach'd,*
> *Withdrawn far, mocking me with mock-congratulatory signs and bows,*
> *With peals of distant ironical laughter at every word I have written,*
> *Pointing in silence to these songs, and then to the sand beneath.*

It is an image of immeasurable effect. And it is, so to speak, a triumph over its own content. Anyone who could construct an image of the higher power—the one he aspires toward—standing far off and mocking him with little satiric bows and gestures, comparing and consigning his verses to the sandy debris under his feet: such a person has already conquered his sense of sterility, mastered his fear of spiritual and artistic death, rediscovered his genius, and returned to the fullest poetic authority. Within the poem, Whitman identifies the land as his father and the fierce old sea as his mother; he sees himself as alienated no less from them than from the real Me, and he prays to both symbolic parents for a rejuvenation of his poetic force, a resumption of "the secret of the murmuring I envy." But the prayer is already answered in the very language in which it is uttered; Whitman never murmured more beautifully; and this is why, at the depth of his ebbing, Whitman can say, parenthetically, that the flow will return.

IV: 1867

If Whitman, by the spring of 1860, had not been "rescued" by his own internal capacity for resurgence, he would, more than likely, have been rescued anyhow by the enormous public event that began the following April with the outbreak of a national civil war. During the war years, Whitman "went forth" more strenuously than in any other period of his life, and he immersed himself more thoroughly in the activities and sufferings of his fellows. The immediate poetic fruit of the experience was a small, separately published volume of fifty-three new poems, in 1865, called *Drum-Taps,* with a *Sequel to Drum-Taps*—containing "When Lilacs Last in the Dooryard Bloom'd"—tacked on to the original in 1866. Both titles were added as an Appendix to the fourth edition of *Leaves of Grass* in 1867, which otherwise contained only a handful of new poems. Several of Whitman's war poems have a certain lyric strength, either of compassion or of sheer imagistic precision; and the meditation occasioned by the death of Lincoln is among his finest artistic achievements. Nonetheless—and however remarkable and admirable his human performance was during the war—it was in this same period that Whitman the poet began to yield to Whitman the prophet, and what had been most compelling in his poetry to give way to the misrepresentation and concealment that disfigured *Leaves of Grass* over the decades to follow.

Until the last days of 1862, Whitman remained in Brooklyn, formally unemployed, making what he could out of earnings from *Leaves of Grass,* and—once the fighting had started—following the course of the war with the liveliest concern. He was initially very much on the side of the North, which he regarded as the side of freedom, justice, and human dignity. But as time went on, he came to be increasingly on the side of the nation as a whole, more anxious to heal wounds than to inflict them—and this, of course, is what he literally turned to doing in 1863. In December of the previous year, he learned that his younger brother Jeff had been wounded. Whitman journeyed south at once, found his brother recuperating satisfactorily near Falmouth, Virginia, and stayed for eight memorable days among the forward troops in the battle area. It was only eight days, but the spectacle of horror and gallantry of which he was the closest eyewitness had an enduring, almost a conversionary effect upon him. He came back north only as far as Washington; and from that moment until 1867, he spent every free moment in the military hospitals, ministering to the needs of the wounded. He became, in fact, a "wound-dresser," though a dresser primarily of spiritual wounds, bearing gifts, writing letters, comforting, sustaining, exhorting; he became, indeed, the physician-priest with whom, in "Song of Myself," he had associated the figure of the poet.

He made a living in Washington through a series of governmental jobs: as assistant to the deputy paymaster for a while; as clerk in the Indian Bureau—a position from which he was summarily dismissed when the bureau chief read *Leaves of Grass* and pronounced it unpardonably obscene; finally in the office of the Department of Interior. Here he stayed, relatively prosperous and content, until he suffered a partly paralyzing stroke in 1873. It was in the same year that, traveling north, ill and exhausted, he settled almost by accident in Camden, New Jersey, where he lived until his death in 1892.

In short, when Whitman went forth this time, or was drawn forth, into the American world of war, he was drawn not merely into New York City but into the center of the country's national life; to the actual battlefields, to the seat of the nation's political power, to the offices of government, to the hospitals, and into the presence of the men who carried on their bodies the burden of the nation's tragedy. It is not surprising that the outer and public life of the country absorbed most of his energy; it is only regrettable that, as a result, and in the course of time, the solitary singer disappeared into the public bard, into the singer of democracy, of companionship, the singer not of "this compost" but of "these States." This was the figure celebrated by William Douglas O'Connor in a book written as an angry and rhapsodic defense of Whitman at the time of his dismissal from the Indian Bureau; a book which, in its title, provided the phrase which all but smothered the genuine Whitman for almost a century: *The Good Gray Poet* (1866).

There had been a faint but ominous foreshadowing of the good gray poet in the 1860 edition: in the frontispiece, where Whitman appeared for the first time as the brooding, far-gazing prophetic figure; in the first tinkerings with and slight revisions of the earlier poems; and in the group of poems called "Chants Democratic," the volume's major blemish. The 1867 edition had no frontispiece at all; but now the process of revising, deleting, and rearranging was fully at work. A number of the "Calamus" poems on manly love, for example, were removed from *Leaves of Grass* once and for all: those which acknowledged or deplored his erotic attraction to another man—including "Hours Continuing." The sexuality of "Song of Myself" and "The Sleepers" was toned down by deleting in particular the orgasmic imagery in both of them. Much of the bizarre and the frantic was taken out of the 1856 and 1860 poetry, in the interest, as Roger Asselineau has put it, of placing "the accent on the poet-prophet rather than on the lover."[8] In a general way, it was the intense and personal *self* of Whitman that got shaded over by the new editing—that self, in its always rhythmic and sometimes wild oscillations, that was the true source and subject of the true poetry. The private self was reshaped into the public person, and the public stage on which this person chanted and intoned became the major subject of the would-be national bard. Whitman became less and less the original artist singing by indirection of his own psychic advances and retreats; he was becoming and wanted to become the Poet of Democracy. No longer the watchful solitary, he was changing into the Poet of Comradeship.

It should not be assumed that, because these were postures, they were necessarily false or worthless; they were simply uncongenial to Whitman's kind of poetry. In the same year, 1867, that *Leaves of Grass* unveiled the prophet of the democratic culture, Whitman also published in the New York *Galaxy* a prose essay called "Democracy," where he set forth much of the evidence that, a few years later, went into the longer essay

8. *The Evolution of Walt Whitman*, p. 196.

"Democratic Vistas"—as cogent and searching an account of the conditions of democracy in America, and of their relation to the life of letters, as any American has ever written. But what Whitman could do with this material in prose, he could not do effectively in verse. The democratic element in the early poems was, as has been suggested, an aesthetic element. It was part of the very stress and rhythm of the verse, implicit in the poet's way of looking at persons and things, in the principle of equality in his catalogues and the freedom of his meters, in the dynamic of his relation to his readers. Tackling democracy head on in poetry, Whitman became unpersuasive, even boring.

In the same way, Whitman's poems about the actual war were least striking when they were least personal. There is critical disagreement on this point, but in one reader's opinion, Melville wrote far more authentic war poetry because he had what Whitman did not—a powerful sense of history as allegory. In "The Conflict of Convictions," for example, Melville could suggest the thrust and scale of the struggle in a frame of grand tragedy and in a somberly prophetic mode that the aspiring prophet, Whitman, could never approach. Whitman, the man, had entered the public arena, but his muse did not follow him there; and the enduring poems culled from the war are rather of the intimate and lyrical variety—tender reminiscences or crisp little vignettes like "Cavalry Crossing a Ford," where the image is everything.

There appears among these poems, however, like an unexpected giant out of an earlier age, the work that is widely regarded as Whitman's supreme accomplishment: "When Lilacs Last in the Dooryard Bloom'd." This poem does not, in fact, have quite the artistic finality of "As I Ebb'd" or "Out of the Cradle"; or, rather, its finality is more on the surface, where it is asserted, than in the interior and self-completing pulse of the verses. But, like the other two poems just named, "When Lilacs Last in the Dooryard Bloom'd"—a string of words, D. H. Lawrence once said, that mysteriously makes the ear tingle—has to do with the relation between death and poetry. The death of Lincoln provided the occasion, and the emergent grief of an entire nation served as large but distant background. What is enacted in the foreground, however, is what so often summoned up Whitman's most genuine power: the effort to come to terms with profound sorrow by converting that sorrow into poetry. By finding the language of mourning, Whitman found the answer to the challenge of death. By focusing not on the public event but rather on the vibrations *of* that event—vibrations converted into symbols —within his private self, Whitman produced one of his master-pieces, and perhaps his last unmistakable one.

V: 1871 and Later

The transformation that both Whitman's figure and his work had slowly undergone was acknowledged by Whitman himself in his Preface to the fifth edition of *Leaves of Grass,* which had two identical printings in 1871 and 1872, while Whitman was still in Washington. The earlier editions, he said, had dealt with the *"Democratic Individual"* (the italics are his); in the new edition, he is concerned instead with the "Vast, composite, electric *Democratic Nationality."* It was never clear just what the latter entity amounted to; and in any case, Whitman was not able to make it susceptible to satisfactory poetic expression. It became the subject not of poetry but of oratory and rant—elements that had always been present in Whitman's work but that, for the most part, had hitherto been sweetened by music and, as it were, liquified by verbal sea-drift.

Oratory and rant were unhappily notable even in the most interesting of the new poems added to the 1871 edition, "Passage to India." But the case of "Passage to India" is peculiar. It was stimulated by several public events (including, for one, the open-ing of the Suez Canal), stimuli usually dangerous for Whitman unless he could instantly personalize them, as here he could not. The poem not only bespeaks the ultimate union of all times and places and peoples but finds in that condition a universal reality; and as Richard Chase has remarked, "Whenever [Whitman] headed for the universal he was headed for trouble." The poem moves swiftly away from the tough entanglements of the concrete that were the vital strength of works as different as "Song of Myself" or "Crossing Brooklyn Ferry" or "As I Ebb'd"; and, arriving at a realm of bodiless vapor, Whitman can only utter such bodiless lines as: "the past—the infinite greatness of the past!"—which is an exclamation without content. Yet "Passage to India" is interesting, because, while providing an example of Whitman's bombast, it is also technically most accomplished. It completes a kind of parabola of Whitman's craftsmanship: from 1855, where consciousness and craft were discovering each other; through 1856 and 1860, where power and technique were very closely fused; to the later sixties, where technique almost superseded content. The technique in question is primarily a manipulation of sound patterns, something too involved to be analyzed here in detail: an extremely skillful distribution of sheer sounds, without any regard for substance. "Passage to India" is interesting too, by way of historical footnote, for the obsessive effect it was to have more than fifty years later on Hart Crane. It virtually supplied the initiating force for *The Bridge,* especially for the "Atlantis" section, the first portion of his symbolist epic that Crane composed.

Whitman spent the last nineteen years of his life in Camden, New Jersey. He made a partial recovery from the stroke of 1873, but then suffered further seizures from time to time until the one that carried him off. In between these bouts, he continued to "go out" as much as he could: to nearby Philadelphia frequently, to Baltimore and Washington, to New York, and once —in 1879—to Kansas, Colorado, and Canada. Otherwise he remained in Camden, writing short and generally trivial poems, a great amount of prose, and countless letters to friends and admirers all over the world. His old age was punctuated by a series of controversies about him in the public press: in 1876, for example, when a clamor from England to raise a subscription for Whitman was countered by a verbal assault upon him in the New York *Tribune* by Bayard Taylor. The charge was almost always obscenity; in the instance mentioned, the charge only aroused the English to greater efforts, and Whitman was so encouraged as to feel, in his own word, "saved" by the contributions —then and later—of Rossetti, Tennyson, Ruskin, Gosse, Saintsbury, and others. Longfellow and Oscar Wilde, old Dr. Holmes and Henry James, Sr., were among the visitors to his Camden home. He became the genius of the city; and his birthday became an annual celebration. It was amid such flurries of support and defamation, idolatry and contempt, that the old man—cheerful and garrulous to the end—succumbed at last to a horde of diseases that would have killed most men many years sooner.

Whitman *was,* as M. Asselineau says of him, a "heroic invalid." But it may be that his physical and psychological heroism as a man was what produced, by overcompensating for the terrible discomforts he felt, the relentless optimism of so much of his writing in the last two decades—optimism not only about himself

and his condition, but about America and about history: for which
and in which every disaster, every betrayal was seen by Whitman
as a moment in the irresistible progress of things toward the
better. The "word signs" of his poetry after 1867 became, as
Whitman himself remarked in *A Backward Glance O'er Travel'd
Roads* (1888), "Good Cheer, Content and Hope," along with
"Comradeship for all lands." Those were also the words that
fixed and froze the popular understanding of the poet.

Mention of *A Backward Glance,* however, reminds one that
Whitman's most valuable work after 1867 tended to be in prose
rather than in verse. The sixth edition of *Leaves of Grass,* printed
in 1876 and called the "Centennial Edition" (America's centennial—America now being Whitman's subject), added almost
no significant new poetry; but it did include the remarkable essay
"Democratic Vistas." The latter poises a noble emphasis upon
individual integrity against the moral squalor of a society that
was already an impossible mixture of chaos and conformity; and
in its plea for "national original archetypes in literature" that
will truly "put the nation in form," it presents one of the great
statements about the relation between art and culture. The next
or seventh edition, that of 1881–82, contained the fine little image
of the copulative collision of two eagles—an image based on a
written description of such an event by Whitman's friend John
Burroughs—and a poem that, with two others, gave cause for
the suppression of the entire volume, following a complaint by
the Society for the Prevention of Vice. But this edition was also
characterized by endless revisions and expurgations and, now
especially, regroupings of earlier poems: the process whereby
the old man steadily buried his youth. In the same year, though,
Whitman also published a separate volume of prose: *Specimen
Days and Collect.* In it, along with *Specimen Days* and the several
indispensable prefaces to *Leaves of Grass,* were "Democratic
Vistas," Civil War reminiscences, and Whitman's annual lecture
on Lincoln. *A Backward Glance* first appeared in 1888; the
following year it served as the Preface to, and was the one
memorable new piece of writing in, the *Leaves of Grass* of 1889.

Though it is indeed memorable and even beguiling, *A Backward Glance* is also somewhat misleading. The real motivations
and the actual achievement of *Leaves of Grass* lie half-forgotten
behind the comradeship, good cheer, and democratic enthusiasm
of the ailing elderly bard. Like F. Scott Fitzgerald, Whitman

could have said, though one cannot imagine him doing so, that he had found his proper form at a certain moment in his career, but that he had then been diverted into other forms, other endeavors less appropriate to his talent. The fact that it was in these other forms that Whitman's reputation got established make the development more lamentable. At his best, Whitman was not really the bard of the democratic society at all; nor was he the prophet of the country's and the world's glorious future. He was, perhaps, the poet of an aesthetic and moral democracy. But he was above all the poet of the self and of the self's swaying motion —outward into a teeming world where objects were "strung like beads of glory" on his sight; backward into private communion with the "real Me." He was the poet of the self's motion downward into the abysses of darkness and guilt and pain and isolation, and upward to the creative act in which darkness was transmuted into beauty. When the self became lost to the world, Whitman was lost for poetry. But before that happened, Whitman had, in his own example, made poetry possible in America.

1961

MELVILLE AFTER *MOBY-DICK*

"Failure is the true test of greatness," Herman Melville remarked in his essay on Hawthorne (1850). He was speaking of the artist's need to risk defeat by constantly attempting more demanding and original creative enterprises; and, like Faulkner in our day, Melville always honored the daring failure over the safe success. "If it be said," he contended (half anticipating Faulkner's remark about Hemingway), "that continual success is a proof that a man wisely knows his powers, it is only to be added that, in that case, he knows them to be small." Melville must have known his own powers to be great ones: he was, at the very moment, in the midst of his most powerful work and spectacular critical failure, *Moby-Dick*. But just as he had a zest for the overreaching artistic effort, so Melville grew to have a special psychological affinity with defeat, almost a bias toward it. "Praise be to God for the failure!" is the motto of one of his slighter stories;[1] and in *The Encantadas* he located his symbol of worshipable humanity "not in the laureled victor, but in this vanquished one," Hunilla, the Chola widow. It is in a context of such affinities and beliefs that the writing here examined is to be measured.

I: Tales and Poems

For the most part, the stories and poems written after *Moby-Dick* represented new directions for Melville's imagination, new challenges to his shaping power; and they were written during what are generally regarded as Melville's long years of failure, neglect,

1. "The Happy Failure: A Story of the River Hudson" (1854).

and silence—following the large misunderstanding of *Moby-Dick* and the critical catastrophe of *Pierre* (1852). Some of the items were no doubt, as Melville said about his book-length poem *Clarel* to an English admirer, "Eminently adapted for unpopularity," given the habits and expectations of the American reading public in Melville's lifetime. But, while the imagery of defeat and of physical wreckage and spiritual ruin abounds, Melville's work after *Pierre* and in media other than the novel comprises an extraordinarily successful achievement. It is a body of work, moreover, that expresses a steadily deepening tone of authority —even, perhaps, of metaphysical and religious authority. In those buried years, Melville came to speak in all eloquence with what Scott Fitzgerald would call "the authority of failure."

Still, it is useful to approach that achievement and that authority from the moment of Melville's encounter with Nathaniel Hawthorne. They met in 1850, not long after Melville, in the immensity of his enthusiasm for *Mosses from an Old Manse,* contributed the essay on Hawthorne to the *Literary World.* Most of what Melville had to say in that essay—his metaphysical expostulations, his insight into Shakespearean tragedy, his passion for paradox as the great vehicle of truth, his search for the robustly native American writer, his sense of the fellowship of creative genius the world round—this tells us, of course, a good deal more about Melville's view of life and of art than about Hawthorne's. But as a result of "Hawthorne and his Mosses," there developed between the two men the most illuminating relationship in the history of American literature; not the less illuminating because it was strained and flawed and doomed to brevity; and not less because, although each had much to teach the other (Melville felt that "this Hawthorne has dropped germinous seeds into my soul"), the writers were in fact moving in almost exactly opposite directions.

Melville's letters chart the course of this curious friendship. "When the big hearts strike together," he wrote Hawthorne, "the concussion is a little stunning." But Melville had a more avid taste than did Hawthorne for intellectual and emotional concussion; as, one feels sure, he did for the "ontological heroics" he speaks of looking forward to enjoying with the older man. On Melville's side, the relationship reached its peak of intensity in the almost uncontrollable and mystical excitement with which he acknowledged Hawthorne's reception (evidently both discerning and sympathetic) of *Moby-Dick*. At that instant, Melville felt Hawthorne to be a "divine magnet" to whom "my magnet responds"; he felt that "the Godhead is broken up like the bread at the Supper," and that he and Hawthorne were the pieces. Hawthorne did not have the temperament to reply in kind; and in the following year, when Melville was being so savagely belabored in the press for *Pierre,* the friendship seems to have gone stale—perhaps, as one or two critics have suggested, because neither Hawthorne nor anyone else could have supplied Melville with the kind of protection and comfort he thought he needed. The last extant letter is dated November 1852; and shortly thereafter Hawthorne went abroad for a long stay. The two men met at least once again in 1856, when Melville stopped off for a few days with the Hawthornes in Liverpool; but Melville was to believe that they had been "estranged in life/ And neither in the wrong." Such was the burden of Melville's "Monody," a poem that is almost certainly Melville's obituary both to Hawthorne and to their friendship.

But, as I have said, these two enormously gifted spirits were moving in opposite directions from the moment they met; and it was only Melville's constant fascination with the mating of opposites that made any friendship at all possible between them. To begin with, Melville, in 1850, had five novels behind him (*Typee, Omoo, Mardi, Redburn,* and *Whitejacket*); he was occupied with *Moby-Dick* and after that with *Pierre;* but his novelistic aspirations were becoming ever more thwarted, and within a couple of years his energies and interests would turn decisively toward the shorter form, toward the story or tale or novella. In 1850, Hawthorne, on the other hand, was done with the shorter form; he had behind him a number of masterful stories and tales, and his endeavors in this vein had reached their climax and end in that very great novella *The Scarlet Letter;* he had, indeed, already advanced into the field of long fiction and had almost completed the first of his "novels," *The House of the Seven Gables.* By the time (in August 1852) that Melville urged Hawthorne to make a tale similar to Hawthorne's own "Wakefield," out of the "Agatha anecdote," the proposal was in every sense anachronistic. Hawthorne was right, in his evasive but kindly way, to suggest instead that Melville should undertake the thing. And Melville did, though without success; it was his first invasion of the short story, and it led swiftly enough to *Bartleby* and *The Encantadas.*

More importantly, Melville and Hawthorne congenitally moved in opposite directions of mental and imaginative inquiry: as one sentence in Melville's letter about "Agatha" reminds us. Concluding his ruminations, Melville tells Hawthorne: "You have a skeleton of actual reality to build about with fulness & veins & beauty." The remark bespeaks Melville's customary method: that of beginning with the actual, the bare bones of the case, often with the personally experienced, and then enlarging by the resources of art toward fullness and beauty. His writing at its best seems to be palpably thickening and stretching, as the actual gives birth to some breath-taking glimpse into the generalized condition of man. Melville's characteristic accomplishment (for example, in *The Encantadas*) was to move from a sort of journalistic immediacy to an exposure of some grave and permanent principle or element that must be at work (even if perniciously at work) in human experience; his creative torment was the awareness, which he often dramatized, that the effort so to expand, to enlarge, was incalculably difficult. Such, however, was neither Hawthorne's accomplishment nor his torment. Although he did of course draw upon the actual and his own experience, nonetheless, and especially in his shorter fiction, Hawthorne habitually began with some perennial human impulse and then sought for the concrete terms by which he might embody it. Hawthorne, in a word, really did approach the allegorical mode, though little that he wrote can be classed as pure allegory; but Melville, for all his allegorical hints and leanings, approached rather the form of the fable. All the difference between them can be suggested by comparing Hawthorne's "Wakefield" (which Melville so admired) and Melville's *Bartleby*. Both are accounts of self-impelled isolates; Wakefield is "the Outcast of the Universe," and Bartleby seems "alone, absolutely alone in the universe." But Hawthorne's capital letters point to a fixed type of human situation that he is, primarily, trying to illustrate; while much of the odd charm of *Bartleby* is its tantalizing escape from fixity. Bartleby remains a mystery just because he is irredeemably an individual, not finally and fully explicable by any general theory of human conduct, toward which the creative effort nonetheless inclines.

Hawthorne must have taught Melville a good deal about the formal possibilities of fiction; and his talent for the dark insinuation must have encouraged Melville in his desire (as he says about Shakespeare in the Hawthorne essay) to express the "deep far-way things in him," to probe "the very axis of reality." Hawthorne's fiction also provided Melville with the major example in America of the poetic resource by which such probing could be attempted—the resource of the complex symbol. On his part, Hawthorne was perhaps reminded by Melville of the inestimable value of the particular, the potent vitality of the immediate: certainly, *The Blithedale Romance,* the only work of fiction that Hawthorne began and completed during the years in question, is by all odds his most "realistic" work, the one most rooted in the actual. But then they moved on, in literally and physically opposite directions—Hawthorne away from the obscurity of a customs house into the bright light of quite considerable popularity; Melville away from his own considerable popularity toward the obscurity of his own eventual job as a customs inspector—and between them there fell a silence.

When Melville said in *The Encantadas* that he worshiped humanity not in the figure of the victor but in the figure of the vanquished, he was giving precise statement to the tragic sense that possessed him in the 1850s. It is a sense that communicates more directly to our own age of wholesale wreckage and defeat —when the laurels go so often and so resoundingly to the worst of men and of causes—than it did to the confident America of Melville's time. Melville, like Albert Camus (who said, via Dr. Rieux in *The Plague,* that "I feel more solidarity with the vanquished than with the saints"), found human dignity in the little dark corners of life; not among the powerful and successful, but among the oppressed, the afflicted, the defeated; among the victims of God or of nature or, simply of "things." In the character of Captain Ahab, Melville had offered a titanic image of magnificent defeat; but in the tales of the fifties, the focus was rather on the touching and forlorn.

Bannadonna, the arrogant Renaissance architect in *The Bell-Tower,* pursues his tragic course in the classical manner; he is the person of exceptional abilities and overweening pride who brings upon himself his own violent destruction. Ironically, this was the only short story of Melville's reprinted during his lifetime —reprinted twice, in fact, and once under the general title of *Little Classics: Tragedy.* Melville's genuinely classic conception of tragedy would find expression in his Civil War poetry; but in the years immediately following *Pierre,* he evinced an unclassical involvement with pathos. More representative than Bannadonna, at this time, are persons like Bartleby, "a bit of wreck in mid-Atlantic"; or Hunilla, with her tearless bleak endurance; or Jimmy Rose, transformed at a stroke from a wealthy man-about-town to a sandwich-filching parasite—"poor, poor Jimmy—God guard us all—poor Jimmy Rose!"; or the blank-looking girls in the infernal papermill, with their pallid cheeks and pale virginity; or Benito Cereno, almost literally shocked to death by his encounter with evil. Vanquished ones like these characterize Melville's collection of short stories, *The Piazza Tales* in 1856, and make incarnate in their variously pathetic ways Melville's then current estimate of life.

Instances of physical collapse or decay are often associated with these cases of human misfortune. The fall of the tower of Bannadonna in an earthquake is sheer melodrama; but elsewhere we observe the "sad disrepair" of Don Benito's ship, the *San Dominick,* which looks as though put together and launched from Ezekiel's valley of dry bones, and the awe-inspiring barrenness of the cindery Encantadas which seem to be Ezekiel's valley itself. We can watch Melville, in his letter to Hawthorne about the proposed "Agatha anecdote," lingering with mournful affection over a projected account of the slow decay of Agatha's mailbox and the post on which it stands:

> To this *post* they must come for their letters. And, of course, daily young Agatha goes—for seventeen years she goes thither daily. As her hopes gradually decay in her, so does the post itself and the little box decay. The post rots in the ground at last. Owing to its being little used—hardly used at all—grass grows rankly about it. At last a little bird nests in it. At last the post falls.

The passage does, indeed, reflect Melville's continuing taste for Gothic moldering, along with his alertness to what he called "the linked analogies"—between the concrete (the post and the box) and the soul of man (Agatha's hopes). But, at the same time, the lines quoted suggest another significant aspect—namely, the source and the nature of Melville's idea of defeat.

It is easy enough to say that Melville's sensitivity to failure in the mid-fifties was the direct consequence of his own "failure" as a novelist, after several years of considerable "success." What is important is Melville's view of just what had happened, of where the failure lay. In his view, the point was not only that his last two novels had failed to sell widely—though this was a fact of great· seriousness to him (dollars, as he said, always damned him). It was not only that American critics did not like his work, or neglected it—though Melville shared with many another American writer a much higher regard for British than for American critics and reviewers. What had really happened, Melville evidently believed, was something rather different. What had failed was an effort at communication. A recurring motif during these years, accordingly, is the motif of the undelivered letter or the misapprehended sign.

In *Benito Cereno,* both the wretched Spanish nobleman and members of his crew attempt to convey by sign language the reality of their desperate situation; and good Captain Delano fails consistently to receive their messages. Closer to the "Agatha" passage above and probably carried over from its rhetoric is the picture of the island "post-office" in *The Encantadas:*

> It may seem very strange to talk of post-offices in this barren region, yet post-offices are occasionally to be found there. They consist of a stake and a bottle. The letters being not only sealed, but corked. They are generally deposited by captains of Nantucketers for the benefit of passing fishermen, and contain statements as to what luck they had in whaling or tortoise-hunting. Frequently, however, long months and months, whole years glide by and no applicant appears. The stake rots and falls, presenting no very exhilarating subject.

A still less exhilarating subject and the most memorable example of this theme occur at the end of *Bartleby,* when the narrator reports the rumor that Bartleby had at one time worked as a subordinate clerk in the Dead Letter Office in Washington. What could be more terrible for a man prone to hopelessness like Bartleby, the narrator asks, than the business of "continually handling these dead letters, and assorting them for the flame. . . . On errands of life," he adds, appalled, "these letters speed to death."

So Melville's letters of life—his novels—had in his view of the matter sped to death, undelivered, unread by the addressee, the public; destined only to be destroyed. Melville felt that he had somehow failed to deliver the messages that shaped themselves so urgently in his imagination; and for a writer as profoundly personal and expressive as Melville, a failure of this kind was apt to be devastating. He could not—like Henry James and to some extent like Hawthorne—rest in satisfied contemplation of his own created objects; nor, once those objects were, metaphorically, destroyed, could he assuage his spirit in contemplation of the ideal that the object had made concrete—as he admires Hawthorne for seeming to say in "The Artist of the Beautiful." But what he could do, and what in these stories he did do, was to convert his sense of the failure of communication into a central fictional theme; and to make expert shorter fiction out of the failure of his longer fiction. It was a courageous undertaking indeed; and it has been properly celebrated by Hart Crane, in his poem "At Melville's Tomb," as the artistic effort by which Melville is to be identified:

> *Often beneath the waves, wide from this ledge*
> *The dice of dead men's bones he saw bequeath*
> *An embassy. Their numbers as he watched,*
> *Beat on the dusky shore and were obscured.*

Crane had to explain to his editor that his intention had been to relate the bones of dead mariners, men who failed to reach the shore alive, with "certain messages undelivered," certain experiences not finally communicated; both the bones and the messages beat on the dusky shore and get obscured. The passage is complex; but it testifies in its oblique way to an essential aspect of Melville, as well as to the sureness of Crane's understanding of it.

To formulate success and failure in terms of communication is, needless to say, to find the focus of human experience in the question of community—that is, of the relation between the individual and community. The tales of the fifties contain some of the most extreme and disturbing images of isolation that modern literature has recorded; and they are the more disturbing because, Bannadonna apart, these luckless men and women are not cut off from humanity through pride, like Ahab ("and Ahab stands alone among the millions of the peopled earth"), or through some sinful act, like Coleridge's mariner. They are rather the victims of a calamity: of a flaw in the psychological mechanism, like Bartleby; of an altogether "absurd" accident, like Hunilla; of the brutality of other men, like Benito Cereno. And, conversely, the one story in the group that breathes an air of perfect contentment is itself an image of perfect community—the account of an evening spent in a London men's club, *The Paradise of Bachelors*. This semifictional fusing of several dinners at the Elm and the Erechtheum Clubs in December 1854 is Melville's worldly, even lip-smacking counterpart to James's "The Great Good Place"; and it offers a Melvillean ideal of genial masculine companionship: "It was the very perfection of quiet absorption of good living, good drinking, good feeling, and good talk. We were a band of brothers. Comfort —fraternal, household comfort, was the grand trait of the affair." One should probably not make too much of the celibate aspect of the English Paradise; for what Melville rejoices in is less the absence of women—of the heterosexual element—than the absence of families ("You could plainly see that these easy-hearted men had no wives or children to give an anxious thought"). And, beyond that, the situation so handsomely set forth is a mode of sexless companionship, in the basic meaning of "companionship" as a deep sharing of nourishment, of both physical and spiritual bread. It is the antithesis of the situation of Bartleby and the others.

In the course of his sketches of isolation and defeat, Melville observes and dramatizes a variety of responses among those for whom there is no Erechtheum Club available. At one extreme is Don Benito, who summons up the courage to plunge out of his confinement and rejoin humanity in the friendly boat of Amasa Delano (a moment reminiscent of the scene Melville selected for special praise in *The House of the Seven Gables,* "where Clifford . . . would fain throw himself forth from the window to join the procession"); but thereafter the Spaniard yields to the horror of his experience and slides helplessly toward death. At quite another extreme is the Chola widow, that "lone shipwrecked soul," whose isolation is absolute, whose plight is the most hideous— and whose fortitude is the most enduring. Somewhere in between is the canny, unashamed adjustment of Jimmy Rose, who emerges from his spell of self-concealment after the disaster, "to crawl through life, and peep among the marbles and mahoganies for contumelious tea and toast"; and Bartleby, who, bit of unsalvageable wreckage that he is, yet continues to utter his brief refusal, who says, "No," to the end—not, "No! in thunder," as Melville imagined Hawthorne saying, but, "No," in a soft intractable undertone.

It has been sufficiently suggested, I trust, that these portraits of the vanquished and victimized are not themselves instances of *artistic* failure or of *literary* defeat. On the contrary, the tales of the fifties represent a very far reach in shorter American fiction: though we have to remove them some distance from the enormous shadow of *Moby-Dick* before their qualities become visible. *Jimmy Rose* may be not much more than an anecdote, though it is carried beyond its slender limits by a surprisingly appropriate verbal vigor. Even *The Bell-Tower,* while "literary" in a bad sense of the word, keeps stirring the edges of our imagination by the hint of a meaning (about cultural history, about race and sex) much more interesting than the moral so heavily insisted on. *The Tartarus of Maids* is a story of perhaps exaggerated reputation that threatens to bore us with the strained comedy of its sexual and anatomical allegory; but, again, the narrative tends to slip out of its frame of contrived fantasy to touch some ultimate in human, and especially in feminine, degradation, some final reduction of the female in a mechanized world to a sexless and, as it were, devaginated thing. These are stories that reward our best attention; once read, they refuse to be dislodged from their little niches in our memory. But three other stories do more than that: they add to our store of imaginative understanding and of beauty; once read, they become part of the way we look into life and appraise it. These, of course, are *Bartleby, The Encantadas,* and *Benito Cereno.*

About *Bartleby,* the least ought to be said; for it is a fable, almost a parable, something that depends, for our satisfaction, on remaining intact. It provides an image in steady slow motion of the gradual extinction of spirit, of the dissolution of all but the fact of will in a single human psyche—not the will *toward* anything, not active desire, but the faculty itself. Bartleby is a voluntary phantom, the dim underside of Captain Ahab. His thinning actuality is perceived in its contrast with the Dickensian fullness of urban life, the Wall Street office, the two volatile clerks and the impish call-boy, the busy activities of the legal profession, and the prudent and well-intentioned narrator. Seen from that vantage point of cozy normality and unquestioning conformity, Bartleby flickers with ever-decreasing light and ever-increasing mystery. The narrator's final exclamation ("Ah, Bartleby! Ah, humanity!") suggests that in the declining person of Bartleby he —and Melville—had identified some type of human character and experience; but all that has been identified is the mystery of life.

The story's mild paradox is that it is the narrator's failure to make contact with Bartleby ("It was his soul that suffered, and his soul I could not reach") that leads him to a sense of common humanity; he feels "a fraternal melancholy." A glimpse of fraternity is thus stimulated by the discovered absence thereof; what is shared is an awareness of darkness; and at the end all we know is that we know nothing.

The Encantadas offers the inquiring reader a more strenuous problem of judgment. If *Bartleby* is all compact, *The Encantadas* is all meandering sketchiness; and nothing is less clear, at first sound, than its exact tone. A contemporary reviewer referred to the work as "a series of charming descriptions," as though it were a contribution to pastoral literature; but we shall not be far wrong if we take it, instead, as a sustained and conscious exercise in the antipastoral mode. The pastoral is an account of the world in its unfallen state, as nostalgically imagined after the fact of the fall (the definition can arguably hold even for the Virgilian pastoral); but Melville's key contention here is that "In no world but a fallen one could such lands exist." *The Encantadas* is not—as was so much American writing contemporary with Melville—an artistic transformation of the actual and fallen world; it is an extension of it. It surveys a certain terrain and certain objects and experiences to conclude, as Cardinal Newman once concluded after surveying human history, that the data collected showed the human race must be "implicated in some terrible and aboriginal calamity."

Melville searches the islands for signs of the absolute consequences of just such an aboriginal calamity; as Charles Darwin, by a suggestive coincidence, had earlier explored the same islands for material to use in his study of the biological rise of man. Indeed, Melville's sketches of the Galapagos archipelago (a thick cluster of islands some six hundred miles west of Ecuador) are at once a scientific description, in the Darwinian manner, and an adumbration of the moral and social world that is the so-called civilized home of modern man. That home is kept present to our minds by the story's allegorical tendency (we should not use a stronger word), which is indicated throughout by the quotations from Melville's favorite allegorical poem, *The Faerie Queene,* and finds its most vivid expression in the hallucination at the end of Sketch First, when a "scene of social merriment" seems to fade into a scene of lonely, haunted woods, and the representative of the Encantadas, a gigantic tortoise, crawls across the ballroom floor. Not only the tortoise with his reminder of mortality, but equally the heroic Hunilla, the Calibanesque Oberlus, the pirates and ghosts and lizards, the "runaways, castaways, solitaries, gravestones etc.": all these beings (Melville suggests) inhabit not only the faraway Galapagos, as a matter of scientific fact; they also inhabit—metaphorically—our modern civilization, they inhabit our drawing rooms, they inhabit our personalities.

The power of *The Encantadas,* in short, derives—as so often with Melville—from its linked analogies, from the creative relation between the abundant concrete and the range of moral and psychological and metaphysical implication. No work of Melville's is so close in its narrative strategy to *Moby-Dick,* a book that was once also praised for being, so to speak, a charming description of whaling voyages. In *Moby-Dick,* we have the leisurely and thorough account of whaling, its history and geography and folklore, the exact dimensions of the various species of whales and their heads and members, the techniques of harpooning; so, in *The Encantadas,* we attend to the skimpily known history of the islands, the reports of visiting frigates, the names and dates of the chief authorities, a survey of the landscape and of plant and animal life, the blurry reports of settlements, uprisings, and freebooting. Like *Moby-Dick,* too, the shorter work—while, similarly, throwing off a steady shower of allegorical sparks—gathers dramatic momentum and bursts into a sudden new vitality toward the end. The dramatic focus of *The Encantadas* is the successive appearances and stories of the Chola Widow Hunilla and the Hermit Oberlus in Sketches Eighth and Ninth, a pairing of images in a sort of dyptich.[2] The opposite possibilities they represent have already been stated fairly flatly at the opening of Sketch Second, where, speaking of the tortoise, Melville remarks that "dark and melancholy as it is up the back, [it] still possesses a bright side. . . . Enjoy the bright . . . but be honest, and don't deny the black. Neither should he, who cannot turn the tortoise from its natural position . . . for that cause declare the creature to be one total inky blot" (compare this with the "Try-Works"

2. The word "dyptich" (which means, of course, a two-paneled painting) has been used by commentators to describe the fictional work in which Melville sets opposite anecdotes or symbols side by side under a dual title. There are several such among the stories of the fifties, *The Paradise of Bachelors* and *The Tartarus of Maids* being perhaps the most memorable.

meditation in *Moby-Dick*). Hunilla and Oberlus were in fact actual human beings, one a Peruvian and the other an Irishman; they come to us as living individuals; but within the prepared atmosphere of allegory they also enlarge into symbols of the human potential—that of grandeur amid defeat and that of bestial degradation. Hunilla, utterly alone except for her dogs and the transient brigands by whom she has been periodically assaulted, embodies what there is of spiritual brightness in the grim hell of the actual; Oberlus has become an animal and an isolate by choice.

Opposition, to speak colloquially, was Melville's middle name; and contrariety is no less central in *Benito Cereno*. Here we have one of modern literature's great enactments of the greatest of all oppositions, to the perennial eye of the poet: that between appearance and reality—concretely, between the apparent situation on board the *San Dominick*, the apparent relation between black man and white man, between slave and master, obedience and command; and the reality of all that. Melville's handling of his story—wherein the slow-witted, kindhearted American, Amasa Delano, boards the Spanish ship, explores it, talks with the Captain and his Negro "servant" Babo, and departs without ever gaining more than the most fleeting impression of the truth—has been much praised. The protective innocence of Delano has been analyzed, and the depths of Babo (the slave who has in fact seized command by means of horrifying violence) have been sounded with various psychological instruments. Melville's exploitation of the element of color in this story has likewise been admired; and his creative techniques studied by comparing the novella to its easily available source in Delano's *Narrative of Voyages and Travels*. But another aspect is still worth considering—that is, whether and how the central opposition is "resolved."

Superficially, the resolution occurs when the narrative of the apparent situation—presented through the undiscerning eyes of Amasa Delano—is followed by the narrative of what had really happened, in the deposition made by the ailing Don Benito at the court in Lima, during the trial of the Negroes. That legal document has caused critical trouble and has resulted, for example, in a hostile verdict on *Benito Cereno* by Newton Arvin, in the best critical study of Melville yet written. The charge is that the deposition is a dry letdown after the murky excitements of the longer section that precedes it, and that in any case Melville had shirked his artistic responsibility by bringing in the (actual) court

t Penn Warren has remarked (*Selected Essays*) in the
on we have of Melville as a poet, while "it must be
at he did not learn his craft, the point is that the craft
earn was not the same craft which some of his more
rtised contemporaries did learn with such glibness of
complacency of spirit." Glibness and complacency
rt in the disturbed, often awkward but sometimes
oetry that Melville wrote out of so much of his craft
manage to acquire.

, the characteristic effect of his best poetry, like that of
rose, is that of a struggle with incompatible materials
ctable language suddenly releasing an insight and an
remarkable poise and beauty. But it was too compound
, too dependent on contrariety, to appeal to Melville's
oraries; *Battle-Pieces,* though not entirely overlooked,
ost indifferent success. Melville's poetic achievement is of
that the present generation, because of historic experience
tical fashions, has learned to appreciate; for it derived
n imagination alert to paradox and contradiction and to
ge mythic action detectable amid the jostling immediacies
That was the imagination summoned to a supreme creative
by the supreme contradiction of a Civil War. It was not only
such, it was fratricidal war, the condition of a whole people
desperate battle with itself, that galvanized the poetic genius
man for whom communal fraternity was so potent an ideal.
s fratricidal war, moreover, seen as a tragic drama of deeply
tional quality and of mythic importance. It was because he
nvisioned the war and because, in *Battle-Pieces,* he gave shape
substance to his vision that Melville deserves to be called *the*
l War poet.

he contrast with Whitman and his *Drum-Taps* is worth paus-
over, since between them Melville and Whitman examined in
etry the two great aspects of the war. The poetry that came out
Whitman's front-line experiences and his service in the military
spitals in Washington is not, strictly speaking, war poetry; it is,
ther, wound poetry, the poetry of hurt, of pain and courage, of
ve and healing and death. *Drum-Taps* records the war in its
nmediate and fragmentary effects upon the bodies and spirits
f individual soldiers, and in its moments of comradeship in the
amp or on the march. Melville, in *Battle-Pieces,* looked at the
errible course of events from a much greater distance; and as the

testimony and laying it down flat in his pages. As to the letdown, the deposition will probably prove engrossing enough, if read without prejudice. But as to the artistic problem, the documentary pages may well comprise one of Melville's happiest strokes. For Melville's point in thus juxtaposing these two so different narrative modes and voices is this: *that neither version of the events contains the truth.* No reader doubts that Delano's version is false, that he got everything wrong way round; but we should recognize, I think, that Benito Cereno's version is equally flawed by an inadequacy of perception, equally remote from the whole reality of the adventure. The remoteness, in the second case, is conveyed precisely by the language of the deposition—by those abstractions of the legal vocabulary that evade all contact with the blood and stuff of experience. We are presumably intended to accept the Spaniard's statements of the external facts, the process of revolt and of massacre, the names and numbers of those that killed or were killed. But for Melville facts were not truth and, wrongly handled, could be an obstacle to truth. The Spaniard was quite unequipped by his aristocratic temperament to grasp the motives at work, the raging desire of the Negroes for freedom, the murderous animosity that slavery begot in them; as Captain Delano was unequipped by his temperament to grasp the force and presence of evil. Neither narrative, accordingly, rises to the truth of the affair; and yet this is a curious instance of two wrongs making a right—or, rather, of two falsehoods making a truth between them. As our minds play back and forth between the two versions, we find each making us more and more aware of what is false in the other. And so the truth comes finally into view, as contained in the continuing tension between alternate versions, in a subtly and knowingly unresolved duplicity.[3]

Another complaint against *Benito Cereno* is an alleged lack of political morality on Melville's part: as though he had failed to indicate sympathy with the Negroes' lust for freedom; as though he were blind to the evil of slavery. But it is Don Benito who is blind to that evil, not Melville. Melville was profoundly aware not only of the slavery issue but of its ambiguities and complexities,

3. Much the same view of *Benito Cereno* has been made persuasively by Allen Guttmann in "The Enduring Innocence of Captain Amasa Delano," *Boston University Studies in English,* 5 (Spring, 1961).

and his awareness is conveyed in a doubleness of narrative mode whereby moral guilt and moral myopia are subtly distributed to all participants in the drama. It can be noted, meanwhile, how frequent is the theme of insurrection in the tales of the fifties; the notion of revolt pressed hard upon Melville's imagination. In addition to the bloody uprising of the slaves in *Benito Cereno,* we recall the mutiny of the lawless mariners against the Dog-King, in Sketch Seventh of *The Encantadas.* Bartleby himself is a sort of passive, unconquerable *homme révolté.* And though, in the uncannily prophetic climax of *The Bell-Tower,* it is the machine that mysteriously turns on the man and destroys him, Melville supplied a motto for the story that points to the analogy intended and relates *The Bell-Tower* unexpectedly and very closely to *Benito Cereno:* "Like negroes, these powers own man sullenly; mindful of their higher master; while serving, plot revenge." More generally still, Melville—as I have been stressing on almost every page—was singularly attuned to conflict as the very definition of experience; to opposition and ambiguity intensifying betimes into frightful collision, and with neither side (to adopt his remark about Hawthorne and himself) altogether in the wrong. No American writer was better prepared to measure the full significance of the quarrel over slavery that led to rebellion and, in 1861, grew into armed conflict with the outbreak of the national Civil War.

But if he was prepared to take its measure, he was only partially prepared to express his understanding of the conflict in the literary genre to which he was now turning—the genre of lyric and narrative poetry. After the failure of *Pierre,* Melville had applied himself to the shorter fictional form; now, after another effort in the longer mode (*The Confidence-Man,* 1857) and another critical and financial failure, he abandoned prose fiction completely and wrote nothing but poetry until, more than thirty years later, he came back to prose for the last time to write that rusty masterpiece, *Billy Budd.*

To be sure, the poetry Melville began to compose in the late fifties was not the very first he had ever attempted. There is evidence that he had tried his hand at verse at least two decades earlier, while the first of his extant poems date from 1849 in the semisatirical poetastings of *Mardi.* But it was in 1859 that his wife wrote guardedly to her mother: "Herman has taken to writing poetry. You need not tell any one, for you know how such

things get around."[4] Jo
ville wrote his sea-capta
[sic] & secret enemy of y
that Tom "had begun to t
sonnet-writing." Melville
himself had been innocen
voyage after which the rum
his brother's guest aboard 7
heard discussing poetry and
light night," as he said in the s
three cables' length of [my] v
presumably among those late
long narrative poem *Clarel* in
the heading "Fruit of Travel c
Timoleon in 1891. But anothe
Melville indicates the source of
"Do you want to hear about the v
McClellan is now within fifteen n
mond. . . . But when the *end*—the
tion is coming, who knows." It was
to General Grant three years late
Melville was to say, to an entire volu
in 1866 as *Battle-Pieces and Aspects*

The author of *Battle-Pieces* had, t
the writing of poetry. But it was a pa
no more than any other gifted contemp
on an established native poetic craft, up
tions and resources he could possess hi
his own purpose. By the early 1860s, Am
worse, not better. After the limited yet
Emerson and Thoreau, the superb but
Emily Dickinson, and the magnificent ach
Whitman (a poet Melville seems not yet to
the evidence is unclear), American poetry w
arts into the dreary decades of dehydrated io
Europeanized sentimentality from which it wo
near the turn of the century, by Edwin Arling

4. Cf. Mrs. Melville again to her mother in 1875:
to *any one* that he is writing poetry [i.e., *Clarel*]—
things spread, and he would be very angry if he knew
and of course I have not except in confidence to you a

final sentence of his prose supplement to the volume declares, he saw the war as a "great historic tragedy" which he prays "may not have been enacted without instructing our whole beloved country through terror and pity." That last phrase tells us that by "tragedy" Melville had in mind something thoroughly specific and traditional: a catastrophe of immense significance, with a traditional rhythm and (so he prays) a traditional outcome. But by referring to the war as a "great *historic* tragedy," Melville was no less precisely locating the area of its tragic action: which was not only, not primarily in what happened to the bodies and spirits of individual soldiers, but in what happened to the body and spirit of "our whole beloved country." The tragic hero of *Battle-Pieces* is America itself.

Battle-Pieces as a whole, therefore, may be thought of as a tragic drama expanding in the direction of a tragic epic, where the fate not of an individual but of an entire nation is fearfully at stake—though an epic composed of more or less separate lyric and narrative poems of varying length and uneven merit. Most of those poems deal with particular moments in the war, but before getting down to particulars Melville establishes a vast setting that reaches almost to a totality of space and time (as epic poets habitually frame their human action in a huge perspective of history and of the gods). He begins with the ominous image (in "The Portent") of the future veiling its face, even as the hangman's cap veils the face of John Brown; goes on to musings about "The tempest bursting from the waste of Time/ On the world's fairest hope linked with man's foulest crime" ("Misgivings"); and from those clashing superlatives proceeds to a sort of absolute spatial and temporal reference in the apocalyptic vision ("The Conflict of Convictions") of "strong Necessity . . . heap[ing] Time's strand with wrecks," of an event so large and convulsive that the very gulfs will bare their "slimed foundations"—whereafter, *perhaps,* "the throes of ages" may "rear/ The final empire and the happier world." But perhaps the dire opposite will come to pass, perhaps "power unanointed may come"—sheer power without grace— and an America that has become mighty by abandoning the dream of its founders. Meanwhile, behind the historic American struggle, Satan and Raphael are glimpsed in the background carrying on their timeless war between evil and good.

Within so universal a context and with such grand alternatives in the offing, the actualities of the war and its aftermath are then dramatized in roughly chronological order, from 1860 through April 1866. After the cosmic tonalities of the opening poems, Melville narrows his focus to the first march into Virginia; to land battles, such as Shiloh, Malvern Hill, the Wilderness; naval battles, such as those involving the *Temeraire;* the draft riots in New York in July 1863 ("The House-top," a powerfully impressive poem); the experience of the prison camp; the fall of the southern capital; the emancipated slave; the returning soldiers and those who failed to return ("The Slain Collegians" from north and south alike); retrospective memorial verses; the confrontation of the postwar American world and an urgent plea for understanding and reconciliation.

We make out—amid these vivid, shocking, and somber particulars—a steadily unfolding "action" of a very familiar kind. It is a movement from youth to age, from innocence to experience, from hope to horror, from life to death; with rebirth, new knowledge and a renewal of hope rather prayed for than affirmed at the end. It is the entire country, as I have said, that is passing through this multiple movement—the country sometimes seen in its manyness, as a northerner or a southerner, a college-boy officer or a dead soldier, a prisoner or a slave, sometimes seen in its oneness, as in the poem called "America" which concluded *Battle-Pieces* proper (before the so-called memorial verses) and which rehearses a good part of this action. But we find a synecdoche of the whole process, an enactment in small, in the last stanza of "The March into Virginia":

> *But some who this blithe mood present,*
> *As on in lightsome files they fare,*
> *Shall die experienced ere three days be spent—*
> *Perish, enlightened by the vollied glare.*

Among other things, the lines testify to a movement from romantic illusion to violent disenchantment, as the young men who marched away "with fifes, and flags in mottoed pageantry" ("Ball's Bluff"), while "The banners play, the bugles call/ The air is blue and prodigal" come up against the reality of the guns on the battlefield. But even more than disenchanted, the young men, in Melville's phrasing, are *experienced* and *enlightened.* The former word reminds us that Melville saw the progress of those chivalric soldiers in the familiar terms he had already dramatized in his fiction; as a development from innocence to experience. The second italicized word, which Melville uses with all the cunning of a metaphysical poet, indicates that in the present instance (as in the case of *Pierre* but not that of *Redburn*), Melville looked upon the development as tragic. For the word "enlightened" not only contrasts ironically with the "lightsome" manner of departure, and not only images the literal and physical lighting up of the scene by the cannon-fire, at the moment of death. It combines both effects with the notion of spiritual illumination, the awareness kindled by experience; and it is, thus, a Shakespearean pun that confirms a Shakespearean sense of tragic action—a catastrophe which, even as it occurs, begets a new perception.

The same traditionally tragic idea—the idea of enlightenment bred out of horror and death either witnessed or experienced—appears at many turns in *Battle-Pieces*. In "The College Colonel," after the splendid simile of the regimental remnant filing home like castaway sailors crawling ashore,[5] Melville goes on to contrast the searing new consciousness of the young officer with the shouts of the welcoming crowds and the wreaths thrown at him from the gay balconies. It is not, Melville says, a mode of self-pity; though he has lost a leg and his arm is in splints, nonetheless "self he has long disclaimed." It is rather an insight into a more general and more terrible truth, the truth that came to him in the Wilderness and the field hospitals; the kind of truth Ishmael arrives at in *Moby-Dick* when he discovers that, although the visible spheres were formed in love, the invisible spheres were formed in fright. A similar point is made abruptly by another brilliantly exploited word in "Shiloh," where, in parentheses, Melville exclaims, "What like a bullet can undeceive!"—not merely kill, but educate; instruct the soul by the removal of illusion. The education achieved in death by the soldiers at Shiloh is what Melville prays will be achieved by "our whole beloved country," when, in the supplement he expresses his wish that "the great historic tragedy may not have been enacted without *instructing"* America "through terror and pity."

Instructed, one notices, not only through terror, but through terror and pity; not only made aware of the horror that lies close to the heart of experience, but simultaneously ennobled by compassion for suffering humanity. By the end of the Civil War, Mel-

5. "Their mates dragged back and seen no more" in the second stanza of "The College Colonel" is probably the immediate Melvillean source of Hart Crane's poem "At Melville's Tomb," quoted above, p. 43.

ville had in fact somewhat revised the formula he had attributed to Ishmael in *Moby-Dick*. He felt now that, if one could indeed penetrate through love to fright, one might also move beyond the discovered fright to a new form of love. The soldiers at Shiloh who were enemies in the morning become friends at eve, as they lie dead together: this is the final accomplishment of the undeceiving bullet. And the collegians who "went from the North and came from the South" as mortal foes end up by lying down "midway on a bloody bed," like lovers after the battle. "Woe for the homes of the North," Melville sighs; and then, after a typographically indicated pause, "And woe for the seats of the South:/ *All* who felt life's spring in prime . . . All lavish hearts *on whichever side"* (italics added).

One of the great qualities of *Battle-Pieces* is its powerful rise toward a comprehensive pity; toward the conviction that, however foul a crime slavery may have been, nonetheless of the two parties to the struggle, of the two halves of America that had been "estranged in life" (again to quote the poem on Hawthorne), neither had been completely in the wrong. "Calvin's creed"— that is, the doctrine of natural depravity—is as much "corroborated" by the northern draft riots (in "The House-top") as by southern slavery; and Melville's sympathy and admiration for the southerners increases through his description of Stonewall Jackson and Sherman's march through Georgia. It is in the intensity of his hope that all America may be so moved, so educated through terror to a new and durable sense of fraternal love, that Melville—after the expressed grief over "all lavish hearts" quoted above—concludes *Battle-Pieces* proper with "America." Here, in a dream of hope, he sees a dead America, a composite of all the dead at Shiloh and Malvern Hill and the other battlefields, returning to "promoted life." The reborn country—so runs the dream— will have been purified through suffering; will have acquired through pain a sobering knowledge; will have reached a certain wisdom that henceforth will ballast its hope. America will represent "youth matured for age's seat"—for, like so many individual heroes in the fiction of Melville and his contemporaries, America itself will have at last grown up.

An America so matured—"its lashings charmed and malice reconciled," to quote once more from Hart Crane's poem— would, for Melville, be like the greatest of poems. In Melville's view, every great poem, like every other genuine work of art, resulted from the artist's struggle to harmonize opposites; every poem involved a sort of creative Civil War. Such is the burden of the remarkable little poem called "Art": where Melville declares that the creation of "pulsed life" and the achievement of form require that "unlike things must meet and mate"; and where, after giving some examples of the meeting of unlike things (love and hate, audacity and reverence, and so on), he concludes:

> *These must mate,*
> *And fuse with Jacob's mystic heart,*
> *To wrestle with the angel—Art.*

Every conflict man endures, accordingly, is analogous to the conflict involved in the creative process; and vice versa. Almost everything that Melville ever wrote—since it was a confrontation of contraries—can thus be taken as a paradigm of the struggle of the artist.

We should keep those burgeoning analogies in mind as we consider the poetry of Melville published after *Battle-Pieces. Clarel* apart, Melville saw to the publication of two privately financed and printed volumes (twenty-five copies each) in the last three years of his life: *John Marr and Other Sailors* in 1888, and *Timoleon* in 1891. The former consisted of twenty-five "sea-pieces," to use Melville's phrase, written during the years when Melville earned his small living as a customs inspector on the New York docks—an appointment he was forced to accept in the year *Battle-Pieces* appeared, 1866. "The Maldive Shark" and "The Berg" were included in *John Marr*. Of the forty-two items in *Timoleon,* a little more than half seem to have been written in the relatively few months remaining to Melville after he was able to retire from the customs job in 1887; among these were "After the Pleasure Party," "In a Garret," "Art," "Shelley's Vision," and "Fragments of a Lost Gnostic Poem." The rest of the book consisted of verses collected under the subtitle "Fruit of Travel of Long Ago" and were presumably written as an immediate result of Melville's travels in Europe and the Near East in the late '50s; "In a Bye-Canal," "Milan Cathedral," and "Greek Architecture" form a part of this group. But a good many of Melville's poems—such as "The Rusty Man," the two Camoens pieces, and "Pontoosuce"—were not published until the Constable Edition of 1924. All in all, Melville's shorter poems comprise a volume of considerable bulk. And when we add to it *Clarel* and finally the novella *Billy Budd* (the latter also not published till 1924), we find in the literary production of Melville's last decades a body of work of great richness, power, and variety—and something that belies the usual impression of long lingering years of creative silence on Melville's part. Melville was a practicing writer quite literally till the day he died.

But he was a writer steadily given to meditation about the drama of creativity, about the nature of the art-work, about the dilemmas of the artist. The first of these provides the subject both of "Art" and "In a Garret"—the key words of each of which are, respectively, "grapple" and "wrestle": robust verbs to suggest the strenuous difficulty of the enterprise, the agony of creation. "Milan Cathedral" and "Greek Architecture" are among several poems in which Melville associates the grand work of art with religious worship, or reverence for the transcendental "idea." Elsewhere, Melville addresses himself to the figure of the artist by taking on the guise of other poets: in "Shelley's Vision," for example, and in the double salute to the sixteenth-century Portuguese writer, Luis de Camoens, whose epic, the *Lusiads,* had so invigorating an effect on Melville's two epic endeavors, *Moby-Dick* and *Battle-Pieces.*

A more characteristic Melvillean statement about the artist, however, may be found slightly hidden beneath the apparent subjects of "The Maldive Shark," "In a Bye-Canal," and "The Berg." For here we encounter again Melville's conviction that the artist must risk disaster by facing up constantly to new challenges. Like the pilot fish, he must be willing, metaphorically, to "lurk in the port of [the maldive shark's] serrated teeth," and find "asylum in the jaws of the Fates." Melville felt, with all justice, that he had done so; and in "In a Bye-Canal," he could claim:

> *Fronted I have, part taken the span*
> *Of portents in nature and peril in man.*
> *I have swum—I have been*
> *'Twixt the whale's black flukes*
>   *and the white shark's fin.*

It is one of the most effective passages in Melville's poetry, or any other nineteenth-century poet; the entire stanza should be read as a superbly compressed chapter of autobiography. But Melville knew that anyone, artist or man, who tried to swim " 'twixt the whale's black flukes/ and the white shark's fin" risked total de-struction; and "The Berg" is a tough-worded dream image of such an event. Yet behind it one feels the force of Melville's persistent belief that, as he said in his essay on Hawthorne, failure —however disastrous—is the true test of greatness.

All these poems bring other highly animated themes into play with the theme of art—for instance, in "The Berg," the idea of nature itself as lumpish, lumbering and, especially, deadly indif-ferent in its massive destructiveness. But probably the richest concatenation of themes appears in what is in other respects as well Melville's finest lyric poem, "After the Pleasure Party." In this easily misunderstood work, preoccupations with art, science, religion, sexual love, and celibacy—each element in various modes—mingle together; and thematic language from other poems turns up here in vitalizing new contexts. The phrase "en-lightened, undeceived" takes us back to "The March into Vir-ginia" and "Shiloh," and to the notion of education through the shocking experience. The line "Few matching halves here meet and mate" echoes the poem "Art" so strikingly as to suggest an intimacy approaching equivalence between the sexual dilemma (the immediate reference here) and the creative dilemma. Despite these guideposts, however, "After the Pleasure Party" is worth a slightly extended look.

The title is itself a mild play on words. "Pleasure party" is a now archaic colloquialism roughly equal to "picnic"; but juxta-posed with the meditation on sexual passion that follows, the word "pleasure" takes on a strongly erotic overtone. The poem's construction, much reduced, is this: after a day's outing on the slopes overlooking the northern Mediterranean, a mature woman who had devoted herself to the intellectual life reflects on the relative value of her celibate devotion to knowledge as against the enjoyment of heterosexual love; for she has been greatly aroused by another member of the party, and has experienced a storm of jealousy over a pretty peasant girl on whom her loved one had looked with obviously physical desire. The woman's tormented interior monologue continues for twelve stanzas. It is followed by two stanzas in which the poet comments directly. Then the monologue is resumed, as at another time and place, in stanza fifteen. The poem concludes with ten last lines of rumina-tion by the poet, and his plea to all virgins to pray for "Urania" and to beware lest, in their virginity, they too offend the love god.

By referring to his troubled heroine as Urania, the goddess of astronomy, Melville evidently intends to indicate the woman's particular scientific profession—she had for long peered through the "reaching ranging tube," the telescope, at such constellations as Cassiopeia. The allusion to "Vesta struck with Sappho's smart" does not mean that this virginal intellectual has been stirred by Lesbian passion; the object of her love is quite plainly (in stanzas eight and nine) a "He," whose presence has the effect upon her of the young person in Sappho's famous ode ("Like to a god" etc.). She compares herself as a "plain lone bramble"—who can yet thrill to the spring—with the allegedly sly girl whose "buds were strung" on briars; and this "floral" imagery reaches its climax in the wonderfully shameless eroticism of the Marvellian couplet: "I'd buy the veriest wanton's rose/ Would but my bee therein repose." As the poem proceeds, the meditation enlarges from the particular incident and the particular erotic surge into a general puzzlement about the fact of sex—or, better, the mystery of sex and its division. And finding that "fair studies charm no more," the woman sets off in search of some other source of physical and spiritual peace, contemplating the convent life and then praying instead to an "armed Virgin," "mightier one," to protect her against the bodily urges the vengeful Amor continues to visit upon her. "Fond appeal," Melville concludes with cleareyed compassion; for there is no escape from the "sexual feud" that "clogs the aspirant life."

The above remarks are merely introductory to this very remarkable poem, and scarcely touch its subtle density of language and symbol—for example, the way the woman's dream of being "throned" alongside Cassiopeia (mythologically, a queen) leads to the realization that in fact she is more like an idiot in a cell "crowned" with straw rather than gold; that she has, so to speak, been uncrowned by sex, so that Melville can later say in parentheses that Rome is a suitable place for her since Rome is "for queens discrowned a congruous home." Nor is there space to inspect the elaborating contrast between pagan and Christian religion and religious art. One can only observe that in "The Pleasure Party," as elsewhere, Melville does not attempt to resolve the fierce contradictions his poem introduces. He holds them in balance, matching and mating them in a form, a pulsed created life that, for Melville, was the perennial ambition of art. Such a form was art's way of representing the ultimate nature of reality, which, as he says in "Pontoosuce" (sometimes called "The Lake"), is itself a mating of opposites, a "warmth and chill of wedded life and death." "Pontoosuce," like "The Pleasure Party," is one of the poems wherein Melville presents his vision of the final truth about things, the very core of his tragically achieved understanding. When we have read works like these and reached that core, we are prepared to alternate Melville's own name with the name of Shakespeare in the final stanza of " 'The Coming Storm' ":

No utter surprise can come to him
Who reaches Shakespeare's core;
That which we seek and shun is there—
Man's final lore.

1962

II: *The Confidence-Man*

The action of this most deceptive and carefully composed of Melville's novels takes place on the first of April, between dawn and midnight on the Feast of All Fools; and by a startling coincidence the book was published on the first of April, in the year 1857. Melville had finished *The Confidence-Man* the summer before, and he was by this date staying at the Hotel Luna in Venice, nearing the end of a long trip through England, the Middle East, and Italy. Very possibly, he was at work on one of the two poems about Venice (the second being the superb lyric "In a Bye-Canal") that he would eventually include in the volume of verses called *Timoleon*. He had, anyhow, already turned from fiction to poetry, and with a kind of finality; until the novella *Billy Budd* more than thirty years later, Melville's statement of the rendingly opposed forces that beset his imagination would find expression only in lyric and narrative poetry. His portrait of a "flock of fools, under this captain of fools, in this ship of fools" —to borrow the wooden-legged passenger's acerbic and echoing words (chapter iii)—thus marked the end of the great fictional period. It had begun in 1846 with *Typee* and reached its apogee with *Moby-Dick* in 1851; had continued through *Pierre* in 1852, *Israel Potter* in 1855, and the remarkable tales of the mid-fifties. Now, by way of rehearsing what he had learned and of displaying the skills he had acquired during that period, Melville, in a mood oddly blended of comedy and controlled ferocity, explored for one final time the human world he had lived through. *The Confidence-Man* was also the last of Melville's writings to gain critical attention. But commentary, if it started late, has in recent years become torrential; it is by now excessive in range and discord of opinion even for Melville criticism. Extraordinary claims have been made for it, extraordinary hostility voiced against it; and extraordinary theories propounded to account for it.[6] Certainly it is not an easy book to read. At first glance, it seems rather to bulge and thicken than to progress; one has the impression of a number of dimly identifiable persons who simply "talk and keep talking," as the character known as the cosmopolitan once puts it; and who "still stand where [they] did." But it is an almost irresistibly easy book to reread. The second or third time round the deck, one enjoyably makes out a good deal of the intricate pattern of the Confidence Man's tricks, disguises, and sophistics. One also makes out something at least of the deeply meaningful artistic trickery of Melville, as he moves his picaresque protagonist through the series of encounters aboard the river steamer named with such apt inaptness the *Fidèle* on that long April day.

The Confidence-Man is in some sort a satire, but of a peculiar variety. Its titular hero, for example, is the agent and source of satire, rather than—as in Voltaire's *Candide,* with which it has been misleadingly compared—the incarnate object or victim of it. The object of the satire, indeed, is hard to determine. In one of the few extant letters that refer to *The Confidence-Man,* Melville reported (September 15, 1857) that he was looking about for "a good, earnest subject" for a lecture, and offered the following underscored possibility: *"Daily Progress of man towards a state of intellectual & moral perfection."* No doubt that recurring

6. Critical opinions up to 1954 have been collected and examined by Elizabeth S. Foster in the invaluable introduction to her own definitive edition of the novel. A second round-up through 1961 has been made by Daniel G. Hoffman in *Form and Fable in American Fiction;* Mr. Hoffman adds some stimulating suggestions drawn from his knowledge of such archetypal figures in American writing as the devil and the confidence man. Among still more recent studies, one should mention H. Bruce Franklin's *The Wake of the Gods,* which argues the case for Hindu mythology as the key to the novel's structure and meaning.

American illusion is being detonated by the book; but only as it existed in the minds of readers in the nation at large, or as it was being noisily asserted in the hustings. Virtually no one of the *Fidèle's* passengers believes in man's moral progress, least of all the Confidence Man. He proclaims it only as a part of his strategy, which resembles the strategy suggested later by Huey Long (a striking modern and real-life descendant of Melville's complex hero); Long, it will be recalled, once said that when fascism came to America, it would come in the guise of antifascism. Misanthropy likewise enters the world of Melville's novel in the guise of its opposite, philanthropy. (In the same way, the Confidence Man, a master of irony and a brilliant satirist, denounces both those modes of discourse—"never could abide irony," he says to Pitch; "something Satanic about irony. God defend me from Irony, and Satire, his bosom friend." And in the midst of his dizzying changes of costume and personality, he pauses to inveigh against inconsistency of character.) Within the novel, a belief in human perfectibility is not an active illusion; it is one of many masks or hypocrisies. And the book's emergent theme, as I shall hope to show, is the theme of charity.

If *The Confidence-Man* should thus be initially distinguished from *Candide,* it is the recognizable and awe-inspiring ancestor of several subsequent works of fiction in America: Mark Twain's "The Man Who Corrupted Hadleyburg" and *The Mysterious Stranger,* for example; and, more recently, Nathanael West's *The Day of the Locust,* Faulkner's *The Hamlet,* Ralph Ellison's *Invisible Man,* John Barth's *The Sot-Weed Factor,* Thomas Pynchon's *V.* Melville bequeathed to those works—in very differing proportions—the vision of an apocalypse that is no less terrible for being enormously comic, the self-extinction of a world characterized by deceit and thronging with impostors and masqueraders, and the image of the supreme tempter (the "super-promiser," as West called him) on the prowl through that world, assisting it toward its promised end. These books and others comprise the continuing "anti-face" of the American dream, the continuing imagination of national and even universal disaster that has accompanied the bright expectancy of the millennium. It is a vast prospect, either way; and *The Confidence-Man* announces at the start the vastness, indeed the totality, of its scope. It will deal, we are told, with nothing less than the entire human race.

After the brief, puzzling view of a flaxen-haired deaf-mute, whose arrival (to which I shall return) coincides with the rumor that "a mysterious impostor from the East" may also be coming aboard the steamer, the narrative turns to inspect the horde of passengers and sees them as including "all kinds of that multiform species, man." They are compared to "Chaucer's Canterbury pilgrims" and to "those Oriental ones crossing the Red Sea towards Mecca;" for a while we are allowed to suppose that these mid-western and mid-century Americans may be intended to resemble the members of St. Augustine's Pilgrim City, the great community of the faithful moving through this earthly world en route to the heavenly and eternal City of God. But we are soon enough disturbed by the awful suspicion that the pilgrim species of this novel is heading in quite an opposite direction.

To chart the course of the pilgrimage, we can begin by noticing the characteristic direction of the book's *prose:* observing what dark periods and unsettling climaxes the prose habitually moves toward. *The Confidence-Man,* I have been trying to insist, is a novel, and should be read as such, rather than as a philosophical dialogue or a contribution to intellectual history (though, like most of Melville's writings, it contains important ingredients of both). It is a novel, moreover, that wears the mask of comedy: primarily, as Melville suggests at the end of the first of several fascinating reflections on the art of fiction (chapter xiv), a "comedy of thought." But the comic technique serves to draw us on through intellectual laughter to something like intellectual panic. Consider, for instance, the description of the woman Goneril, in the story about her in chapter xii:

> Goneril was young, in person lithe and straight, too straight, indeed, for a woman, a complexion naturally rosy, and which would have been charmingly so, but for a certain hardness and bakedness, like that of the glazed colors on stone-ware. Her hair was of a deep, rich chestnut, but worn in close, short curls all round her head. Her Indian figure was not without its impairing effect upon her bust, while her mouth would have been pretty but for a trace of moustache. Upon the whole, aided by the resources of the toilet, her appearance at distance was such, that some might have thought her, if anything, rather beautiful, though of a style of beauty rather peculiar and cactus-like.

The whole tone, purpose, and strategy of *The Confidence-Man* are in those sentences, with their parade of notations and counter-notations, and the final flurry of phrases that modify, hesitantly contradict, and then utterly cancel one another out, leaving not a rack of positive statement behind. Goneril is in fact repellent: flat-chested, with a baked face and matted hair, heavily made-up, moustached and prickly-looking: *or is she?* As her physical actuality is blurred and dissolved by Melville's prose, we belatedly remember that Goneril probably does not even exist, but is simply an invention of the Confidence Man himself in his guise as "the man with the weed."

Or take Melville's analysis of the gentleman with the gold sleeve buttons in chapter vii. He had, Melville tells us with a straightforward air, the "very good luck to be a very good man"; although, Melville adds, he could not perhaps be called righteous, and righteousness was indeed—St. Paul is cited as the authority —a quality superior to goodness. Still, Melville goes on, the gentleman's goodness, if falling short of righteousness, should even so not be regarded as a *crime;* or anyhow (pressing the argument onward) not a crime for which the poor fellow should be sent to jail, since after all he might have been innocent of it. This is mental and moral sabotage. Amid all those pre-Jamesian qualifiers and circlings, Melville is of course insinuating that the gentleman with the gold buttons is not good at all: that his alleged goodness is no more than willful, self-protective innocence, thus reinforcing an earlier hint that the gentleman was the kind who refused to dirty his hands in the dilemmas of ethical choice, and was moral brother to history's most notorious hand-washer, "the Hebrew governor"—Pontius Pilate. Before Melville's prose is through with him, this very good man is lumped with those responsible for the crucifixion of Christ; and Melville has delivered himself of a very searching moral insight.

In short, the first and most accomplished of the confidence men in the novel is the author; and his first potential victim is the inattentive reader. The drastic aim of Melville's comedy of thought is to bring into question the sheer possibility of clear thinking itself—of *knowing* anything. The aim is a sort of intellectual derangement, by arousing and deploying what Whitman called the terrible doubt of appearances; doubt every which way; doubt of the gold-buttoned gentleman's goodness and of Goneril's beauty, and then doubt of that doubt. Out of these particular and playful doubts, there gradually arise the more fateful ones, those which shake our foundations: doubt about goodness and beauty as existent realities anywhere in the world of man; doubt about the benevolence of God and of nature, or, for that matter, about the cruelty and hostility of either; doubt, in the outcome the most desperate of all, about the remaining capacity for genuine friendship or charitable love between man and man.

The prose is perfectly designed to bring into view a world of dubious and mutually doubting humanity; one that is dominated, though by no means exclusively populated, by cheats and impostors. As we move about the *Fidèle,* we catch a glimpse of riverboat gamblers. We meet an old soldier whose physique was ruined by a long stretch in the tombs, but who passes for a heroic and charity-imploring veteran of the Mexican war. We encounter a mean-spirited miser, and a callow, conceited college student (needless to say, a sophomore, or wise fool). We are introduced to swindlers, hypocrites, and falsifiers, like Charles Noble and Mark Winsome and Egbert; and, in Egbert's perverse moral fable, we hear of the unspeakable Orchis and his relentless ruination of his no less oddly named "friend," China Aster. We witness the efforts of a young boy who is skilled in corruption beyond his years. So suspicious are the passengers of each other and so expert is Melville at infecting us with a nearly universal skepticism, that we cannot be sure but what some of the apparently decent and goodhearted persons, like the two clergymen in chapter iii, may not also be practitioners of pious fraud.[7]

Most of these are types one could find on a Mississippi steamer something over a century ago, products and representatives of the bustling, greedy, inventive American Middle West; the book's solid sociological basis should never be neglected, nor its running implicit contrast with other times and manners in the American East. But the passengers surveyed are also representative of the pilgrim species, man, in Melville's immeasurably disenchanted —yet not altogether hopeless—view of him. They are the constituents of an appalling human world: a radically "fallen" world, and a splintered one; a wolfish world, wherein the crafty and utterly self-regarding denizens are intent chiefly on fleecing one another. In this world, as in the apocalyptic vision of Albany in *King Lear,* humanity has at last begun to "prey upon itself/ Like

7. H. Bruce Franklin has explored the evidence for this possibility and for comparable ones.

monsters of the deep." It is our world in the process of becoming our hell. And, what is the same thing, the pilgrimage on which the species, man, has here embarked is a pilgrimage not to the Christian shrine or the Moslem Mecca but to a midnight hell on earth of man's own devising. Moving through that cosmos, eventually towering over it, is another figure, the book's ambiguous hero: *the* Confidence Man, for whose visitation the race of small-time confidence men has made itself ripe and ready.

The Confidence Man makes eight appearances in all: seven in fairly rapid succession over the first half of the book, and continuing in the single majestic role of the cosmopolitan throughout the latter half. As Black Guinea, a crippled Negro with a tambourine (in chapter iii), he names the roles he will go on to assume, in a pretence of naming people who know him and will vouch for him: "a werry nice, good ge'mman with a weed, and a ge'mman in a gray coat and white tie, what knows all about me; and a ge'mman wid a big book, too; and a yarb doctor . . . and a ge'mman wid a brass plate" and so on. In the course of time, we meet most of the gentlemen named and in the order listed. It is a part of Black Guinea's guile (or, more simply perhaps, of Melville's forgetfulness) that he also includes several references —to a soldier, a man with a yellow vest, other unspecified "ge'mmen"—who do not show up or, if they do, are not masks of the title figure.[8] But the others appear, ply their trade, and disappear with a sort of rhythmic dishonesty.

In each of his early guises, the Confidence Man exerts one distinctive kind of appeal, represents a parody or debasement of one phase of humanity and performs one sort of symbolic function. The developing pattern would be worth examining in detail, but here we need only remind ourselves of the general progression. The man with a weed in his hat—a spurious emblem of mourning—wears the mask of private misfortune; he spins his melancholy tale of domestic misery (including the bizarre depravities of his "wife," Goneril) and touches the kindly merchant

8. Melville helps us detect the so-to-speak genuine masks of the Confidence Man by a number of devices: for example, by showing the man with the weed in possession of a business card we have seen Black Guinea surreptitiously acquiring; by having the various *personae* loudly vouch for each other; by a similarity of names—John Ringman (a man who is a ringer of changes), John Truman, Frank Goodman.

for money. The man in the gray coat and white tie is the enthusiastic spokesman for the highly organized and public "business" of charity, and for the profit that can accrue from exploiting the multiple pains of mankind; he works effectively on the gold-buttoned passenger and on a "charitable lady." The representative of the Black Rapids Coal Company bespeaks another phase of the business world; he sells stocks to a miser, a sophomore, and the merchant and writes their names in his big book (which we suspect of being the ledger of the damned). The Herb Doctor is the healer as fraud; he plays gainfully on the terrors and the sentiment of the miser, a sick person, and an old soldier; but he is rebuffed by a suffering backwoods "Titan" and by a staunchly morose Missouri bachelor named Pitch. Returning as a sycophantic Philosophical Agent wearing a brass plate, the Confidence Man has another go at Pitch, this time by a more devious and appropriate (because more intellectual) brand of salesmanship, and manages to sell him a nonexistent lad who will be the perfect boy-of-all-work on Pitch's plantation.

The Philosophical Agent concludes the first half of the adventure by announcing his departure from the *Fidèle* at a "grotesquely-shaped bluff" known as "the Devil's Joke"; and it is shortly after this that the Confidence Man re-enters in the role he will retain, that of Frank Goodman, a fantastically garbed "cosmopolitan." Nudged by these proper names, the essential question about the Confidence Man comes into full and alarming prominence. *Are* all his tricks and bluffs and bilkings the grotesque April Fool's jokes of the Devil? The question "grows in seriousness" as the masquerade goes forward; partly because the cosmopolitan himself (Melville twice uses the phrase about him in the later portions of the book) grows in seriousness—and in stature and mystery. For it is this book's ominously joking version of the question that energized Melville's writings, drove and destroyed his Ahab, and unremittingly obsessed his mind. Is the supreme force in the universe a force of good or one of evil? Does one find love at the heart of things, or does one find horror? Is the Confidence Man a devil, or is he a savior? Pitch uses the precise adjective about him when he calls him (chapter xxiv) not a moral but a *"metaphysical* scamp"; for he seems, as the chapters pass, to loom above us, demanding nothing but the largest and most ultimate interpretations. We confront him in his role as cosmopolitan the way Axel Heyst confronted the mysterious trio approaching his remote island in Conrad's *Victory;* their appearance, Heyst felt, was:

> like those myths current in Polynesia, of amazing strangers, who arrive at an island, gods or demons, bringing good or evil to the innocence of the inhabitants—gifts of unknown things, words never heard before.

The Confidence Man—who was "in the extremest sense of the word, a stranger," as Melville says about him—is also an amazing and ambiguous creature of myth; though it is a main feature of the world he invades that it has little innocence left in it and only scattered examples of moral conscience. *As* a creature of myth, the Confidence Man is to some extent Melville's American embodiment of one of the most engaging of the great archetypal figures: namely, the trickster god, especially as that figure took the name of Hermes in Greek mythology. Hermes was a god of travelers, and in this capacity he also escorted the souls of the dead into the underworld. He was, to use modern terms, the god of gambling, and the deity of financial profit, the one involved in commercial dealings—particularly in shady ones. Hermes was the muse responsible for inspiring the rhetoric of salesmanship; he had a modest musical talent; and he was an adept of the daring and elaborate prank.[9] The resemblance to the Confidence Man is impressive; and Melville's hero (like the fictional descendants mentioned earlier) can be related in similar terms to other avatars of the trickster god in European folklore. But the Confidence Man is somehow a more dangerous, at once a twistier and a more portentous figure than Hermes; and his multiform character contains archetypal aspects of quite different orders.

In a book dense with diabolic hints and allusions, the Confidence Man seems to be at least a species of devil: say, a Protestant and even Miltonic devil. His voice is seraphic; and he quotes, sometimes slyly misquotes, Scripture to his purpose. Time and again he is associated with the figure of the snake: so frequently, indeed, that one inevitably begins to doubt the implication. As the cosmopolitan, he appears—like Satan in Melville's favorite biblical text, the book of Job—from coming and going on the earth, and from walking up and down in it; he is "king of

9. See, for example, the *Larousse Encyclopedia of Mythology,* introduction by Robert Graves (New York, 1959), pp. 133 ff.

travelled good-fellows." But the fact is that Melville is of this devil's party: more knowingly than Milton was thought to be by William Blake; and we recall that Milton's Satan is honored by Melville (in chapter xliv) as one of the few radically "original characters" in literature, along with Hamlet and Don Quixote.

The Confidence Man was evidently conceived by Melville as just such an original character: as, when we meditate the matter, the results he achieves can indicate. If the Confidence Man's intention is to deceive for profit, he is only indifferently successful. The man with the wooden leg spots him at once as a sham: "some white operator betwisted and painted up for decoy." The Herb Doctor is assaulted by the Titan. Pitch resists the Confidence Man in two of his disguises, and recognizes him at the third encounter for what he is: "Jeremy Diddler No. 3." Charles Noble is horrified when the cosmopolitan beats him to the draw in asking for a loan (they have been trying to get each other softened up by drink); and Mark Winsome and his disciple combine in a long and chilling refusal of financial assistance. There is a kind of cynicism, a kind of hard-won moral harshness, a kind of moody intelligence, and a kind of rock-like egotism against which the Confidence Man's deviltry seems powerless. But of course the Confidence Man is not really interested in money, though he is extremely interested in the interest evinced in money by others. The wooden-legged man touches a part of the truth when he rebukes the passengers for thinking, as he puts it, that "money . . . is the sole motive to pains and hazard, deception and deviltry, in this world. How much money did the devil make by gulling Eve?" The Missouri Bachelor adds his own similar and bemused reflection: "Was the man a trickster, it must be more for the love than the lucre. Two or three dirty dollars the motive to so many nice wiles?"

The human species in the novel, and in this respect it is emphatically the American species, is intensely money-minded; and it is in fact money-mindedness (rather than, say, optimism or innocence) that is the important first half of the book's theme and the first object of its satire—an evidently ineradicable money-mindedness that plays steadily though obliquely into the Confidence Man's hands. For the motive of *his* nice wiles is something different. His motive is to trick, beguile, maneuver, or force each and every person he accosts to declare himself: to announce, whether consciously or not, his own fundamental moral and

intellectual nature. In this, Melville's hero is unreservedly successful every time: and no less successful with the Titan and Pitch,
with the wooden-legged man and with Mark Winsome, than he
is with his more obvious victims. He has, in short, exactly the
same prodigious effect as that attributed by Melville to the great
original in literature.

The latter, Melville claims, "is like a revolving Drummond-
light, raying away from itself all round it—everything is lit by it,
everything starts up to it (mark how it is with Hamlet)."[10] Mark
how it is, too, with the Confidence Man. His own consciousness
may or may not be a darkened one; but his effect upon others
is incandescent. Everyone he meets "starts up to him," the moral
reality of each is lit by contact with him. This man of many masks
is after all the great unmasker; this unrivaled obfuscator is the
great illuminator; this customarily bland mock optimist is a great
satirist in action. And if the spectacle uncovered by his wiles is
for the most part a dreadful one, several more goodly qualities are
also forced into the open. The merchant's essential if flawed
kindliness is made apparent. The stricken Titan, as we have seen,
is driven to exhibit his outraged integrity. And Pitch, an attractive
figure throughout, is stung by the Herb Doctor's mealymouthed
statement of his position on slavery (chapter xxi: a splendid instance of self-erasing prose) into a passionate and prophetic
expression of political morality:

> "Picked and prudent sentiments. You are the moderate man,
> the invaluable understrapper of the wicked man. You, the
> moderate man, may be used for wrong, but are useless for
> right."

The passengers on board the *Fidèle*, we may say, get the Confidence Man they deserve. And this, I venture, is the explanation
of the novel's opening chapter, and the simultaneous appearance
of the deaf-mute and of the placard describing the impostor from
the East. The Confidence Man is prepared to offer himself either
way. When he appears in the first sentence "suddenly as Manco
Capac at the Lake Titicaca," in the guise of a lamb-like defective,

10. From the OED: *"Drummond light.* 1854. The lime-light or oxyhy-
drogen light (invented by Capt. T. Drummond, R.E., *c* 1825), wherein a
blow-pipe flame, *e.g.* of combined oxygen and hydrogen, impinges on a
piece of pure lime, and renders it incandescent."

intimations of divinity hover in his features and conduct and in the metaphoric language used about him.[11] The deaf-mute, pleading for charity, is manhandled, rejected, and forgotten. He retires to his spot on the forecastle with an aspect "at once gentle and jaded," a sort of weary and disillusioned but still gentle-spirited Christ. After a brief interval (long enough, one presumes, to "betwist" and paint himself), the Confidence Man returns in his alternative or trickster role; and from Black Guinea to the Philosophical Agent, he performs as impostor, outconning the con-men and deviously eliciting those occasional declarations of intellectual and moral firmness.

As the cosmopolitan, however, the Confidence Man is more and other than an impostor. He becomes a figure of almost palpably greater dimension; as though now composed of larger and more resplendent versions of the two alternative roles he had previously practiced. He is, we may suppose, an outsize embodiment of the major contradictions in the universe and in man: or so he is willing to insinuate (in chapter xlii) when the barber, startled by what for an instant he had taken for "a sort of spiritual manifestation," exclaims in relief that the cosmopolitan "is only a man."

> "*Only* a man? As if to be but a man were nothing. But don't be too sure what I am. You call me *man,* just as the townsfolk called the angels who, in man's form, came to Lot's house; just as the Jew rustics called the devils who, in man's form, haunted the tombs. You can conclude nothing absolute from the human form, barber."

All the enigmas are there—human versus inhuman; angel versus devil—and we can conclude nothing absolute. But that is not the same as saying that we can conclude absolutely nothing. Melville has offered a long-range advance hint in the multiple analogy suggested at the end of the second chapter: between the crowd of passengers—"these varieties of mortals [who] blended their varieties of visage and garb;" mid-America—"the dashing and all-fusing spirit of the West;" and the great river—"the

---

11. Elizabeth S. Foster informs us that Manco Capac was a Peruvian god, a child of the sun—the deaf-mute, we remember, appears at sunup— and the legendary founder of the Inca Empire. His earthly career began with his sudden manifestation at Lake Titicaca.

Mississippi itself, which, uniting the streams of the most distant and opposite zones, pours them along, helter-skelter, in one cosmopolitan tide." We have to learn, as the novel unfolds, never to place complete trust in any individual statement by author or character; but it is impossible not to add a fourth term to the analogy. It is, needless to say, that of the dashing and confident cosmopolitan himself, with his garb of many colors, his shifting visage, his all-fusing character, his multizoned citizenship. He really is Everyman—that is, Everyman as All-men; manifesting to a splintered world the grand human potential for demonism or divinity, summoning mankind to choose.

It is, finally, exactly in his all-fusing personality that the cosmopolitan bespeaks and tests the human capacity *for* fusion: for friendship, for the intimate and organic relation between man and man, for free participation in a human community. No one of his tests is failed more absolutely; and it is that failure that darkens and renders more deeply "serious" the closing sections of the book. One way, indeed, to trace the growth in seriousness from the first half of the novel to the second is to follow the development in focus from what the man in the gray coat calls the *business* of charity to what we ourselves might call the *virtue* of charity. Of all the interrelated words and terms and themes that are central to *The Confidence-Man*—confidence, faith, trust, nature, goodness, and so on—it is probably charity that is the chief victim of Melville's dialectical battering. This is hardly surprising: for charity in its traditional Christian or Pauline sense—the self-giving love between man and man—had always been for Melville the supreme human resource, the supreme human counter-measure, in a wolfish and maddeningly ambiguous world; and Melville's commitment to it was passionately manifested in his fiction, his letters and his marginalia, as well as in his life. He was all the more alert to the way charity had been reduced to its narrower and materialistic if no less traditional meaning, not of self-giving but of money-giving (as the man in the gray coat indicates, institutionalized money-giving). Charity in this lowly sense is the source of much of the hoaxing in the earlier episodes, when money is handed over and withheld with all the air of a debased ritual. But meanwhile, in addition to those sordid exposures, the many debates about the degree of goodness in man, in nature, and in God have been pointing up the urgency of the issue of charity in its higher sense. This is what is finally at stake in the cosmopolitan's encounters, in the relationships enacted, and in the long anecdotes exchanged.

The most fully dramatized form of charity is the displayed capacity for genuine friendship; and it is of this that the stories both of Charlemont (chapter xxxiv) and Orchis and China Aster (chapter xl) provide such bleakly negative demonstrations. The lengthy report on Colonel John Moredock (whose historic career is adjusted to Melville's fictional needs) is a more generalized example: that, namely, of obstinate if courageous and honorable hatred toward an entire segment of the human race, the whole breed of Indians; the latter appear as so many devils to be exterminated, and in dealing with them Colonel Moredock exhibits extreme versions of all the qualities opposite to the virtue of charity. The fascinations of Colonel Moredock's adventurous career and the complexities of his character are such that his story, for a while, runs away from the novel, and becomes uncommonly absorbing and memorable for its own sake. But the other two tales are more sharply related to the book's major theme. Charlemont—and the cosmopolitan tells his story immediately after his "boon companion" Charles *Noble* has agitatedly rejected a request for money—was a man too much possessed of a fragile dream of friendship. In the crisis, he does not dare put his ideal to the test, and so vanishes till he has recovered those material fortunes upon which, as he secretly and desperately believes, all friendship is actually grounded. The story of Orchis is, in itself, an extended study in the hypocrisies of friendship; but it gets its vibrations from the comically bewildering dramatic context within which it is being recited.

Egbert offers his account of the systematic destruction of one friend by another as a moral lesson against borrowing or lending among friends. Part of the dramatic irony at work here is that Egbert is as it were the human application of the idealism of his master Mark Winsome:[12] an idealism that, though opposite in force, has curiously similar consequences in practice to the reported idealism of Charlemont. At the same time, and at the

12. At some remove, the figure of Mark Winsome seems to be a satire on Emerson, or on the Emersonian kind of idealist. But Winsome no more represents Melville's rounded view of Emerson than the Colonel Moredock story represents his view of Indians—or, for that matter, Black Guinea his view of the Negro.

cosmopolitan's request, Egbert has assumed the role of Charles Noble: that is, of the false friend whose recent conduct had given rise to the story of Charlemont. The various scenes and stories thus mirror and parody each other; and in the dialectical squeeze that results, the sheer possibility of the most minimal of friendships seems altogether to evaporate. It is the fulfillment, the final confirmation, of what had been implicit in the novel's opening scene: when the deaf-mute's plea for charity—a plea carried by scribbled phrases from St. Paul—was greeted with derision and violence.

We come thus to the novel's ending: to the solitary pious old man discovered reading the Bible by the light of a single and strangely decorated lamp. A mysterious boy, a sort of apprentice devil apparently, sells the old man protective devices against the world's deceitfulness and thievishness, in which, the old man has only just declared, he does not believe; while a voice from one of the bunks cries out about the Confidence Man and about the apocalypse. The last lamp is extinguished; and the Confidence Man "kindly [leads] the old man away" into the darkness. There is without doubt a sense of terrible and total finality about the scene. The closing questions of *King Lear,* those uttered by Edgar and Albany, come insistently to mind: "Is this the promis'd end?/ Or image of that horror?" An already darkened world had shown itself radically devoid of the one human impulse that might relight it and redeem it: the impulse of charity. The last scene, with its heavily and somberly ceremonial atmosphere, seems to be enacting a ritual of cosmic obliteration. Perhaps it is; perhaps the Confidence Man, having induced the human species into freely choosing its own damnation, is now ready to escort it with all courtesy down to the underworld.

But Melville does have one more thing to say: that "Something further may follow of this Masquerade." There is no implication here that Melville contemplated writing additional episodes; it is hard to name a novel that so completely comes to its end as does *The Confidence-Man.* It is not the novel but the Masquerade it has been describing that may continue. The ambiguous power represented by the Confidence Man may make another visitation: may at some future time enact again what Hart Crane called God's "parable of man." *This* visitation could scarcely end anywhere except in absolute darkness; for though the human species did not know it, it had been edging into darkness all along. The next time may be different: but Melville does not encourage us to think so. He only makes it clear that the Confidence Man is not the bringer of darkness; he is the one who reveals the darkness in ourselves. Whether this is the act of a devil or an angel may not, when all is said and done, really matter.

1964

HAWTHORNE AND JAMES:
THE MATTER OF THE HEART

The Bostonians is Henry James's single major effort at a novel not only set entirely on the American scene but populated exclusively by American characters; and it is hardly surprising that, when he came to write it, James's imagination should be more than usually hospitable to the good influence of his major American predecessor in the art of fiction. The Hawthorne aspect of *The Bostonians* is pervasive: so much so that James's novel seems at times to be composed largely of cunning rearrangements and inversions—on a lower mimetic level (to borrow Northrop Frye's category) and at a later moment in history—of ingredients taken over from Hawthorne. The several similarities between *The Blithedale Romance* and *The Bostonians,* as between novels dealing respectively with the New England reformist temper before and after the Civil War, have been sufficiently pointed out, and we may accept them as among the valid commonplaces of American literary history. But what is striking is that *The Bostonians* carries forward and downward more interestingly yet from *The Scarlet Letter,* and that it significantly perverts elements derived from *The House of the Seven Gables.* I even suspect that James, for the fullness of his artistic effect, may have depended upon our having the novels of Hawthorne in mind: as, for example, Thomas Mann in *The Magic Mountain* depended upon the reader's recollection of the *Odyssey* and the *Divine Comedy,* on each of which he was ringing a number of ironic and terrible changes. If my suspicion of James is correct, it was splendidly continental and un-American of him: the more so because, when the American writings are juxtaposed, they bring into prominence compulsions and strategies that have become generic to American fiction, in good part because Hawthorne made it possible for James to see those phenomena as generic to any imaginative view of that American world which, in *The Bostonians,* James for the first and last time explored in depth.

They bring into view, among other equally absorbing things, what I find no way to avoid calling the American theme; in James's case, we might call it his own local treatment of the intranational theme. One likes to assume that American fiction has displayed a sufficient variety of themes; none of the novels in question is inclined to reduce reality to a single phase or anything as abstract as a theme, still less a theme transfixed and further reduced by a patriotic adjective. But it remains true that one idea more than another has agitated American novelists from Hawthorne's generation to our own, and that this idea is what Hawthorne defined as "the sanctity of a human heart." We should cling to Hawthorne's remarkable and precise wording of the formula, and not shrink the matter to a mere question of "identity" or some polemic for the rights of personality. Understood as Hawthorne and James understood it, wrapped in unmistakable if ambiguous religious connotations, the formula has had an almost explosive power of suggestion for the novel in America (and, from Whitman onward, for poetry too).

It has appeared there, persistently, as a kind of touchstone for human behavior and social organization. True and false human relationships have been identified by appeal to it. It is what is at stake when everything is at stake: what has most aroused novelists when they seek to dramatize the periodic clash between new ideas and old; the real issue in fictionalized moments of historic social crisis and ideological change. It is or has been made to seem the measure of progress and reaction, what threatens the old and is threatened by it. It is or has been made to seem the first of all sacraments in any vital religion, what blasphemes the established order and is blasphemed by it. It is even implicated in the distinction of genres to which American fiction has been prone: allegory, legend, romance, satire, the realistic novel. To these large contentions, a whole range of American writers could testify, though I shall not summon them to do so. I want only to reflect, by means of a few notes and notations, on the extent to which Hawthorne and—following him—James felt the radical force of the heart's sanctity; and on how, by making that force palpable in narrative, they showed what the American novel can grapple with and how much it can accomplish. I shall be addressing myself to what Hawthorne's generation called a writer's talent as much as to his genius, his craft as much as his vision; nor do I expect to say anything very new. But the occasion is ceremonial: a time for reaffirmations.[1]

I

In *The Scarlet Letter*, as in *The Bostonians*, the theme of the heart's sanctity is closely associated with a question about the condition of women, and that question in turn arises out of a supple play of historical perspectives. The patterning becomes evident in the course of the opening scene: though fully so, I shall suggest, rather to the attentive reader than to the actors in the drama. Among the latter, it is Dimmesdale who, for his own mixed private purposes, comes closest to sounding the theme: when, according to John Wilson's report, he argues that "it were wronging the very nature of woman to force her"—as Hester Prynne is being forced—"to lay open her heart's secret in such broad daylight, and in presence of so great a multitude." Hawthorne has already let us know that he shares Dimmesdale's attitude and goes beyond it, and that in his opinion enforced public exposure wrongs not only the nature of woman but human nature generally, that it violates some urgent, perhaps some sacred, principle of life: "There can be no outrage, methinks, against our common nature . . . more flagrant than to forbid the culprit to hide his face for shame." Unlike Dimmesdale, who is wholly encased within what he believes to be a changeless theocratic structure, Hawthorne is there speaking out of a historical perspective. His voice is that of the humane nineteenth-century New England spirit as it broods over the New England of two centuries earlier; and it is the same spirit that had been quick to observe, and from the same historical vantage point, the awesome dignity as well as the cruelty of Hester's punishment: "On the other hand, a penalty, which, in our day, would infer a degree of

1. The occasion was the centenary of Hawthorne's death—May 16, 1964—and a gathering in Columbus, Ohio, sponsored by the Ohio State University Press, which also honored the date by publishing a volume of *Centenary Essays*. The present essay was read at the morning session; in the afternoon Professor Lionel Trilling read his fine essay "Our Hawthorne."

mocking infamy and ridicule, might then be invested with almost
as stern a dignity as the punishment of death itself." Hawthorne
then goes on to enrich the whole matter by some remarks about
the female Bostonians of the 1640s that throw a fascinatingly ambiguous light, in advance, over Dimmesdale's appeal.

As he looks at the females pushing and crowding around the
scaffold and watches them "wedging their not insubstantial persons . . . into the throng," as he runs his eyes over their "broad
shoulders and well-developed busts" and listens to the startling
"boldness and rotundity" of their speech, Hawthorne is led to
conclude that: "Morally, as well as materially, there was a coarser
fibre in those wives and maidens of old English birth and breed-
ing, than in their fair descendants, separated from them by a series
of six or seven generations." For Hawthorne, at least in this novel,
the nature of woman is susceptible to historical definition. These
seventeenth-century New England women, like everything else in
the book, are identified within a long process of physical and
moral transformation. Hawthorne traces the process backwards
half a century and across the waters to sixteenth-century England
and the age of "man-like Elizabeth"—an epoch of "beef and ale
. . . [and] a moral diet not a whit more refined;" and forward
through the years to Hawthorne's time, noticing how "every successive mother has transmitted to her child a fainter bloom, a
more delicate and briefer beauty, and a slighter physical frame,
if not a character of less force and solidity."

The passage reveals the characteristic narrative tactic of *The
Scarlet Letter,* even though the tactical aim reveals itself more
slowly. The temper of the Puritan men during the period of the
novel's action is, like the nature of the women, established by the
tracing out of a historical process, and one which again stretches
back to the Elizabethan age, forward into the later generations of
Puritans, and on into the nineteenth century. Hawthorne (in
chapter xxi) pauses in his account of the holiday games
to insist that "the great, honest face of the people smiled grimly,
perhaps but widely too." For they were, he reminds us, "not born
to an inheritance of Puritan gloom. They were native Englishmen,
whose fathers had lived in the sunny richness of the Elizabethan
epoch." They were men, in fact, who by 1645 were only "in the
first stages of joyless deportment;" it was not they but their "immediate posterity, the generation next to the early emigrants,
[who] wore the blackest shade of Puritanism, and so darkened

the national visage with it, that all the subsequent years have not sufficed to clear it up."

What Hawthorne is doing by means of this recurring dialectic of historical epochs is to create the terms—the very sources of meaning—of the drama he is engaged in describing; and the achievement is a remarkable one. Hawthorne knew, better than any writer of his time, that existence for the Puritan "was completely dramatic, every minute was charged with meaning."[2] In his own words, the Puritans tended to speak of human existence as simply a state of "trial and warfare"—the scene of the great war between God and the devil; a scene overwhelmed by allegory. It was just this quality of Puritan life that made it so attractive a subject for a novelist of Hawthorne's dramatic persuasion. But the crucial point is this: that the meaning with which every minute of the action in *The Scarlet Letter* is charged is never quite the meaning assigned to it by the characters involved; nor could it be. For surrounding the meanings so confidently attributed to events and relationships by the magistrates and the clergymen, the matrons and the maidens, is the creative play of Hawthorne's historical imagination. This is, so to speak, the charging force of the novel; and this it is that invests what I take to be the supreme moment in the story, the swift exchange between Dimmesdale and Hester in the forest, with something like a revolutionary significance.

Between the opening scene and that encounter, much had been happening and much a-building; one of the many things Hawthorne taught James was to let narrative power accumulate at a fairly measured pace, so as to give maximum resonance to those otherwise slender moments when the entire drama is asked to change course and, in doing so, to yield up its central meaning. Among the several developments in *The Scarlet Letter,* we may mention the two most obvious ones. There is, on the one hand, the long patient effort of Chillingworth to drag Dimmesdale out of his psychological hiding place and onto a private scaffold, a place of moral exposure, of Chillingworth's own making. And on the other, there has been the strange career of Hester's interior musings. The exchange in the forest is the created compound of these two developments—and of Hawthorne's handling of them.

2. Perry Miller and Thomas H. Johnson, *The Puritans* (New York, 1938), p. 60.

In her lonely cottage by the sea, Hester has come into touch with the array of new ideas that, as Hawthorne says, were stirring the minds of Europe and toppling the systems of "ancient prejudice" ("wherewith," he characteristically adds, "was linked much of ancient principle"). But she is able to do so because, in her tragic freedom, she is gifted with the mode of imagination that informs the entire narrative—the historical imagination—and she is the only person in the book to be so gifted. Hawthorne permits Hester to share a little in his liberated perspective: she alone envisages the possibility of significant historical change, and she alone is allowed thereby to escape some real distance from the allegorized world of fixed and changeless meanings and conditions and relationships which all other figures in the book inhabit. As Hester reflects upon "the whole race of womanhood," she arrives at the vision of social and sexual revolution to which, Hawthorne implies, women in her position are always liable.

> As a first step, the whole system of society is to be torn down, and built up anew. Then, the very nature of the opposite sex, or its long hereditary habit, which has become like nature, is to be essentially modified, before woman can be allowed to assume what seems a fair and suitable position. Finally, all other difficulties being obviated, woman cannot take advantage of these preliminary reforms, until she herself have undergone a still mightier change.

The consequence of all this—as Hester, at the book's end, is still telling the unhappy women to whom she ministers—would be to "establish the whole relation between man and woman on a surer ground of mutual happiness." But until it is revealed to her by Dimmesdale, Hester does not truly perceive the ground of that ground.

Hawthorne reminds us how appalling Hester's speculations would have seemed to the Puritan authorities: "as perilous as demons." He reminds us, too, how genuinely dangerous, how gravely unsettling, such speculations can be for the person who entertains them: they can quite literally, he suggests, draw one on toward madness. But what Hawthorne most deeply distrusts is not Hester's revolutionary dream, but the essentially intellectual source and nature of it. It is too much a product of the head; and "a woman," Hawthorne declares, "never overcame these problems by any exercise of thought." The remark is by no means condescending, for *The Scarlet Letter* is animated by the belief that these problems can be overcome, or at least that the overcoming of them should be among the supreme goals of human effort. Hawthorne so far believes that a woman will lead the way, if anyone will, that he grants the woman Hester the unique privilege of entering into his own historical perspective. But his dominant conviction is that the solution must come from the heart; that the problems will themselves vanish when, and only when, the heart "chance to come uppermost." And this, of course, is what does happen during the meeting in the forest.

There, for a brief and perhaps illusory moment, the relationship between Dimmesdale and Hester, between the man and the woman, stands upon that surer ground of mutual happiness that Hester has dreamed of. One even conjectures that for a few seconds the scarlet letter betokens those words—"angel" and "apostle"—with which Hester hoped to associate herself as the destined prophetess of the new revelation. Such religious titles and allusions are, in any event, not out of place. For what comes flickering into view, what the whole course of the novel has been preparing for, and what terrifies Dimmesdale when he catches a glimpse of it, is something much more far-reaching than social reform. It is, indeed, a religious revolution. "May God forgive us both!" Dimmesdale says sadly. And then:

> "We are not, Hester, the worst sinners in the world. There is one worse than even the polluted priest! That old man's revenge has been blacker than sin. He has violated, in cold blood, the sanctity of a human heart. Thou and I, Hester, never did so!"
>
> "Never, never," whispered she. "What we did had a consecration of its own. We felt it so! We said so to each other! Hast thou forgotten it?"
>
> "Hush, Hester!" said Arthur Dimmesdale, rising from the ground. "No; I have not forgotten."

In context, the implication is almost breath-taking. It is just because neither of them had violated the sanctity of the other's heart that what they had done—their entire relationship—had had a consecration of its own. Dimmesdale's words release Hester's extraordinary contention and give all her wandering meditations a sudden coherence. It is from the implications of Hester's answer that Dimmesdale shies back in a kind of horror, for he is equipped to appreciate the enormity of them. He had been trained to pursue his priestly calling among a people for whom "religion and law were almost identical, and in whose character both were . . . thoroughly interfused." But latent in his attribution of sanctity to the human heart, and still more, in the suggestion it leads to, that of the sanctification of lawless love, is the seed of a new sacramental order; and one that, from the Puritan standpoint, is altogether blasphemous. No wonder that Dimmesdale rises to his feet, cuts short the exchange, and commands Hester to hush. It is a moment characteristic of Hawthorne —the short glimpse and the speedy covering over of the world-disturbing truth—and Hester hushes. But she does not relinquish her vision, nor will she for the rest of her fictional life.

She takes no steps to bring that new order into being, except for her humane ministrations to the forlorn who come to her door. But Hawthorne tells us that, had matters been otherwise, Hester "might have come down to us in history hand in hand with Anne Hutchinson"—"sainted Anne Hutchinson," as he has called her earlier—"as the foundress of a religious sect." It is the very substance of that projected and unrealized religion that is gradually created by the novel's historical dialectics; and Hester's limited eligibility to lead it can be measured by the limited but real degree of her participation in those dialectics. It would be a religion founded on the doctrine of the inviolable sanctity of the individual human heart; and one in which the human relation—above all the relation between man and woman—itself shaped by allegiance to that doctrine (by the mutual reverence of heart for heart), would become the vessel of the sacred, the domain of the consecrated. It would have provided a sacramental basis for a genuine community, of the kind envisaged, for example, by Henry James the elder in *Society the Redeemed Form of Man*. Indeed, it is tempting to look beyond Hawthorne across a dozen decades, to notice how, from the two Henry Jameses onward, writer after writer has reflected the same curious but persistent brand of religious humanism—and usually in an escape from traditional religious institutions and dogmas, and in despite of the world's irreverent practices. But no writer ever succeeded in making this epochal possibility as compelling as did Hawthorne: for no American writer possessed the vision, both historical and transcendent, to set the new possibility amid and against the stiffening vigor, the hard historical actuality, of the older order. In the clarity of his perception and in his unsentimental compassion, Hawthorne was able, as well, to do honor to both the old and the new, while seeing each as an absolute challenge to the other. If Hester had become the destined prophetess, she "might, and not improbably would, have suffered death from the stern tribunals of the period, for attempting to undermine the foundations of the Puritan establishment." Within the world of *The Scarlet Letter,* the establishment triumphs; but within the novel as a novel, its foundations are constantly and quietly undermined by a play of perspectives to which only Hester is privy; and the fusion of religion and law is giving way to a new conception of sanctity.

II

About *The House of the Seven Gables,* there is for present purposes less that needs to be said; but we can begin by remarking that its narrative method to some extent reverses that of *The Scarlet Letter,* and that the Hawthornian formula emerges here from a different direction. In *The Scarlet Letter,* an action set in the past completes its meaning under the pressure of a shifting later-day perspective; in *The Seven Gables,* events occurring in the present—or anyhow in "an epoch not very remote from the present day"—draw much of their force from the shifting pressure of a long past, through a series of what seem about to be fated re-enactments and turn out to be reversals. *The Scarlet Letter* projects forward, beyond the consciousness of its characters, from the 1640s to Hawthorne's own time; *The Seven Gables* reaches backward from Hawthorne's time almost to the age of *The Scarlet Letter,* touching upon happenings that took place in or around 1670 (Hawthorne's arithmetic is casual), 1707, 1820, and 1850. In *The Scarlet Letter,* Hawthorne, observing the robust physiques of the Puritan matrons, glances ahead to the fainter bloom and briefer beauty of their descendants. In *The Seven Gables,* almost everything is described as diminished or decaying, and contrasted with the heartier qualities of earlier times. Even Jaffrey Pyncheon, for all his wicked strength, carries in his face the marks of a physiological decline:

> The Judge's face had lost the ruddy English hue that showed its warmth through all the duskiness of the Colonel's weather-beaten cheek, and had taken a sallow shade, the established complexion of his countrymen.

The brother and sister are dreary relics: Hepzibah is a "far-descended and time-stricken virgin," and Clifford, until the book's climax, is no more than an elderly wreck of what had been a beautiful and brilliant young man. Their habitation, the moldering house with its garden-plot "so unctuous with two hundred years of vegetable decay," and its "ugly luxuriance of gigantic weeds" is dismally appropriate, an objective correlative for their weedy spirits. It is within such an atmosphere that Hawthorne's historical imagination—working with no less agility than before, but, as it were, reversing its direction—once again brings into dramatic play the principle of the heart's sanctity.

The principle is no doubt less central here than in *The Scarlet Letter:* ideas in general are less central in *The Seven Gables* than in its much more dramatic predecessor. But it does make its important appearance, and it is, as formerly (though less tightly), related to a cluster of "new ideas." Given the time-laden atmosphere of the story, we may expect the new ideas in this case to be mainly ideas about newness itself: about getting rid of the past which, as the daguerrotypist Holgrave proclaims oratorically, "lies upon the Present like a giant's dead body," in every conceivable physical, psychological, social, legal, and religious form. Holgrave's rhetoric is, of course, excessive; it warrants the recoiling comment of Phoebe about the ferocity of his hatred for everything old; and it is countered by the very figure of Clifford, by the infinite pathos of a man who really has gotten rid of the past, or been bereft of it. It is Holgrave's personal destiny, in the novel, to come to terms with the past, including his own genealogy. Nonetheless, Holgrave (and Hawthorne goes on to say as much) deserves our attention and that of his fellow characters; for more than anyone else in the novel Holgrave understands the necessary basis of any new system of life: a quality he himself possesses and which Hawthorne—in the milder and properly more modern but still religious idiom of *The Seven Gables*—describes as "the rare and high quality of reverence for another's individuality."

The phrase occurs (in chapter xiv) at a moment when Holgrave has very nearly mesmerized Phoebe by his histrionic reading of the story about Alice Pyncheon. The latter, one remembers, was herself completely mesmerized by one Matthew Maule, grandson of that Matthew Maule who had been executed for witchcraft upon the false testimony of Colonel Pyncheon; and who thus takes his family's revenge upon the wicked Colonel's granddaughter. Alice is held in thrall until Matthew's marriage, where-upon she wakes from her "enchanted sleep" and straightway dies —leaving Matthew "gnashing his teeth, as if he would have bitten his own heart in twain," not unlike Chillingworth on the occasion of Dimmesdale's death. This is the supreme instance, in *The Seven Gables,* of the violation of Hawthorne's first principle, a literally murderous invasion of another person's individuality: Maule "had taken a woman's delicate soul into his rude gripe, to play with—and she was dead!" Retelling that story almost a century and a half later, another Maule (who temporarily calls himself Holgrave) comes to the verge of re-enacting that earlier sin and of casting a similarly fatal spell over the susceptible spirit of young Phoebe Pyncheon. "A veil was beginning to be muffled about her"—one thinks of the veilings and mesmerizings of *The Blithedale Romance*—"in which she could behold only him, and live only in his thoughts and emotions." Holgrave's gesture at this point not only liberates Phoebe's potentially enslaved self; it is a victory over his own dangerous and inherited power—and insofar a reversal and a rejection of the past.

> To a disposition like Holgrave's, at once speculative and active, there is no temptation so great as the opportunity of acquiring empire over the human spirit; nor any idea more seductive to a young man than to become the arbiter of a young girl's destiny. Let us, therefore,—whatever his defects of nature and education, and in spite of his scorn for creeds and institutions,—concede to the daguerrotypist the rare and high quality of reverence for another's individuality. Let us allow him integrity, also, forever after to be confided in; since he forbade himself to twine that one link more which might have rendered his spell over Phoebe indissoluble.

And, with a gesture of his hand, he restores Phoebe to herself. It is because he refuses to repeat his ancestor's blasphemous act and to make his spell over the girl indissoluble, that Holgrave becomes fitted for that highest kind of human relationship: a marriage, based not on human empire but on mutual reverence, a modest example, one supposes, of the right relation between man and woman prophesied by Hester Prynne. Holding back from the indissoluble spell, Holgrave makes possible the indissoluble union, something that will have a consecration of its own.

Quite the opposite, needless to say, is the case with Jaffrey Pyncheon.

The Judge is totally bent on acquiring "empire over a human spirit"—a diabolic empire over the spirit of poor Clifford—and he acquires it by repeating the actions of his ancestor, by a combination of murder and false testimony. Those crimes were monstrous enough, but the final sacrilege, the very sin of the crimes as it were, is the utterly debilitating spell the Judge has cast and continues to exercise over Clifford: "That strong and ponderous man had been Clifford's nightmare. There was no free breath to be drawn within the sphere of so malevolent an influence." Clifford is released from his psychic imprisonment only by Jaffrey's death. Jaffrey, who had believed too much in the past, who believed that the past could endlessly repeat and re-enact itself and who even believed in the inherited tale of buried treasure: Jaffrey is himself destroyed by the past, by the inherited disease—"the physical predisposition in the Pyncheon race"— and he dies with the legendary blood on his lips. The Judge, as we may say, is defeated by the legend, as he ought to have been: for in the deepest sense, it was a heartless legend, and he is a heartless man. By his defeat and death, Clifford is released from the legend, enough at least to recover something of himself. Holgrave escapes further still from the confines of the legend, as Hester Prynne—in her thoughts and in her gentle advices to the wretched—had moved somewhat outside the confines of allegory. As a work of fiction, *The House of the Seven Gables* moves similarly away from the legendary and toward the more modern and realistic; and arrives at a form, the Romance, in which Hawthorne could present his steadiest belief about human nature and its relationships not as an ideal dimly visible in the far future, but as an immediate possibility among the modern realities.

III

"Every one will, in his way—or in her way—plead the cause of the new truths. If you don't care for them, you won't go with us."

"I tell you I haven't the least idea what they are! I have never yet encountered in the world any but old truths— as old as the sun and the moon. How can I know? But *do* take me; it's such a chance to see Boston."

The new truths to which, in the opening scene of *The Bostonians,* Olive Chancellor so passionately appeals and of which her kinsman from Mississippi Basil Ransom, makes courteous mock, are, like those of *The Scarlet Letter,* ideas bearing chiefly upon the unhappy condition and possible future status of women. There are times, indeed, in *The Bostonians* when Olive Chancellor (though her surname more suitably if very faintly echoes that of Chillingworth) markedly resembles Hester Prynne. Or, more accurately, there are times when James is plainly drawing both his rhetoric and his subject matter not from contemporary historical developments but—as literary artists tend to do—from existing literature, and especially from *The Scarlet Letter.* "The unhappiness of women! The voice of their silent suffering was always in her ears, the ocean of tears that they had shed from the beginning of time seemed to pour through her own eyes." That is Olive, in James's articulation of her. "Women . . . —in the continually recurring trials of wounded, wasted, wronged, misplaced, or erring and sinful passion,—or with the dreary burden of a heart unyielded, because unvalued and unsought,—came to Hester's cottage, demanding why they were so wretched, and what the remedy." That, of course, is Hawthorne; and if Hester has once "imagined that she herself might be the destined prophetess," so "it seemed to [Olive] at times that she had been born to lead a crusade." It is, like the movement meditated by Hester, to be a religious crusade: "This was the only sacred cause; this was the great, the just revolution." And the nature and scope of it, as they form themselves in Olive's overheated mind, resemble those of the social upheaval Hester had pondered, with sacrificial death once more the probable and even desirable outcome:

It must sweep everything before it; it must exact from the other, the brutal, blood-stained, ravening race, the last particle of expiation! It would be the greatest change the world had seen; it would be a new era for the human family, and the names of those who had helped show the way and lead the squadrons would be the brightest in the tables of fame. They would be the names of women weak, insulted, persecuted, but devoted in every pulse of their being to the cause, and asking no better fate than to die for it.

In the near-hysteria of tone and the savagery of attitude toward the male race, the passage diverges markedly from the passage quoted earlier from *The Scarlet Letter*. It is, indeed, the meaningful differences between the two novels that I eventually want to stress—and that James himself, as I believe, wanted to stress; for James (to repeat my remark) seems to have counted upon our remembering Hawthorne and to have striven for his ultimate effects by means of a combined echo of and contrast with Hawthorne. But we should notice, meanwhile, that if *The Bostonians* shares with *The Scarlet Letter* an interest in revolutionary ideas about the condition of women, those ideas palpitate in *The Bostonians* within a general atmosphere of decline oddly similar to that of *The House of the Seven Gables*. In James's novel, as in Hawthorne's romance, almost every item participates in a pattern of diminution. The historical distance spanned in *The Bostonians* is nothing so large as that of *The Seven Gables:* it is at most the four score years of the saintly Fool, Miss Birdseye; and James's impressionistic and allusive evocation of even so short a stretch of history illustrates perfectly the remark of T. S. Eliot that Hawthorne's sense of the past "exercised itself in a grip on the past itself," but that "in James it is a sense of the sense." To which we should add, I think, that James had in particular a sense of Hawthorne's sense; and this made it possible for James to include in his own pattern of decay a much larger variety of elements than Hawthorne, and to cover a great deal more of the national landscape.

To begin with, the reformers who gather in Miss Birdseye's rooms appear aimless, bemused, rhetorically corrupted by comparison with "the heroic age of New England life," the age before the Civil War, an age "of plain living and high thinking, of pure ideals and earnest effort, of moral passion and noble experiment." And the social crusade, the marshaling of the feminist squadrons, sounds suddenly almost tawdry when James invokes "the simple emotion of the old fighting-time," the war itself, escorting us, with Basil Ransom and Verena Tarrant, into Harvard's Memorial Hall and remarking upon the "singularly noble and solemn effect" of the "temple" for the fallen soldiers, its symbolism of "duty and honor . . . sacrifice and example." But the conservative temper in *The Bostonians* is in no less sorry a state than the reformist: there is, on the one hand, the virtual medievalism of Ransom and, on the other, the mere muddled snobbishness of Adeline Luna, who, though she liked to think that the word "conservative" was "the motto inscribed upon her own silken banner" (the motto, in short, of her own crusade), limited her conservatism to prattle about the inferiority of republics and the bad manners of servants.

Places share in the general decay and are analogues of it. The entire Boston area is seen as disappearing into the spreading jungle of factories and engine shops. In James's famous and eloquent description of the western view from Olive's apartment on Charles Street, there is observed "something inexorable in the poverty of the scene," something

> shameful in the meanness of its details, which gave a collective impression of boards and tin and frozen earth, sheds and rotting piles, railwaylines striding flat across a thoroughfare of puddles, and tracks of the humbler, the universal horsecar, traversing obliquely this path of danger; loose fences, vacant lots, mounds of refuse, yards bestrewn with iron pipes, telegraph poles, and bare wooden backs of places.

(It is characteristic of Verena that she thinks this view lovely, just as at first she had secretly wished to emulate Adeline Luna rather than her sister Olive.) But if the northern landscape is thus being devoured by an industrial version of those ugly gigantic weeds that smothered the terrain in *The House of the Seven Gables,* the postwar South—"the poor, dear, desolate old South," as Ransom calls it—lies in utter ruin; and swift recollections of its former splendor sometimes flash through Ransom's consciousness and into ours, as a measure of its present desolation. Within the novel, in fact, and by a pattern of allusion more intricate than I can here suggest, the entire country is represented as having suffered some strange and terrible reversal of fortune (to borrow the phrase used about "the great drawing-room of Europe" in *The Wings of the Dove*). And this aspect is perhaps best summed up in the picture of the Cape Cod town of Marmion (i.e. Marion) which "was a good deal shrunken since the decline in the ship-building interest; it turned out a good many vessels every year, in the palmy days, before the war," but now Ransom gathers the impression "that it had had a larger life, seen better days." The larger life, the better days, stand everywhere behind the elements of the novel—persons, places, movements, ideals, interest—and testify to the present unhappy shrinkage.

In a much-quoted notebook entry for 1883, James wrote that—as his novel's main concern, and as "the most salient and peculiar point in [American] social life"—he had chosen "the decline in the sentiment of sex." That, certainly, is a major phenomenon in *The Bostonians,* and one which many of the other instances of "decline" explain and illuminate. But it is, I think, as much a symptom as a cause; and what the novel's action as well as its rhetoric more profoundly reveals is the decline of the religious sentiment—that is, of the specific religious sentiment to which, with and following Hawthorne, James was himself most profoundly committed. What is happening in this regard is indicated at a stroke, a single casual remark, almost an aside: when James reports that the Harvard library was "a diminished copy of the chapel at King's College," and that Verena Tarrant introduces Basil Ransom into it "with the air of a person familiar with the sanctified spot." These are lines that, in the theater idiom, James is quite willing to "throw away," and we miss nothing but a momentary pang of aesthetic pleasure and admiration if we fail to notice them. Nonetheless, in context, they fairly bristle with meaning.

We can best formulate that meaning by reference once again to *The Scarlet Letter.* There, Hawthorne set his action among a people—the Bostonians of the 1640s—for whom "religion and law were almost identical, and in whose character both were . . . thoroughly interfused." James set his own American novel among a people—the Bostonians of the 1870s—for whom *religion and ideology* were becoming almost identical, and in whose character both were already dangerously confused.[3] And both pairings are portrayed as the absolute enemy of the fundamental religious sentiment: the sense of the sanctity of the individual human heart. *That* is the sense that characterized "the heroic age of New England life"; that is the sense that has most fatally declined; and that is the sense which the novel seeks in its own subtle and dramatic manner to re-establish—though the characters in it do not.

Olive Chancellor, as we have seen, regards her feminist crusade as a sacred cause. Later in the story, she is made by James very tellingly to reflect that "without Verena's tender notes, her crusade would lack sweetness, what the Catholics call unction"; and with Verena, all during the winter of 187–, she looks forward across "the solemn vista of an effort so religious as never to be wanting

3. In his fine introduction to the Modern Library edition of *The Bostonians* (New York, 1956), Irving Howe makes a similar point within a somewhat different context.

in ecstasy." Basil Ransom—who in this regard as in others may be thought of as a deliberate inversion of Hawthorne's Holgrave —invests his own reactionary ideas, and especially his passionate antifeminist speeches, with no less ardent a religious quality; and though with much of what he says James would probably have agreed (in a quieter tone of voice), still Verena responds for James and for us when she is impressed "by the novelty of a man taking that sort of religious tone about such a cause." These are persons, Olive Chancellor and Basil Ransom, who really are violated by ideas, to draw again upon T. S. Eliot's inexhaustibly useful commentary and phrasing; who corrupt their feelings with ideas (the language is still Mr. Eliot's); who "produce the political idea, the emotional idea, evading sensation and thought"—and who make a religion out of the result. They are, in short, ideo-logues; and worse still, they are ideologues in action. They are not only violated by ideas, they use ideas to violate others; and in particular, of course, they violate, and fight to the death for the privilege of violating, the vulnerable individuality, the susceptible human heart, of Verena Tarrant.

The process need not be spelled out; to do so would be to rehearse most of the book's plot, for the plot turns exactly upon the effort and countereffort of Olive and Basil to possess them-selves of Verena, and each in the name of Verena's perfect free-dom and the holiness of the conflicting creeds. Two moments may stand for many. When Verena comes to live with Olive, the latter emphasizes the fact that the younger girl "should be as free as air, to go and come." But by that time, James informs us,

> Verena was completely under the charm. The idea of Olive's charm will perhaps make the reader smile; but I use the word not in its derived, but in its literal sense. The fine web of authority, of dependence, that her strenuous companion had woven about her, was now as dense as a suit of golden mail.

The literal sense of "charm" is, of course, a magic spell or in-cantation; and the suggestion of spells and webs carries us back instantly to the story of enchanted Alice Pyncheon in *The Seven Gables*. That masculine suit of mail, anyhow, retains its power, and its nature is reinforced by frequent allusions to actual or metaphoric cloakings and imprisonments: until, on an early spring afternoon in New York's Central Park, Basil Ransom casts his potent counterspell over the impressionable Verena. The sexual element is here all the more notable, since the ideas Basil expounds to her are, from her viewpoint, monstrous. The girl's reflections

> softly battled with each other as she listened, in the warm, still air, touched with the faraway hum of the immense city, to his deep, sweet, distinct voice, expressing monstrous opinions with exotic cadences and mild, familiar laughs, which, as he leaned toward her, almost tickled her cheek and ear. . . . there was a spell upon her as she listened.

As a dramatic construct—combining as it does the oratorical statement of social theory and of attitudes to history with a sort of psychological-cum-sexual hypnosis—the whole scene derives without much doubt from the long scene between Holgrave and Phoebe that extends from chapter xii through chapter xiv in *The Seven Gables.* The resemblance is worth emphasizing because in certain essential aspects James is carefully reversing Hawthorne, and the force of his accomplishment depends in no small part on our awareness of this. It is not only that all of Basil Ransom's eloquence goes toward getting rid of the present in the name of the past, rather than, as with Holgrave, the other way round. It is also that, Holgrave, for all his temptation to acquire "empire" over Phoebe's spirit, does have the high quality of reverence for her individuality, and releases the girl from her momentary enslavement. Ransom persists in his imperial design, to the end of the scene and the end of the novel.

That kind of reversal characterizes the relation consciously aimed at (as I am maintaining) and achieved between *The Bostonians* and the novels of Hawthorne. In the same way, the social revolution proposed by Olive Chancellor would in its consequences reverse those of the movement that Hester Prynne might have led. Hester's new sect would bring with it a relationship between man and woman grounded on mutual reverence; Olive apparently would like to see that relationship destroyed once and for all. The relationship Olive does establish in the novel (and even she perhaps comes to realize this) is a sort of paradigm of falsehood: it is sexually wrong, morally wrong, even politically wrong; and from the Hawthornian viewpoint of Henry James, it is religiously wrong. Its radical wrongness is one justification for Basil Ransom's ambiguous victory in the denouement; he is, after all, a man and a manly man. And beyond that—though Basil's crusade to "rescue" Verena from "ruin" is deeply suspect (there are too many examples in James's fiction of the lethally selfish nature of the rescuing impulse)—there is in Basil some faint occasional glimmer of the distinctive value of another person's individuality, or at least of Verena Tarrant's.

But "value" thus circumscribed is the strongest word we can use. There is no one in *The Bostonians* who, like Hester or Dimmesdale (for his moment of insight) or Holgrave, has and acts upon a clear sense of the heart's sanctity. The person who most nearly does is Miss Birdseye: she, as Verena exclaims, is "our heroine . . . our saint," exactly because she thinks only of others. There is evidence that James adjusted his attitude of Miss Birdseye as the novel progressed: in the early pages she is the victim of some of James's most brilliant comic writing; but from the second book onward she grows into truly heroic and saintly proportions, and in her final moments she is affectively larger than the life about her. But she *is* the ancient relic of an older epoch, the old heroic age; and in the book's most portentous scene, she does die. And that, of course, is James's point and the motive of his reversals: the antiquity and the death of the old selflessness, the old sanctity, the old sense of sanctity.

James, in *The Bostonians,* is exploiting Hawthorne to suggest a view opposite to Hawthorne about the fundamental *course* of human affairs, at least as those affairs were being conducted in America. James saw the American character moving away from, not toward, a belief in the sanctity of the human heart; away from, not toward, relationships consecrated by that belief. Where Hawthorne, in *The Scarlet Letter,* made tragic drama out of the possibility of religious legalism yielding to reverence for the individual, James in *The Bostonians,* in an equally impressive display of prophetic power, describes individual reverence yielding to a religion of ideology. The world in which that is happening is, as James makes almost appallingly clear, a world without sacrament, without any sort of sacramental sensibility: a world, from the point of view of the literary artist, unavailable to either allegory or legend, and fit primarily for satire and realism.

This is James in mid-career. During his major phase twenty years later, James for various reasons felt himself liberated in part from the clutch of the contemporary. He was then able to return to something like Hawthorne's tragically hopeful vision, and he would then adopt in consequence symbolic devices reminiscent of Hawthorne, along with a Hawthornesque atmosphere of the legendary and remote: precisely to suggest how a sacramental consciousness like that depicted in *The Scarlet Letter* could be quickened into being even within a world characterized by a lust for violation. But in *The Bostonians* James made his comment upon the American scene by casting a Hawthornian eye upon a non-Hawthornian world: by reassembling themes and motives and language from Hawthorne and by twisting and reversing them. It was James's comment as well upon American literature, upon what the novel in America had once done and could now do.

1961

HOLD ON HARD TO THE HUCKLEBERRY BUSHES

The search for religious elements in literature, especially in American literature, has become a phenomenon in recent years that would have startled and bewildered Matthew Arnold, who did not have this sort of thing in mind at all. An increasing number of books address themselves to the subject, courses and symposia are given over to it, and I believe a university department or two have been established to make the undertaking permanent. Some of the work, like some of the workers, displays a high degree of cultural relevance; but in general practice the study of "religion and literature," as the phrase usually is, exhibits several rather disturbing oddities, the first of which is implied by the phrase itself. It is theologically correct but aesthetically perilous: in a way which might ultimately damage the theology. Absolutely speaking, as between religion and literature, religion no doubt comes first; but in the actual study of a particular literary text, it probably ought to follow, and follow naturally and organically and without strain—for the sake of the religion as well as the literature. Or so I shall try to suggest. We may perhaps recall the remark made to Emerson by an old Boston lady who, talking about the extreme religious sensibility of an earlier generation, said about those pious folk that "they had to hold on hard to the huckleberry bushes to hinder themselves from being translated." Their instinct was as sound as their impulse was proper.

I

It was characteristic of Emerson to have quoted those words, for he knew well enough that his own hold tended to slip from time to time. He was articulately dedicated to the actual; he embraced, as he said, the common and explored the low and familiar, both in life and in literature. But the Over-Soul drew him like a magnet, and he was regularly prone to premature translation into the vast, unindividuated realm of the One. The atmosphere he found there was invariably sunny and smiling; and it is by stressing the sunshine and disregarding the translatability, that Randall Stewart, in *American Literature and Christian Doctrine*,[1] is able to condemn Emerson to the sixth circle, the place reserved for the burning tombs of the heresiarchs. "Emerson is the arch-heretic of American literature," says Professor Stewart, "and Emerson-ism [sic: a foreshortening rhetorically equivalent to the phrase Democrat Party] the greatest heresy. By no dint of sophistry can he be brought within the Christian fold. His doctrine is radically anti-Christian, and has done more than any other doctrine to undermine Christian belief in America." There is a kind of health in the hardness of Professor Stewart's saying. But I confess that it has for me a pointless irrelevance which it would not be easy to measure, though it may be important to define.

Professor Stewart's little book is amiably unambiguous in state-ment, and engagingly direct in style; it is sprinkled with nice personal reminiscences of a long and honorable academic life for which many of us have cause to be grateful. The book belongs, in its slender way, to the number of studies which have sought to examine the whole of American literature from a single organiz-ing viewpoint; and in this respect it follows a path opposite to the one followed by Frederick I. Carpenter in *American Literature and the Dream*[2]—a neglected work, in which Emerson appears as the high priest and dream purveyor rather than the arch heretic. But Professor Stewart's title is radically misleading, just as his method is revealingly—one is tempted to say, importantly and usefully—ill advised. By Christian doctrine, Professor Stewart means Protestant doctrine; by Protestant doctrine, he means American Puritan doctrine (in a manner that rather confirms than refutes the contention of the great Protestant historian of dogma, Adolph von Harnack, that there can be no such thing as Prot-estant dogma); by Puritan doctrine, Professor Stewart means very simply the doctrine of Original Sin; and by the doctrine of

1. Baton Rouge, La., 1958.
2. New York, 1955.

Original Sin, it is no longer clear what he means, since the matter has grown too small to be visible. He seems to mean even less, so far as one can make out, than T. E. Hulme meant thirty-five years ago, when he said—in a sentence that has done as much harm to the cause of cultural good sense as any that one can rapidly remember—that "dogmas like that of Original Sin . . . are the closest expression of the categories of the religious attitude." Separated from the rich theological framework within which it historically evolved, the concept of Original Sin is not much of a concept at all; it is more an image of unredeemably depraved human nature shivering somewhere in the void. In any case, this is the image that provides the single instrument by which Professor Stewart gauges the value of American writers from Edwards to the present. By the use of it, he denounces the villains, those who seem unaware of Original Sin (Paine, Franklin, Jefferson, Emerson, Whitman, Dreiser, Lewis), and salvages the elect (Edwards, Hawthorne, Melville maybe, James, Eliot, Hemingway, Faulkner, Warren). But the writings of both heroes and villains suffer a sort of total defeat. The latter are blown into oblivion by the author's rumbling southern rhetoric; and the former are blotted out behind an enormous O S, as Hester Prynne's image was lost behind the gigantic A reflected in the convex surface of the shining armor.

In Professor Stewart's case, the translation was effected before the huckleberry bushes were ever taken hold of. The actualities of the works in question—their actions, their words, their concrete embodiments, their sensuous images, their characters, their incidents—seem to have evaporated before a single glance descended on them. This is the likely consequence of the doctrinal approach to literature. If Professor Stewart had taken a more generous view of Christian doctrine, he might have composed a more interesting book; but I am not sure that it would have been a more pointed and purposeful book, or that it would have done better service to the field of literature or of religion; for the issue of priority would still remain. This issue is whether one scrutinizes literature for its univocal formulations of particular historical doctrines one cherishes or whether one submits for a while to the actual ingredients and the inner movement and growth of a work to see what attitude and insight, including religious attitude and insight, the work itself brings into being. Emerson continues to be a valuable case. Proceeding from Emerson's words as he uttered them, Newton Arvin—who is anything but a sophist, and is on the contrary one of America's most intelligent, tactful, and scholarly critics—has managed to bring Emerson some slight way "within the Christian fold."[3] Emerson, Mr. Arvin says, did after all have a knowledge of evil and an awareness of human sin; his famous cheerfulness was for the most part an achievement, a matter of discipline and hard intellectual choice. But Emerson could not convey his conceptions in the theological vocabulary available to him, because it was not comprehended within that vocabulary; and he was not in command of the vocabulary which could, in fact, convey it. He set it forth in tropes and figures, in shadings and insistences, in asides and repetitions of his own; and he emerged with a view of evil so profoundly different from that of his contemporaries that of sin itself he has seemed to have been simply and blissfully unconscious. For Emerson's sense of the problem was surprisingly similar to the older and more really traditional Christian attitude: the one that held firm from St. Augustine to the Reformation: the view of evil as non-being, as a privation, as a negation and an absence of good. Emerson normally preferred to talk about something rather than nothing, about being rather than non-being and affirmation rather than negation; he lacked the special taste and affection for evil of so many modern intellectuals. But (here I am pushing Mr. Arvin's argument beyond anything he would wish to claim for it) it might be salutary to reflect that, as regards the doctrine of sin, it is Hawthorne who was the heretic and Emerson who was working toward the restoration rather than the undermining of Christian belief in America.

Emerson did not knowingly aim at the restoration of anything: except of the soul's fresh and immediate perception of certain aspects of the universe, getting rid of the linguistic and institutional clutter in which those aspects had gone stale, and relating them anew to the instant of experience. "They only who build on Ideas, build for eternity. . . . The law is only a memorandum. We are superstitious, and esteem the statute somewhat: so much life as it has in the character of living men is its force." That is Emerson's authentic voice, or one of his authentic voices: the voice of a man disentangling the Idea from the historical record of it, and allowing it again to invigorate the present. But it is

3. "The House of Pain," *Hudson Review, 12* (1959), 37–53.

a suggestive and representative accident that, in pursuit of that aim, Emerson's metaphysical gaze lighted just occasionally and without historical awareness upon the essences of certain moral and religious doctrines that had been given their fullest elaboration in pre-Reformation Christian theology. It is this essential (or, may one say, essentializing) quality in Emerson that should dictate the method and scope of any significant religious inquiry into his writing; and it is this quality that relates him as an American of his time to his most talented contemporaries.

The same faculty for arriving by mistake at the very heart of some ancient doctrine, long since smothered by Calvinism, is observable in the two Henry Jameses, and to a greater or lesser extent in Hawthorne and Poe. The elder James, for example, wrestling in New York with the secret of Swedenborg, emerged with his own version of the Augustinian concept of the *felix culpa,* the notion that the fall of man was a happy and a fortunate event. Not a syllable of James consciously echoes either St. Augustine or the medieval *Exultet* which celebrated the fortunate fall; nor was his statement of the idea (Adam's fall was "an every way upwards step indeed, pregnant with beatific consequences") buttressed by the traditional theological scheme that lent some measure of logic to the paradox. But there he was, driven by his personal intellectual momentum and his private tropes, at the naked center of the old doctrine. Henry James, Jr., is a much more complex and awe-inspiring case, deserving lengthy analysis elsewhere. Here let us say only that either James is a cultural miracle, or else he had devoured (as seems distinctly improbable) almost all of Aristotle, St. Augustine, St. Thomas, St. Bonaventura, and Dante Alighieri. And as to Poe, his root idea, according to the persuasive essay by Allen Tate,[4] the one idea he did not merely "entertain" but which actually pushed and bedeviled him was the grand old heresy of attributing to human beings the intellect and imagination that God had reserved for the angels. It is a heresy, to be sure, but one form of it was indispensable to the scholastic thinking of the twelfth century, and in particular to St. Anselm, of whom Poe is unlikely to have heard. And so on.

The American Protestant analyst, if sufficiently limited in viewpoint, is apt to miss these strange appearances and theological throwbacks. He tends to go at the business wrong way round,

4. "The Angelic Imagination," in *The Man of Letters in the Modern World* (New York, 1955), pp. 113–31.

looking for unmistakable recurrences of key terms and neglecting
the cumulative suggestive power of the terms or images or special
private meanings of the individual writers; while the doctrine
accidentally echoed or latent in the work inspected may not be
a part of the American Protestant stock in trade. Hawthorne
tried out *his* version of the fortunate fall by having Kenyon, the
sculptor in *The Marble Faun,* broach it to conventionally Protestant Hilda; and "Oh, hush!" she tells him, shrinking away
"with an expression of horror," saying that she could weep for
him, she is shocked beyond words, his "creed" makes a mockery
"of all religious sentiments . . . [and] moral law"—that is, the
sentiments and the law drilled into her back in New England.
Kenyon hushes.

II

I have probably not escaped, in the preceding few paragraphs,
from seeming to honor in Emerson, Hawthorne, and the others
their rediscovery of "pieties that are older and more solid than
the Puritan ones"; but, much as I respect those older pieties, the
pieties of age-old Catholic Christianity, that is not precisely what
I am trying to do. It *is* what is attempted in *American Classics
Reconsidered,* from which the last quotation above is taken. This
book, edited by Harold C. Gardiner, S.J.,[5] brings together essays
by ten Roman Catholic writers on the major American men of
letters in the early and middle nineteenth century. It is by no
means a work of systematic expropriation. The intellectual standards are Catholic ones, and the approach is explicitly theological;
but there is a reasonably sustained effort to deal with the writers
as writers and as Americans, and very little effort to scold or
convert them. "Quite literally, I think," says Michael F. Moloney
in a creditable essay on Thoreau, "[Thoreau] went out to Walden
Pond to write a book. . . . He went . . . to strike a blow in defense
of the poet's right to existence. . . . He must be evaluated primarily
as a creative artist rather than as a thinker." Mr. Moloney does
so evaluate him; yet it is a sign of a certain uneasiness, as of
one who has muddled a little the right order of the goods, that
Mr. Moloney's title is "Christian *malgré lui.*" The phrase luckily
has almost nothing to do with the essay's content; for if it were
Mr. Moloney's intention to Christianize Thoreau despite himself,

5. (New York, 1958).

it would be a serious misdirection of energy. A similar sense of strain is detectable, or seems to me to be, in most of the other essays; and I shall offer some hints about the possible reasons for it, by looking in some detail at the essay by Joseph Schwartz on Hawthorne.

The latter is not necessarily the best contribution to the book. Although the volume is almost inevitably uneven, the level of critical and scholarly accomplishment strikes me as pretty high. The treatments of Longfellow, Poe, Melville, and "the literary historians" are perfunctory, perhaps because the writers in question are perfunctory themselves, like Longfellow, or because they have been drained of blood, like Melville, by the interminable critical surgery of the past few decades. (I digress to wonder with a certain anxiety how long the relatively small store of American literature is going to survive the writing about it, and especially the writing about the whole of it. Our production has fallen badly behind our consumption, as Henry James foresaw seventy years ago when he told a summer school on "the novel" at Deerfield, Massachusetts, that "We already talk too much about the novel in proportion to the quantity of it having any importance that we produce.") But the long analysis by Robert C. Pollock of Emerson's "single vision," for example, is a work of genuine scholarly composition; it composes something (a view of reality), and it is about the effort to do so. Mr. Pollock makes good overt use of Charles Feidelson's brilliant *Symbolism and American Literature* to clarify Emerson's long struggle "to free men from the delusion of a split universe, which, as he knew, had reduced human life to a fragmented state." Perhaps Mr. Pollock presents Emerson as achieving too completely what Emerson only succeeded in aiming at, and when he says that Emerson "steadfastly refused to recognize any split between the higher and lower worlds," he may have chosen the wrong verbal. What Emerson refused was to accept a split that he did recognize; he remains, in fact, America's most knowing and moving portrayer of the failures of connection in human experience—of the appalling lack of context, in modern times, for action and for judgment.

In addition to the chapters on Emerson, Thoreau, and Hawthorne, several other items in *American Classics Reconsidered* are to be commended. They include Ernest Sandeen's sometimes awkwardly phrased but compassionate and suggestive examination of Whitman ("He must accept even the social and moral outcast because he is himself an outcast asserting his claim to be accepted"); Alvan S. Ryan's intelligent survey of Orestes Brownson and his dialectical involvement with New England idealism; Charles A. Brady's informed and even loving study of the life and writings of James Fenimore Cooper—in my opinion, the most valuable as well as readable essay in the book, rather unexpected considering not Mr. Brady but James Fenimore Cooper, and rising to a poetic evocation of Leather-Stocking as a godlike figure similar to Oberon and Herakles ("Hawkeye and Chingachgook . . . become twin numina, two great *genii loci,* two waiting presences, tutelary deities of the American continent, joining hands in amity over a coil of motives and cross-purposes, the Green Man and the Red Manitou");[6] and Father Gardiner's brief introductory chapter, which establishes the theological perspective and makes up for a debatable salute to Colin Wilson's *The Outsider* by citing the special relevance, for his volume, of Charles Feidelson's book.

Father Gardiner urges, in his introduction, that "modern criticism would do well to minimize somewhat its preoccupation with techniques and return to more theological approaches." With that advice, I am personally very largely in agreement, up to what is for me a crucial point. And it should be added, especially on the evidence of this volume, that *most* Catholic writers, unlike *some* Protestant writers, are aware that in the theological approach some account must be taken of God. There is an extraordinary contemporary intellectual reluctance to utter the name of God, or even to allude to God in any definite way at all: a phenomenon peculiarly notable in books and courses on religion and literature. This is a current characteristic of the highest significance, though it does not, I believe, mean that God is dead in the consciousness of the present time (the report of God's death has been very much exaggerated). It means something rather different, my main suggestion about which I shall shortly and belatedly come round to. But in much of the purportedly "religious writing" of the day, God is treated, if at all, in the

6. Like Henry Bamford Parkes, in an extremely valuable essay published in *Modern Writing* No. 3 (New York, 1956), Mr. Brady emphasizes the organic continuity between Leather-Stocking and the hard-eyed private detective of recent years, affirming the claims of morality in the midst of cross-purposes more frightful and treacherous than any Leather-Stocking knew of.

manner dramatized time and again by Graham Greene (who is, I am aware, a Catholic of sorts)—as a married man's mistress, someone who must never be mentioned openly, is only thought about with a far corner of the mind, and is met briefly and on occasion in dark and hidden places, for illicit reasons. God, in short, is associated primarily with the sometimes titillating modern sense of sin and guilt. Hence it is that the entire range of Christian doctrine can be narrowed down to a belief in Original Sin, and Emerson, who had a more sublime view of the universe and its creator, dismissed as a corruptive influence on young minds and one who made the better cause appear the better. Even certain American forms of Roman Catholicism, I am told, are not always free of this bleak reductive tendency. But Father Gardiner's volume of essays is. When Michael F. Moloney wants to distinguish between Thoreau's humanistic mysticism and that of an authentically Christian religious mystic, he says rightly and flatly, "Man is Thoreau's primary concern, not God"; and Father Gardiner's own list of the great issues that he regards as central to the theological approach includes "the indwelling of God in the soul" as well as "the nature of sin and responsibility and the role of free will in responsibility." It also includes "[God's] Providence and salvific will . . . detachment from created goods, the communion of saints . . . and the real and proper 'divinity of man.' "

Those terms (especially "salvific," which I had to look up, and which means "tending to save" and is listed as obsolete) are not ones that an outsider in the non-Wilsonian sense can feel very easy with. But that they partake of a comprehensive and unmistakably theological vocabulary is hardly open to doubt. What is open to doubt is not the value of a theological approach to literature, but the value of approaching this particular body of literature with any set of terms and doctrines that has been fully and finally elaborated, historically, once and for all. That is just the question perhaps unwittingly pushed into prominence by Joseph Schwartz, in his essay on Hawthorne: an essay in this case appropriately titled "God and Man in New England."

Mr. Schwartz begins with the proposition that "the history of literature has been an attempt to put such abstractions ["free will, the natural desire for God, fatalism, and providence"] into concrete statements for the benefit of mankind"; and hence that it is proper to seek out in Hawthorne his concept of "the moral and religious character of man." The crux of the problem may be right there. Mr. Schwartz's principle runs counter, of course, to the most influential critical convictions and prejudices of the past few decades, according to which literature does not "put abstractions into concrete statement," but, rather, generates a special kind of idea by the special processes of the creative imagination. The basis of those critical convictions has been the observation that modern literature, at least, can be shown to be doing just that: which has led to the suspicion that maybe the greatest literature in all ages has been up to the same poetic business. Hawthorne is an uncommonly tangled and contradictory case. From time to time, he most certainly did put abstractions into concrete form, and his notebooks let us watch him as he does so. But at other moments, he seems rather to have begun with a particular image or incident and to have allowed it to expand in his mind till it reached its maximum suggestiveness.[7] Similarly, while the conclusion of "The Artist of the Beautiful," published in 1844, declares that the symbol which makes beauty perceptible becomes at last of little value for the artist who has "possessed himself . . . of the reality," the conclusion of "The Antique Ring," published a year earlier, argues that the artist "can never separate the idea from the symbol in which it manifests itself." The two statements have different contexts, and they are not strict opposites in any case. But they illustrate the magnificent hedging of which Hawthorne was a master, and which was radically necessary under the cultural circumstances in which he found himself. The same thing shows up still more revealingly in his habit of dramatizing a humane resistance to the metaphysical and theological concepts he has at the same time splendidly acknowledged. So, at least, I read tales like "The Birthmark" and "Ethan Brand," neither of which would readily yield their full and echoing discordance to the critic who searches for the abstractions made concrete in them.

Mr. Schwartz knows, at any rate, the right abstractions to look for: the conception of God and of God's relation to man. As he attempts to make these things visible, he (I think persuasively) disengages Hawthorne from the legend of an uninterruptedly

7. Ronald Gray's little book on Kafka (Cambridge, 1958) traces in scrupulous detail an analogous development in the composition of *The Castle,* and manages thereby to demonstrate the relative unsoundness of the Christian or Jewish doctrinal attack on that novel.

Puritan ancestry. Militant orthodoxy seems to have vanished from
the Hawthorne family by the mid-eighteenth century; Nathaniel's
mother, who had exclusive charge of him from the time he was
four, was an unemphatic Unitarian; Hawthorne was never, on
the evidence, indoctrinated or proselytized; and when he arrived
at Bowdoin, he gravitated instinctively toward persons "of the
same noncommittal temperament." Mr. Schwartz draws the picture of a man with a strong religious impulse and an intense religious curiosity who yet had the opportunity of choosing the
forms in which his sense of religious experience might get itself
articulated and who disliked and distrusted all the forms available to a nineteenth-century New Englander—all the gradations
of orthodoxy and the varieties of "liberal Christianity." He then
makes too little of the form Hawthorne finally did choose for his
purposes: the form of the narrative art.

If he slights that eventuality, it is probably because the art of
narrative does not appear to Mr. Schwartz as one of the forms
accessible to the religious impulse. For a person to whom none
of the modes of Protestant Christianity in the nineteenth century
were satisfying, only one other religious mode—Mr. Schwartz
seems, not unnaturally, to assume—could be possible. He becomes explicit only at the moment when he relates Hawthorne's
account of Donatello's "way to the Lord" to a sermon by St.
Thomas Aquinas for "The Feast of Saint Martin," and expresses
"amaze[ment] at Hawthorne's knowledge of Catholicism as it affected a character drawn from that tradition." The religious pattern which Hawthorne is here found to be slowly fulfilling is the
pattern of traditional Catholicism. Central to that pattern and to
Hawthorne's fiction as studied by Mr. Schwartz is the image of a
God of love and of hope.

It is a useful counterbalance to the occasional description of
Hawthorne as presenting a hopelessly depraved human nature
cowering away beneath the imminent chastisement of a coldly
angry deity. And for about half of his essay, Mr. Schwartz holds
on pretty hard to Hawthorne's huckleberries, to the human and
artistic elements sensibly at work in the notebooks and some of
the earlier stories: but then the process of translation sets in, and
nothing further hinders it. The remainder of Hawthorne's writings, including *The Scarlet Letter* and *The Marble Faun,* are
translated out of their unique existence into the (for those writings)
deforming emphases of Catholic Christianity. An entire inter-

pretation of *The Scarlet Letter* rests on the theory that "Dimmesdale's fundamental weakness . . . is his failure to recognize that
God is a God of love"—an excellent notion for a psychoana-
lytically trained confessor to try to inculcate into a real-life
Dimmesdale, but not the one central to the realized stress and
strain of the novel itself. And a bundle of quotations about "the
promises of a blessed eternity" and "O beautiful world! O benefi-
cent God!" leads Mr. Schwartz to identify Hilda, who sometimes
does talk like that in *The Marble Faun,* as "winningly virtuous."
Hilda comes at us in fact, from the fictional context she inhabits,
as a girl so bloodlessly virtuous as to be well-nigh terrifying, and
partly because of the way she talks. That Hawthorne, or a part
of him, thought of Hilda as such is indicated by his references
elsewhere to his belief that the words " 'genteel' and 'lady-like'
are terrible ones," and to "the pure, modest, sensitive and shrinking woman of America—shrinking when no evil is intended, and
sensitive like diseased flesh that thrills if you but point at it."

This is not to say merely that Hawthorne reveals more fertile
contradictions in his work than Mr. Schwartz acknowledges; it is
to say, rather, that the contradictions that give Hawthorne's work
its particular mood and movement are not entirely translatable
into traditional Christian terms—because they are moving away
from rather than toward a demonstration of the relevance of those
terms. Like Emerson, Hawthorne was largely free of the exact
religious formulas of his own time (though he regarded them more
closely, and always with a fascinated and creative skepticism).
Hawthorne's gaze, too, in its curious range and freedom, rested
betimes upon the essence of some central pre-Puritanical piety
—an image of God, perhaps, a deep conviction about human
responsibility. But those elements remained unrelated except in
the quick of Hawthorne's imagination; they were unfortified by
anything like a theology, much less a definitely Christian theology.
There is no dramatic use (I do not say, no mention) in Hawthorne
of the determining items in such a theology—no use whatever of
the idea of an intermediary between man and God: of Mary, of
the Holy Ghost, and, most crucial of all, of the figure and role of
Jesus Christ. There is an important sense in which Hawthorne
was not a Christian writer at all.

Hawthorne's view of religious experience is to be found only
by following the actual evolution, in each work and from one
work to the next, of his persistent images and patterns of relation-

ship. I am not making one more pedantic defense of the absolute integrity of literature; I am trying rather to say something about American and modern literature and the forms of religious expression in our times. As regards Catholic *or* Protestant Christianity, as in his relation to any other major historical development, Hawthorne was neither an outsider nor an insider: he was an in-betweener. His writings and his habitual concerns and responses lie somewhere in between the Christian epoch and an epoch (our own) which, with due modifications, we have to call post-Christian; and Hawthorne's imaginative energies bent forward, not backward. The direction in which he was bending is made clearer by his logical successor, Henry James; for James is probably the representative or at least the introductory figure in the post-Christian epoch.

James was post-Christian in somewhat the way that Virgil seems to us pre-Christian—James could dimly remember about as much of the substance of Christianity as Virgil could dimly foresee. The two men stand at opposite ends of the most enormous cultural curve in Western history, and almost everything they wrote had to do with their sense of where they stood. Each was beautifully shaken by premonitions of some gigantic disaster and by opaque hopes of an eventual transformation scene in the affairs of the cosmos. James's fiction, R. P. Blackmur once remarked in a singularly tantalizing sentence, was his reaction to "the predicament of the sensitive mind during what may be called the interregnum between the effective dominance of the old Christian-classical ideal through old European institutions and the rise to rule of the succeeding ideal, whatever history comes to call it." To the phrase "sensitive mind" in Mr. Blackmur's remark, I should like to add "religious imagination"; for James was, I believe, a religious writer, and his fiction was increasingly caught up in the web of circumstances investing and indeed creating the relationship between man and God.

James never put it that way: he was American and modern. Both the human and the literary problem of the present epoch was summed up by Merton Densher in *The Wings of the Dove,* when, trying to make good his lie to Maude Massingham about having been on his way to church on Christmas morning, he asked himself miserably, "To what church was he going, to what church . . . *could* he go?" He went, finally, to the Oratory on Brompton Road, but we must not make too much of that decision, any more than Merton did. It was no more than a transient effort to find a traditional Christian form in which to acknowledge what Merton had long before realized was nothing less than a religious experience. That realization was compounded altogether of Merton's sense of Milly Theale and of the course and meaning of his relationship with *her*. It was this that was "too sacred to describe," just as it was the genuine sacredness of the relationship that James had spent some seven-hundred-odd pages in describing: or, rather, in creating. The creation is achieved while carefully avoiding any direct utterance of the name of God; we have instead the names of Milly Theale, Merton Densher, and the others. This is the point of a reverent witticism made by a friend of mine who, when asked whether he thought that Milly Theale is a Christ-figure, replied, "No, but perhaps Christ is a Milly-figure."

It was, in short, characteristic of James, as representative of the post-Christian epoch, to have conveyed his religious sense by intensifying the human drama to the moment where it gave off intimations of the sacred. And it was characteristic of him to have done so almost exclusively by the resources of the narrative art, generating the "vision" *within* the developing work of art, and with almost no help from and perhaps very little knowledge or recollection of the traditional Christian doctrines. (Hence, by the way, the strange and baffling quality—strange and baffling, at least, for those who probe them from a systematic theological viewpoint—of James's mainly self-begotten symbols.) It was toward the Jamesian position and method that Hawthorne and his contemporaries were heading in an earlier generation. Perry Miller was luminously right when he claimed, in his introduction to *The Transcendentalists,* that Emersonian transcendentalism was "a religious demonstration" in which, however, the persons concerned put their cause into the language of literature rather than of theology. But it must always be added that when that is done, as I have suggested elsewhere, something happens to the cause as well as to the language. There is a deep propriety in searching for religious elements in works of literature, since that is where they often appear with the greatest urgency in the modern epoch; but there is a certain impropriety and perhaps an irrelevance in searching for historically grounded doctrinal elements. Christianity itself may very likely *not* be a historical phenomenon, or at least not in any decisive manner a purely historical phenomenon. But its institutions and its vocabulary are historical phenomena, and they may in some instances become as unusable for our present religious purposes as Anglo-Saxon is to our linguistic ones. The analogy is intended to be reasonably precise, for in both cases some very important use yet remains. James is representative in this respect as well, for he is post-Christian in the sense of coming after and making scant dramatic use of the finished frames of doctrine: while various essences of Christianity continue to work in his prose and to color and flavor the forms he finds and the forms he creates in human experience.

1959

HENRY JAMES: THE THEATER OF CONSCIOUSNESS

Among the great artists in narrative, Henry James is the most persistently, even the most obstinately dramatic—though to say so will make restive a certain class of readers for whom he has never seemed anything of the kind. It is just the complaint of those who have tried to read him and failed, or who have been forced to read him and hated it, that virtually nothing *happens* in a novel by Henry James. As against, say, *The Charterhouse of Parma,* with its fund of passionate heroics, or *Nostromo,* with its series of desperate enterprises, a novel like *The Wings of the Dove* (it has been argued) appears long-windedly devoid of the sharply visualized incident, the daring gesture, the heartfelt outcry, the electrifying encounter—devoid of those "dramatic" moments that seize and compel a reader's imagination. But a contention of this sort, though by no means unreasonable or naïve, derives from an association of the dramatic with the overt, the sensational, the abrupt; with crises that intensify beyond endurance and then explode. There are explosive elements in James's fiction, and there is a good deal of (often surreptitious) passion; there are moments of sudden and extraordinary illumination, and there is perhaps a larger degree of sheer melodrama than one would like. These are aspects of James's essential dramatism, but the latter is not adequately defined in terms of them and even works, paradoxically, to reduce their traditional "dramatic" effect. James's dramatism was above all a principle of fictional form—but a principle rooted in a vision of human life.

James was a dramatist in fiction on the formal side because he sized up life as dramatic on the human and experiential side. He composed his best novels according to the principles of dramatic construction—almost, one sometimes feels, according to the principles of Aristotle's *Poetics*—because he believed it to be the purpose of fiction (as he once told a symposium on "the novel") to give an impression of life. And it was his impression that life—life truly lived, and not squandered or simply not attempted at all—revealed the shape, the rhythm, and the slow relentlessness of classical and especially of neoclassical drama. James's formula for the novel, "an impression of life," was almost his modern and American version of Aristotle's formula for tragedy, "the imitation of an action" (and, as it were, vice versa, since for Aristotle human life *was* a mode of action). But there was a difference, due to historical circumstances as well no doubt as to a limitation of personal experience and a lack of talent (that is, of the talent for plot-making). In any event, the most intense and accessible action for James was that of the aroused consciousness, as it expanded and came into focus through conflict with the consciousness of others. The ground of experience, in the Jamesian view, was the theater of consciousness, and the person most fully alive was the one who saw himself as a histrionic participant on that stage. The achievement of that special Jamesian kind of histrionic awareness and vitality is at the same time—so the discussions that follow try to suggest—an act of transcendence that partakes of the religious.

I: The Sense of Fair Play[1]

Again the good lady [Mrs. Brigstock] looked hard at her young hostess. "I came, I believe, Fleda, just, you know, to plead with you."

Fleda, with a bright face, hesitated a moment. "As if I were one of those bad women in a play?"

The remark was disastrous.

The Spoils of Poynton, chapter xv

Writing in the New York literary monthly, the *Galaxy,* in May 1877, Henry James—reporting from abroad—offered a small anecdote to explain his feeling that the London stage was in a

1. This brief discussion was written for an American Literature session in December 1960 at the Modern Language Association meeting. The subject of the session was the concept of beauty in the work of four American writers—the other writers being Dreiser, Pound, and Stevens.

poor way. His story had to do with an American visitor James
had observed one day in a London grill-room and who, upon
leaving, took with him innocently enough a copy of the bill of
fare, no doubt as a memento for his wife. One of the English
customers immediately rushed to the manager in a blaze of moral
indignation to report the theft, and was overheard arguing, as
James put it, "in the name of outraged morality.—'You know
he oughtn't to have done that—it was very wrong in him to do
it. . . . You know I ought to tell you—it was my duty to tell you
—I couldn't *but* tell you.' . . . It is not easy," James continued,
"to point out definitely the connection between this little episode
. . . and the present condition of the English stage; but—it may
have been whimsical—I thought I perceived a connection. These
people are too highly moral to be histrionic, I said; they have too
stern a sense of duty." It is not easy for me in turn to point out
the connection between this passage and the topic to which we
have been asked to address ourselves; but I think there is one,
and I shall suggest that for Henry James the question of beauty
was located somewhere amid that lively anecdotal dialectic of
the moral and the histrionic.

The latter word indicates at once James's own reordering of
the entire moral issue. In common with many of his contemporary
men of letters, James was repelled by the static, declamatory
moralism of the middle class. When he used the word "conscience," he normally meant the philistine conscience, and often
presented it as a mode of self-satisfied treachery; while the phrase
"good conscience" in his fiction could define a temperament that
was positively lethal (as in the case of that man of good conscience, Lord Mark, in *The Wings of the Dove*). But James did
not follow some of his English and continental peers in simply
replacing the Victorian cult of morality with a *symboliste* cult
of beauty. His view of things fused the moral *with* the beautiful;
and the not unfamiliar form of moral beauty that resulted was
given a peculiar vitality by what was, in James, an essentially
histrionic imagination.

The process shows James hanging on to a family legacy, and
at the same time crucially modifying it. In his autobiography,
James recalled with immense pleasure the cheerful paradoxes
of a father and a family all dedicated to the moral and all intensely
opposed to the moralistic or priggish (just as he remembered "the
particular crookedness of our being so extremely religious without

having, as it were, anything in the least clarified or striking to show for it").

I can scarce sufficiently express how little [our family life] could have conduced to the formation of prigs [he wrote in *A Small Boy and Others*]. Our father's prime horror was of *them*—he only cared for virtue that was more or less ashamed of itself; and nothing could have been of a happier whimsicality than the mixture in him . . . of the strongest instinct for the human and the liveliest reaction from the literal. The literal played in our education as small a part as it perhaps ever played in any, and we wholesomely breathed inconsistency and ate and drank paradoxes . . . the moral of all of which was that we need never fear not to be good enough if we were only social enough: a splendid meaning indeed being attached to the latter term.

Thus we had ever the amusement, since I can really call it nothing less, of hearing morality, or moralism as it was more invidiously worded, made hay of in the very interest of character and conduct; these things suffering much, it seemed, by their association with conscience—that is, the *conscious* conscience—the very home of the literal, the haunt of so many pedantries.

To the word "moral," Henry James the elder thus opposed the word "social," "a splendid meaning indeed being attached to the latter term"; and to the notion of the self, he opposed his privately understood notion of humanity. The acquisition of selfhood, the birth of moral conscience, the formation of the ego—all this represented the capital sin in the father's universe: though it was a necessary and even a fortunate sin, a critical step in the individual psychic career beyond that mindless Adamic innocence in which the career took its start. But it was one of the father's ideas that the passage from innocence to conscience was an altogether self-ish affair; and to arrive at genuine human maturity there must occur a shattering of the ego, followed by a rejuvenation as a member of what he called "the divine-natural humanity," that being the elder James's phrase for the ideal socialism, the paradox of perfect individual integrity with perfect harmony, that he celebrated in 1879 under the telling title, *Society the Redeemed Form of Man*. In the doctrine of Henry James Senior, there was already a certain dramatic quality; he seemed to detect a plot in experience, a dramatic form of a tragic variety in the life that was really lived. The accomplishment of his younger son was to push and tighten the analogy; to implicate the moral in the social, but then to implicate both within the histrionic—so that the well-lived life had some of the formal beauty of the well-made play; and even the word "character"—as in the phrase "character and conduct"—carried with it something of the playwright's as well as the moralist's meaning.

The development of this attitude can, I think, be marked with sufficient clarity. Like his father, Henry James Junior had "the strongest instinct for the human." As a humanist, he was a strong moralist; but the human situation focused itself most sharply for anyone who regarded it as striving toward the conditions of art: that is, of an art-*work*. It is a clue to Merton Densher's potential for salvation in *The Wings of the Dove* that he can see himself as "but a sentence of a sort in the general text"; and the soundness of his moral aspiration is contained in his hope of avoiding the spiritual poverty of "reading the romance of his existence in a cheap edition." In the years following James's unhappy foray into the actual world of the English theater, during the nineties, the genre of art to which human experience was analogized tended increasingly to be the play rather than the novel. About her ailing young friend Milly Theale, Susan Stringham has the impression that she is not simply a princess, but "a princess in a conventional tragedy." And in *The Spoils of Poynton,* Fleda Vetch reaches a kind of peak of insight when she shocks Mrs. Brigstock by venturing that the older woman had come to plead with her about Owen Gereth "as if," Fleda says, "I were one of those bad women in a play."

It is a rich and cunning moment. The play both Fleda and Henry James had in mind was *La Dame aux Camélias* by Alexander Dumas the Younger: a play about which James had written at some length and with reverent memories of seeing Eleanora Duse as Marguerite, during the same year, 1896, that he completed and published *The Spoils of Poynton*. To Mrs. Brigstock, the allusion is unpardonably frivolous and downright immoral; in fact, however, the theatrical comparison is a main sign of Fleda's profoundly moral alertness. But Mrs. Brigstock is as insular as she is priggish: if she is too moral to be histrionic, she is also too British to appreciate the special histrionics of the French. The Jamesian analogy of human conduct with the conduct of persons on stage did not hold for any sort of play; he had in mind the play that grew out of the traditions of the French theater, and in particular the French neoclassic theater. What James admired in *La Dame aux Camélias* was "its combination of freshness and form, of the feeling of the springtime of life and the sense of the conditions of the theatre"—conditions James was emphatic in contending obtained almost exclusively in France. In such drama, James felt an ideal expression of life: which is to say that his father's ideal socialism, his redeemed form, became the son's ideal theater; to the extent that one sometimes imagines that God, for Henry James, was primarily the supreme dramatist—only to discover, in his story "The Birthplace" of 1903, that he voiced that very suggestion by converting William Shakespeare into at least a powerful local deity. In the ideal life, in any case, individual characters perform like persons in a French neoclassic drama: they are very distinctly *persons,* in gesture and speech, but they are engaged—and consciously engaged—in a single, binding social action; or, in stage language, in what is here called ensemble acting. The moral equivalent is of persons decidedly themselves who are yet thoroughly aware of the reality of others: are poised, so to speak, *toward* others. It is in this context that behavior is judged not so much as good or bad, but as beautiful or ugly; and James's tribute to Eleanora Duse—that for her, "the most beautiful thing is always the great thing"—could be applied to instances of actual or fictional behavior. There is thus a special twist and accent, even a kind of pun, in one of James's favorite phrases for defining any kind of honorable conduct: he liked to refer to it as "fair play."

It is in *The Spoils of Poynton* and specifically in the relation between Fleda Vetch and Mrs. Gereth, the widowed mistress of Poynton, that the Jamesian concept is most luminously rendered. The two women come together on the common ground of their love of beauty; or, more accurately, their revulsion from ugliness —from "the aesthetic misery of the big commodious house" of the Brigstocks at Waterbath. They are, as James says, spirits of the same family; and the narrative point of view in the early chapters makes no distinction between them. Throughout this section, indeed, the novel seems to promise us a familiar late

Victorian conflict between vulgarity and greed, supported by a
crafty moralism, on the one hand (the Brigstock world), and an
aesthetic devotion, on the other, that amounts nearly to the
religion of beauty (the world of Poynton, where Mrs. Gereth
says of its treasures that "They were our religion, they were our
life!"). But what James calls his "little drama" unfolds in a manner absolutely characteristic of him; and that initial conflict
suffers a radical change at the very moment it reaches its own
climax—when the representative of Waterbath, Mona Brigstock,
enters the world of Poynton to sit among its exquisite possessions
like a bored tourist. On the instant, the movement shifts and
deepens; for the spectacle of Mona so horrifies Mrs. Gereth that
she bursts out with the suggestion that her son insure the safe-
keeping of the precious spoils by marrying Fleda Vetch instead.
The proposal reveals Mrs. Gereth as, suddenly, a representative
far more terrible than Mona Brigstock of everything the James
family meant by moralism—that is, of the conscious conscience,
of lethally self-satisfied egotism—and precisely in her role as
the high priestess of the cult of beauty. In her fanatical regard
for her beautiful things, it is now Mrs. Gereth who assumes attributes formerly associated with the Brigstocks; and when Fleda,
after her hostess's outburst, turns on her with a scorching, "How
could you," Mrs. Gereth shows a face (as James observes) of
"perfect blankness" that was "a sign of her serene conscience."

The conflict thereafter is between the two one-time spirits of
the same family; and it is reflected exclusively in what James
designates as Fleda's "intenser consciousness." Within that consciousness, the truth about Mrs. Gereth and the ultimate value
of her kind of aesthetic devotion become fully recognized: especially when Mrs. Gereth intuits Fleda's secret—that she has fallen
in love with Owen. Fleda then tells herself, apprehensively, that

There were things for which Mrs. Gereth's *flair* was not so
happy as for bargains and "marks." It wouldn't be happy now
as to the best action on the knowledge she had just gained. . . .
There were ways in which she could sharply incommode a
person, and not only with the best conscience in the world, but
with a sort of brutality of good intentions. . . . She was nothing
if not practical: almost the only thing she took account of in her
young friend's soft secret was the excellent use she could
make of it.

The language is exact, particularly in the seeming casualness of the repetition of the word "thing." Mrs. Gereth had, it is said elsewhere, "a maniacal disposition to thrust in everywhere the question of 'things' "; and when, as here, out of a perfect conscience which is just the symptom of her immense spiritual greed, she seeks to make use of other persons, she is treating human beings not as persons but, literally, as things.

If Fleda can appraise Mrs. Gereth so correctly, it is because of the nature of her own consciousness. She is the only one in the novel to possess that histrionic awareness that James so honored. When the parlormaid at Ricks comes flying out to announce the arrival there of Owen Gereth, "she became"—in Fleda's mind—"on the instant an actress in the drama." At this point, Fleda still assumes "that she herself was only a spectator," and she has the sense of looking "across the footlights at the exponent of the principal part." By the time, eight chapters later, that Mona Brigstock's mother calls to plead with her in London, Fleda has realized that she herself has had to take on the principal part, and she can even hint, lightly, at the content of the play they are engaged in. Such an awareness is the very basis of her moral sensibility; for, seeing all of the other persons as caught up, with her, in the central action of a carefully shaped play, she is peculiarly alive not only to her own desires but to the motivations and hopes and significance of each of the Brigstocks and the Gereths as well.

Her sense of the beautiful, as a consequence, is not less but far more refined than that of Mrs. Gereth, for it is always involved with the human and the histrionic. When she discovers at the little cottage at Ricks that Mrs. Gereth has transported there most of the Poynton treasures, she finds that they have lost their beauty for her. Surveying them, Fleda "was impressed anew with her friend's genius for composition . . . [but] there was no joy for her" in the spectacle. "She couldn't care for such things when they came to her in such ways; there was a wrong about them all that turned them to ugliness." The beauty of the *things* had been destroyed by Mrs. Gereth's violation of a higher beauty: the principle of fair play, of beautiful conduct between human individuals. That is what Fleda requires of Owen, even after they have confessed their love to one another: that he play fair with Mona, that he give her a final chance. Mona, of course, seizes that chance greedily; and Fleda's secret hopes disappear in the ultimate holocaust of the Poynton estate. Her very loyalty to her principle is her practical undoing; at the end she is totally and irrevocably alone; but she has, at least, been constant and faithful to the Jamesian vision of beauty in action.

1960

II: *The Wings of the Dove*

There is no small talk, there are scarcely any manners. . . . Well in the very front of the scene lunges with extraordinary length of arm the Ego against the Ego, and rocks in a rigor of passion the soul against the soul.

Henry James on *John Gabriel Borkman* (1897)

James's uncommonly spirited remark about *John Gabriel Borkman* gives us our best working hypothesis for *The Wings of the Dove*. Almost everything James said about Ibsen can be applied, with a little stretching or reduction, to himself—even though, when he wrote Gosse in the first enthusiasm for the Norwegian that "you must tell me more about I.," he added, "That is not in this case female-American for *me*." But in a sense it was; it always was; and as his feeling for Ibsen deepened, James began to admire in the plays the very quality that distinguishes his own later novels—the ability to arrive "for all his meagerness at intensity." The achievement of *The Wings of the Dove* (or the one, at any rate, I want here to consider) was the product of intensity; and it was something for which the only word that will do is "religious," and that word will not do very well. For the religious experience to which the adventure rises is very meagerly supported; it cannot depend upon creed or doctrine, upon church or institution; it is a matter of mounting intensity, an affair—however artfully beclouded—of the passionate lunging of soul against soul, in an absence of small talk and a transcendence of manners. James held to the belief (historically exaggerated but prophetically sound) that, in the world he knew, there was little left for the artist to manipulate save the rocking and the lunging; and through them he regathered in his pages the forces of a recognizably traditional event of all but the highest order.

In one of his prefaces, James would define experience itself in social terms, as the apprehension and measure of the self in its social being. But in 1902, when he was composing *The Wings of the Dove,* he had been smitten by a characteristic American uncertainty over the actual possibility of that kind of experience. Milly Theale has hardly settled in London before it is hinted to her that, for all her desire to become "involved," there may be precious little to become coherently involved *with*. Were there even (Lord Mark, that man of good conscience, raises the question) such things as social sets any longer? "[W]as there any thing but the senseless shifting tumble, like that of some great greasy sea in mid-Channel, of an overwhelming melted mixture?"[2] A good many weeks and books later, the hint is confirmed by poor Merton Densher when he contemplates the Venetian pavements "greasy now with the salt spray." In the context of his disturbing drama, Venice is an image of a declining, perhaps even a shattered culture: "the whole place, in its huge elegance, the grace of its conception and the beauty of its detail, was more than ever like a great drawing-room, the drawing-room of Europe, profaned and bewildered by some reverse of fortune" (chapter XXX). *The Wings of the Dove* is about senselessness and collapse, about both dissociation and confusion; and it is a triumph over them. It shows what can be done—or what James could do—to give value and meaning to experience when those qualities were no longer discoverable in social terms. And what James could do, in the face of profanation and bewilderment and out of the observed battle of the spirit, was to recover something like a sacramental sensibility. This is what happens within the texture of the novel; and this is what happens, in the story, to Merton Densher.

At the same time, James's imagination, like that of his father, was two-edged. It was, as he said, an imagination of disaster; but there was also the dim imagining of what, in describing his father's most vigorous expectation, he called "a transformation scene in human affairs." There might be emerging, James felt, a different society altogether from the one visibly declining in Europe and the one struggling to be born in America. Associations between and among the members of both societies "have created"—he argued, in the preface to *Lady Barberina*—"a new

2. (New York, Scribner's, 1902), chapter VII. Subsequent references to this edition—identical in pagination to the Modern Library edition—are cited in the text. In the New York Edition, James revised the above passage to read: ". . . was there anything but the groping and pawing, that of the vague billows of some great greasy sea in mid-Channel, of masses of bewildered people trying to 'get' they didn't know what or where?"

scale of relations . . . a state of things from which *emphasized* internationalism has either quite dropped or is well on its way to drop." And so the subject of *The Wings of the Dove* and *The Golden Bowl* could in each case (James continued) "have been perfectly expressed had *all* the persons concerned been only American or only English or only Roman or whatever." This points toward a different and a more delectable kind of melting and mixing. It too is hinted at in *The Wings,* and leads similarly to a perception religious in its peculiar energy: when Milly, in the most ardently alert moment of her life, feels "the elements melt[ing] together," feels at Matcham that "Once more things melted together—the beauty and the history and the facility and the splendid midsummer glow: it was a sort of magnificent maximum, the pink dawn of an apotheosis" (chapter XI). And she knows, confronting the Bronzino painting, that she will never again be better than this.

It should be said that the social and cultural ties had in fact not slackened as much by 1902, the distinctive natures of persons and things not become as mixed and melted—to an end either sanctified or profaned—as James appeared to believe. His account is essentially prophetic. It is more accurate as a picture of our immediate condition, after the great drawing rooms of Europe and America have been more radically bewildered by a couple of wars and an assortment of betrayals and misalliances, and following our stumbling, ill-conceived, but not ill-motivated efforts to stage some sort of transformation scene. Both processes have become accelerated; and now our vague hopes for an apotheosis alternate with the dull conviction that the great greasy sea is upon us. This is a major reason why we can detect and honor James's bold achievement, and why it is an almost poignantly appropriate moment to do so—to honor this bequest as an earnest of what can yet be accomplished in the melting season.

As to the source of James's prophetic power, I hazard the following—a personal variation on a pretty old tune. When he left America and settled in Europe, he departed from a culture which had, or thought it had, to build afresh, from the ground up, with new tools and new blueprints, constructing new kinds of relationships with new names. It could give James little to travel with, and he brought with him nothing but the inexhaustible fertility of a uniquely creative consciousness. The culture he then inhabited was slowly loosening at the joints; his consciousness was sufficient to make him aware of the loosening, but not enough to get really in touch with what still held firm. In Europe, he celebrated the artistic availability of the famous list of items lacking to the American scene; but because he was so American, or rather because he was so incorrigibly a native of the James family, the items presented to his inspection only their surfaces. What lay beneath— all the crowded history that had gone into them and that Hawthorne responded to so warmly—remained invisible; but the surfaces suited James very well, for by genius and by the "sensuous education" foisted on him and William by their father, he was an insatiate devourer of surfaces. It is recorded that, to the consternation of his elders, he could recall in detail the surface of a monument he could only have seen (in Paris) when he was less than two years old; it is not recorded that he ever knew to any depth what the monument stood for. His early fiction gleamed with its bright notations of the outsides of things—surfaces humanized into manners—but when he worked his way inward, he could discover only what his fertile consciousness had put there— the rocking of the souls, the lunging of the egos. And that was quite enough; he saw so small an amount of what was present that he could powerfully envisage what might be in the future; his blindness was the very instrument of his vision.

The Wings of the Dove recapitulates its author's career by working its way through and beyond surfaces to the collision of psyches, and through the achieved intensity thereof to a fleeting glimpse (the most, after all, we humans are ever vouchsafed) of the divine. The plot, or "letter," of the novel is conventional enough, especially as sketched in James's notebooks: the wicked scheming of youth, and its fatal effect upon a radiant, consumptive, and enormously rich young woman whose whole desire is to live, out of the very warmth of her affection for the schemers. It was when the plot was elaborated in the novel and the effect of the scheming began to work both ways that it took on its remarkable substance, its relentless momentum. It acquired, first of all, a series of suggestive surfaces—the most striking of which is the assortment of homes and houses, the variety of drawing rooms which represent the great drawing room of Europe. The vast act of profanation is reflected in the arc along which those surfaces may be plotted. It ascends from "the vulgar little room" of Lionel Croy, with its shabby sofa, sallow prints and soiled centerpiece; to the dreary residence of Marian Condrip in "comfortless Chelsea"; to Lancaster Gate; to Matcham (the high point, the scene of creative melting and the dawn of apotheosis); to the Palazzo Leporelli; to Merton Densher's "shabby but friendly" faded old rooms (here the descent is marked) in Venice; to Marian Condrip's once again; and finally comes to rest on a note of total dissociation in Merton's dim London lodgings. As the tale moves from setting to setting, we witness one of the supreme instances in modern fiction of what Kenneth Burke calls "the act-scene relation," the tactic whereby settings are made to explain and comment on the actions that occur in them.

It is not merely that the dark and dismal vulgarity of Lionel Croy's room and the Chelsea household help us to sympathize with Kate's hard aspiration to go (as her aunt puts it) "high, high up—high up and in the light" (chapter IV), and to understand her enjoyment of the "high retreat" in which she is installed at Lancaster Gate. It is also that inanimate things bespeak, in this novel, the forces that invade them—forces which are human and other than human—and they do so by their own mute dialectic, by the contrasting messages they seem to issue to the minds that observe them. To Kate, a person to whom "material things spoke," Lancaster Gate spoke all of charms and pleasures; but to Merton, for whom "it was the language of the house itself that spoke," it hinted of something "ugly—operatively, ominously . . . cruel." The division between the lovers will not be clearly sensed by them until the encounter in Venice and not acknowledged until two months after the following Christmas; but it is foreshadowed at once in the difference between their responses to the power of surfaces.

The moral pressure of material things and the ambiguity of their language are so important in *The Wings of the Dove* that Lord Mark, though as tenaciously obtuse as ever, may have been only superficially wrong when he misunderstood the murmured plea of Milly Theale in Book Seventh. "Ah, not to go down— never, never to go down!" (chapter XXV) she had strangely sighed, gazing from the high window of the Palazzo Leporelli; and Lord Mark thought she meant descending the tremendous old staircase to the courtyard and the canal. Milly referred to a decline into unconsciousness, into death; but her visitor unwittingly grasped the way such an action is rendered or resisted in the fiction he inhabits: going down, in his meaning, would insure not going down in hers. Milly's inability any longer to go down the staircase is as suggestive as Merton's inability (during most of the ninth book) to go up into her presence. The quality of moral beauty personified by Milly Theale exists only in the high places; it may walk briefly in Regent's Park, but the atmosphere there is fatally thick; it is truly at home on an Alpine plateau or in the upper story of a great palazzo. There only it can live, and, given the conditions of actual morality, it can only die there, felt by but above the reach of a Merton Densher.[3] Milly cannot go down; and Kate Croy can do nothing else. The distance of her fall is measured by the descent from her high retreat in Lancaster Gate to the obscurity of the rooms where we last indistinctly see her; and it is due to a tough but faulty judgment of what might constitute a worthy and acceptable height—to her "dire accessibility to pleasure" from material things and from the kind of loftiness Mrs. Lowder planned for her.

But surfaces in *The Wings of the Dove* are—as has perhaps been indicated—so deeply penetrated by consciousness that little tangible or palpable remains of them. That is why we can say about *The Wings* what James said about *John Gabriel Borkman:* that there are, in fact, scarcely any manners, in the formal sense, as there is certainly no small talk at all. There are manners enough to conceal for a while the horror of the action; their function is to keep the action furtive, to subdue, as it were, the shout of appalled recognition to a soft murmur; but they tend to yield rather early in the game to the impact of the lunging Egos. And what, in their place, is gradually begotten by the drama is best illustrated (I suggest) by the novel's evolving definition of marriage—of marriage and its calamitous relation to money. Marriage means so little when the novel opens that it can mean almost everything before it closes; and here again we notice the singular value of James's view of the contemporary cultural condition—his curious remoteness from the historical actuality of institutions. A comparison with Jane Austen is useful. Marriage was the key event and the constant goal in the characteristic Austen novel: it could be assumed as a known thing, permanent in its nature, before the novel began; and nothing that happened during the narrative could or did affect its significance. In the world of Jane Austen, marriage may no longer have been what it once primarily

3. The phrasing here is itself a tacit acknowledgment of R. P. Blackmur's essay, "The Loose and Baggy Monsters of Henry James," in *The Lion and the Honeycomb* (New York, 1955), pp. 268–88.

was—a sacrament—but it was still an honorable estate; it was altogether à la mode. By the end of the century, James suspected (and, as usual, he was historically wrong but prophetically right) that marriage as such meant little or nothing; what it *could* mean would be produced in each instance by the conflict of consciousness. That conflict is so intense in *The Wings of the Dove* that marriage, which starts with considerably less meaning than it had for Jane Austen, ends up with very much more. It is enabled to recover not so much its honorable as its sacramental character; it is made vulnerable to blasphemy.

Kate Croy and Merton Densher are in love when the story opens; they become engaged; they wish to marry. For Merton, with his as yet uncreated conscience, there is no great mystery about marriage; he is simply impatient over the delay. But Kate has a more complex sense of the matter, owing to her family experience of it and the vigorous but still undefined ambition that experience had stimulated in her. Marriage had been a suffering for her mother, and connected with something horrid and unknown; Mrs. Croy had had to learn that her husband was "a terrible husband not to live with." And as to her sister Marian and the snuffling dejection to which marriage had reduced her— "If that was what marriage necessarily did to you, Kate Croy would have questioned marriage" (chapter II). With her severe inherited actuality, Kate contemplates marriage within the dangerous drama of poverty and wealth, power and freedom, habits of conduct and the energies of relationships; and she sets herself to mastering the dangers for the future well-being of Merton and herself. Marriage becomes a source of friction between the lovers as it is pushed thus into the midst of Kate's tough-minded strategy —which, upon the entrance of Mrs. Lowder, doubles into a pair of hostile strategies—and it enlarges steadily in significance till it appears the crucial event, the determining condition of life and value.

But it is still further enlarged, and now beyond the limits of ordinary human measure, with the arrival of Mildred Theale. For at this point the two strategies of Kate and her aunt no longer touch merely each other—touch, that is, robust and worldly people; they touch a fragile and fatal image of moral beauty; they touch a princess, a seraph, a dove, an image doomed to destruction and doomed to destroy: little Miss Theale from New York, the fatality in the lives of everyone. All the lunging, all the maneuvering, all the meditation and the talk over nearly six hundred pages—the exploratory discourses of Kate and Merton, the gossipy planning of Maude and Susan, the delicate fencing between Sir Luke and Milly, the more guarded conversations between the latter and each of the lovers, and the inward ponderings of them all—work to produce and invest the epiphanic moment in Book Eighth when Merton understands that he is being urged toward sacrilege. The quotation follows, but the force of it is not in its language, but in the dialectical movement that leads toward it. Kate's fully evolved plan emerges at last, as she talks with Merton at the party in the Palazzo Leporelli; but she requires of him that he name it: "If you want things named, you must name them."

> He had quite, within the minute, been turning names over; and there was only one, which at last stared at him there dreadful, that properly fitted. "Since she's to die I'm to marry her?"

Kate is brave enough to repeat his words. He continues, puzzling it out, in a deepening sense of the prodigious. "So that when her death has taken place I shall in the natural course have money?"

> It was before him enough now, and he had nothing more to ask; he had only to turn, on the spot, considerably cold with the thought that all along—to his stupidity, his timidity—it had been, it had been only what she meant. Now that he was in possession, moreover, she couldn't forbear, strangely enough, to pronounce the words she had not pronounced: they broke through her controlled and colourless voice as if she should be ashamed, to the very end, to have flinched. "You'll in the natural course have money. We shall in the natural course be free."
>
> "Oh, oh, oh!" Densher softly murmured. (chapter XI)

That soft murmur is James's subdued, still partly ironic, even very slightly playful version of tragic terror—the acknowledged awareness of the source of Kate's energy. It marks the closest approach possible in James to a religious experience: except for the silence, a response too deep even for the softest of murmurs, with which both Merton and Kate greet the smile thrown at them from across the room, a few moments later, by Milly Theale. It had already been observed, from Susan Stringham's point of view, that Milly's smile was a public event; the smile she now suddenly flashes at the two lovers who are conspiring to betray and destroy her, transcends even that. If inanimate things are the elements by which James renders what Dante called the tropological or moral meaning of his story; and if the historical or allegorical dimension is revealed in what the conflict of consciousness can do to revitalize institutions historically drained of importance; then Milly's smile, like that of Beatrice, gives a piercing glimpse of the anagoge. To Merton—in his excruciatingly heightened state, dazzled by Milly's pearls (to which Kate had insistently drawn his attention), beside himself with desire for Kate and quavering on the edge of some abyss—it expresses the quintessential quality of everything that harried and excited him, the very core of all mystery:

> . . . they watched a minute in concert. Milly, from the other side, happened at the moment to notice them, and she sent across toward them in response all the candour of her smile, the lustre of her pearls, the value of her life, the essence of her wealth. (chapter XI)

It is Merton's sense of "the reality she put into their plan" that later breeds in him his "consecrated idea"—of renouncing the money—that in fact consecrates the idea that gets bred and that he takes reverently into the Oratory on Christmas morning and then down to the house in Chelsea. He sees himself now as "a young man, far off yet dimly conscious of something immense and holding himself, not to lose it, painfully together. . . . Something had happened to him too beautiful and too sacred to describe" (chapter XXXIV). It was indeed indescribable in the language available, or seemingly available, to a novelist writing in English in 1902: it was the terrible and totally unprepared-for fragmentary vision of grace. *That* was something Merton Densher could not begin to express coherently. It could be expressed only in the manner James did express it—by dialectic made flesh, by the dramatized struggle of unenlightened but illuminating passion.[4]

1957

4. It was only after delivering the above paper that I succeeded at last in finding Dorothea Krook's essay on *The Wings of the Dove*. I warmly recommend this essay—as well as Miss Krook's study of *The Golden Bowl*—to all students of James and indeed of modern fiction. My agreement with her is so substantial that some of my remarks seem now to be as it were anticipatory echoes.

EDITH WHARTON AND
THE HOUSE OF MIRTH

The House of Mirth, published by Scribner's in 1905, is the first
of Edith Wharton's longer writings to win any kind of sustained
critical approval; and for many readers it remains the most satisfying of her novels. It is the account of the last nineteen months
in the life of Miss Lily Bart, a singularly engaging young woman
of twenty-nine when we first meet her. But it is also a rapidly
shifting image of certain segments of American society in New
York and Long Island and on the French Riviera at the time the
novel was written. The story's action consists in the interplay
between those elements—between, that is, Lily Bart's contradictory aspirations and the contradictory worlds in which those
aspirations seek fulfillment. "What she craved . . . was a situation
in which the noblest attitude should also be the easiest." But what
Miss Bart is offered in fact is not the convenient blend she feels
entitled to, but the alternative on the one hand of "a selfish
crowded world of pleasure," the realm named in the book's title,
a place where attitudes are easy; and, on the other, a presumably
nobler and yet curiously arid domain described by Lily Bart's
sometime lover, a lawyer named Lawrence Selden, as "the republic of the spirit."

The dilemma thus established is familiar enough both in literature and in life; it is as old as the conflicting temptations of matter
and spirit. Mrs. Wharton's narrative treatment of the dilemma,
however, is decidedly original; and it is the more unfortunate that,
in this novel and in others, Mrs. Wharton's writing has evidently
struck a number of commentators as anything *but* original. Critics,
especially those in recent years who have proposed theories about
the whole range of American fiction, either have not bothered to
notice Edith Wharton at all or have implied that her work repre-

sents something done earlier and more resolutely by Henry James, and later and more suggestively by Scott Fitzgerald. Certainly, a clear line (perhaps the clearest line of development in the history of the novel in America) connects Mrs. Wharton with the other two writers just mentioned. All three are artistic historians of manners, particularly of the widening breach between manners— the palpable externals of behavior—and a significant morality, Mrs. Wharton's major accomplishment in this mode being *The Age of Innocence* (1920). Elsewhere, however, the focus of her imaginative energy results in a very different kind of book, distinctly un-Jamesian and indeed closer in nature to American novels since the second World War. At such a moment, her narrative form approaches the picaresque—the episodic ramblings of the morally ambiguous personality through an unstable and discordant world—and in this mode Mrs. Wharton's masterpiece is *The Custom of the Country* (1913), the career of Undine Spragg, literature's most indomitable female rogue since Becky Sharp. It is the unique and almost accidental achievement of *The House of Mirth* to have successfully combined both modes into a genre that Mrs. Wharton can be said to have made her own.

I have no name for this genre except that of its ablest practitioner, Edith Wharton herself. But I have no doubt that it was invented, or stumbled upon, during the apprentice years, to convey her sense of life; her sense of what was happening, historically, to the conditions of the social and moral and psychological life. And I have no doubt that the combination described is the very source of the remarkable and enduring features of *The House of Mirth:* the mysterious appeal of its often vexatious heroine, its odd but engrossing changes of narrative pace, its mixture of the vivid and the crepuscular, its dramatized realization of the fateful consequences for *both* matter and spirit when they are divorced from one another, and, above all, its steady command of our moral and emotional sympathy. To justify those claims and to identify the fictional genre of *The House of Mirth,* we may begin by reminding ourselves who Edith Wharton was.

I

She was the former Miss Edith Newbold ("Pussy") Jones, and, as a friend remarked, she was a true daughter of New York City, having been born there on January 24, 1862, of a well-established and reasonably prosperous upper-middle-class family.[1] She was also or, rather, she became, as someone else remarked in a different rhetorical vein, "a self-made man." In her adult years, the two sides of her nature—the feminine side begotten by the conventions of the older New York and the masculine side begotten by personal ambition—engaged in just the sort of internal quarrel that, as Yeats has famously pointed out, can lead to poetry; for example, in Mrs. Wharton's case, to the poetry of *The Custom of the Country,* where the two sides appraise each other as the handsome and notably unfeminine Miss Spragg moves like a tornado among the debilitated daughters and sons of New York City. Later, of course, Mrs. Wharton fell unhappily to quarreling with others, in the way that Yeats equally observed led only to rhetoric: to her increasingly frequent lectures to twentieth-century America on its gross cultural deficiencies. The daughter of New York was in the ascendancy at times like that; but during much of Edith Wharton's life, and starting early, the self-made side was a deep necessity.

There is good, apparently incontrovertible evidence that she believed herself to be illegitimate: the daughter of New York only in part and via her mother; the offspring, paternally speaking, not of that heavy nonentity Mr. Jones, but of some man of distinguished intellectual and artistic qualities, someone who had spawned her and vanished—leaving her to develop those inherited qualities by her own energies, as it were self-creatively.[2] This may well have been only the restless romanticizing of a young girl whose talents found no outlet within the milieu in which she was reared. The fact remains (and reappears as a

1. Her mother had been a Miss Rhinelander, of the solid Dutch stock that is regularly honored and smiled at in Mrs. Wharton's fiction; and she was a descendant of Ebenezer Stevens, a veteran of the Revolution and later a successful merchant. Edith's father, George Frederic Jones, had a less socially illustrious but no less firmly respectable background; he was an independently wealthy and thoroughly conventional gentleman.

2. Mrs. Wharton's papers, some of which may possibly shed light on the question of her origins, are locked up in Yale University Library and will not be available until 1968. One unsubstantial rumor has it that Mrs. Wharton once searched in England for traces of her father. Meanwhile, it is perhaps worth noting that, although illegitimacy is an occasional theme in her fiction—a minor one in *The Age of Innocence,* and a central one in the novella *The Old Maid* (1924)—there is no example in her writing, so far as I know, of that grand archetypal theme of the search of the child for the father.

fertile tension in her work) that Mrs. Wharton while still Miss Jones did feel that way about her own milieu: in it, as the saying goes, but not altogether of it; obscurely illegitimate, in such a manner as to make her at once, in her private estimation, secretly dubious *and* secretly superior. The New York "high" society of the 1870s and '80s comprised a world that she belonged to and did not belong to or want to belong to. She could assert its importance with all the excess and the uncertainty that betoken the perfect snob, but she could also see its dullness, its obstinate defenses against reality; she could feel in her throat its oppressive and sterilizing effect, and she could feel herself feeling it. New York society was a kind of home, and it was a kind of trap, or cage. "She was everything that was right and proper," observed a visitor to the Jones family, "but the young hawk looked out of her eyes."

The right and proper young lady, at the age of twenty-three, made a suitable marriage with Edward Robbins Wharton of Philadelphia and Boston, a gentleman of considerable private means and no literary interests. The young hawk chafed under the bondage of charming banality, fell sick, took to travel and, later, to writing; and even as the marriage was crumbling (because of various calamities, ending in Mr. Wharton's incurable mental illness), she formed a relationship of an as yet undefined intimacy with one Walter Van Rennsalaer Berry.[3] Berry was an international lawyer, an American residing in Paris, a lifelong bachelor and an austere amateur—something more than a dilettante—of the arts. It was his shadowy distinction that Marcel Proust regarded him as "a Greek of the Golden Age," found his face "beautiful . . . to look upon," and dedicated to him a volume called *Pastiches et Mélanges*. Berry was not popular among Mrs. Wharton's friends. But for more than thirty years he was a valuable literary counselor, giving her the most sustained encouragement and the most searching advice she was to receive from anyone. He seems indeed (though the evidence is not quite clear) to be the first to have sensed a crucial portion of the untamed in Edith Wharton's imagination, and to have urged her not to hold that element too firmly in check—not to cage the young hawk too absolutely in her writing.

3. Thus, a psychologist might conceivably argue, replacing one sort of "father-figure" for another—the false one for the secretly true one.

Her first publications had been as right and proper as any publications could be, from the disapproving point of view of her parents. In 1878, when she was sixteen, there had been *Verses,* courteously supported (and influenced) by Longfellow and printed privately in Newport. Almost twenty years later, after the marriage and a series of illnesses and the recourse to writing as therapy, she collaborated with the architect Ogden Codman on a book called *The Decoration of Houses* (1897). At that same moment, Louis Sullivan, as he was to report later in his autobiography, was contemplating with despair the near-fatal setback to a native American architecture in the triumph of the European and the eclectic, and of Stanford White, at the 1893 Chicago Fair. Mrs. Wharton, however, wholeheartedly joined Stanford White in an expressed reverence for "the best models"—"models . . . found in buildings erected in Italy after the beginning of the sixteenth century, and in other European countries after the full assimilation of the Italian influence." It is hard not to feel that the phrase "best models" is a variant of the phrase "best people," and that her perfectly genuine and richly informed admiration for Renaissance villas and gardens came in part from the application of social snobbery to the aesthetic question: a right and proper attitude. Still, as we shall see, Mrs. Wharton had a developing sense of what we might call the *drama* of houses, a creative insight that went far beyond snobbery and would serve her imaginative purposes well—beginning, as its very title implies, with her first significant novel.

The same addiction to Italy and its historic culture led, after three volumes of shorter fiction between 1899 and 1901, to her first *published* novel, *The Valley of Decision* in 1902. This was a tediously long narrative about the Italian *sette cento,* in which an eloquently described background smothers, even while it partly atones for, an inert foreground plot of love, renunciation, and inexorable propriety. There followed another set of short stories and another novella; and then two more forays into the Italian scene. The latter—*Italian Villas and their Gardens* (1904) and *Italian Backgrounds* (1905)—are still quite readable, and they confirm Mrs. Wharton's eminence in that minor but often fascinating if loosely defined genre, "travel literature." Few American writers have tried their hand at this genre, and fewer still with the knowledge and ability of Edith Wharton. But now, in 1905, she seems to have begun meditating the comment Henry James made to a correspondent about *The Valley of Decision:* "The little lady . . . *must* be tethered in native pastures." James had already become her friend, her mentor, and her gossip; his advice had to be listened to. She set to work on a novel located in her own contemporary New York; and within six months she was able to offer *The House of Mirth* for serialization in *Scribner's Magazine.*

II

It had not always been called *The House of Mirth.* Mrs. Wharton experimented with two other titles before settling on that now familiar phrase, and the shifts involved provide some clues both to the content and to the eventual emphasis and the unusual form of the novel. The manuscript title was *A Moment's Ornament.* This was changed in typescript to *The Year of the Rose*—until that phrase in turn was struck out by hand and replaced with *The House of Mirth.* The two earlier titles share the same connotation: namely, of something beautiful and yet evanescent; and the emphasis in each case is, of course, upon the heroine, on Lily Bart herself and the final period of her blooming and fading. Lily, moreover, is associated alternately in those phrases with something artificial (an ornament) and something natural (a rose); but, while there is a running opposition throughout Book I between the natural and the artificial, the common defect of the two original titles lies in the fact that Lily characteristically possesses a degree of *both* qualities. The third title transfers attention from the heroine to the world—or one of the worlds—in which she seeks her fortune; and suggests at once the reason why (given her divided nature, her attraction to the spiritual as well as the mirthful) she is pathetically destined to fail.

Mrs. Wharton's ultimate choice was typical and revealing. In her published titles, she customarily focused upon a context for action, rather than on the human actors concerned or the meaningful shape of the drama to be enacted. Her books speak to us initially of a valley, a house, a milieu, a time, a city, a river (*The Valley of Decision, The House of Mirth, The Custom of the Country, The Age of Innocence, Old New York, Hudson River Bracketed*)—with a quality or function added on as generally indicative of just that kind of context. *Ethan Frome* is an exception and it is Jamesian; for Henry James, by contrast, habitually pointed to his chief characters (*Roderick Hudson, Daisy Miller*) or to the dramatic or symbolic function of his characters (*The American, The Ambassadors, The Wings of the Dove*). This does not mean that Edith Wharton was uninterested in characters and action, or inept in the handling of them; and it certainly does not mean that her novels were no more than fictionalized additions to her informative discourses on Italy and interior decoration. What it means is that Mrs. Wharton's view of motive and of causality in human affairs was rather different from that of James. The latter's dramas were driven by a deadly but mainly human and individual dialectic; for while James felt that society, almost by definition, was the very arena of experience, nonetheless he did not see society as a thing apart. In his view, life itself, the significant life, consisted (to borrow his comment on Ibsen) in the lunging of ego against ego, of soul against soul—no matter how socially located the lunging might be. There are instances of just such lunging throughout Edith Wharton's fiction, but there is, one feels, usually a third party to the contest. Her characters tend to be affected not only by each other but also by pressures in the atmosphere; by the more general and pervasive temptations and taboos, by the inexplicable conventions and the vague ex-pectancies of the social setting in this place or that time. No doubt there is in this novelistic perspective of Mrs. Wharton a trace of what literary historians sometimes call "naturalism"—the per-spective according to which environment (metaphysical as well as physical) is the major force that determines human activities. But the parallel should in no way be insisted upon, since, as Mrs. Wharton describes it, the environment—society—is itself an extract of human attitudes; and the warmth of human possibil-ity rather than the dry coldness of impersonal force is always her main subject.[4]

The so-called James aspect of Edith Wharton is worth pursuing for a moment: partly to examine further the composition and revision of *The House of Mirth;* but chiefly to insist that this aspect was largely a superficial one, a matter literally of occasional sur-face items. Mrs. Wharton's work kept veering, so to speak, back toward James's, even to touch it tangentially from time to time;

4. For an extended and thoroughly cogent discussion of Edith Wharton and "naturalism," see Blake Nevius, *Edith Wharton: A Study of her Fiction* (Berkeley and Los Angeles, 1953). I have occasion to cite this excellent study below.

but there was never any real degree of duplication of substance. *The House of Mirth,* for example, may seem to incorporate some of the essential stuff of *The Wings of the Dove* (1902), but one useful and negative way to define the former would be to show that in fact it does not. Both are stories of marital intrigue, and in both the plot turns on the ill-fated effort of an impoverished young woman—Kate Croy, Lily Bart—to combine marriage, material prosperity, and personal satisfaction. The two heroines are comparably poised between instances of well-being (in the form of shrewd and wealthy patronesses) and of the dingy dreariness of unrelieved poverty (warnings incarnate in their own families—sister Marian Condrip, cousin Gerty Farish). Both narratives conclude in the complete and final separation of the women from the men they love. But all of that belongs to the mechanics of staging; the structure and stress, the very theory of life at work in the two novels, are radically different. We are left with a misleading accumulation of echoes by Mrs. Wharton of Henry James: echoes of plot details, of allusion, of names, of phrasing.

"The continued cry that I am an echo of Mr. James," Edith Wharton wrote her editor in the year before *The House of Mirth* was published, "makes me feel rather helpless"; and she added that James's "books of the last ten years I can't read, much as I delight in the man." The remark is disingenuous or muddled (as Mrs. Wharton's observations on writing often tended to be). The plain fact is that she *had* read the later James; and the evidence is exactly in the number of surface echoes. An utterly unimportant character in *The House of Mirth* is given a name—Kate Corby —that is almost an anagram, or a misspelling, of Kate Croy. The Veronese painting that is invoked at the Venetian dinner party in *The Wings of the Dove* and the reference to which is arguably the key to the entire "meaning" of that novel is presented as a *tableau vivant* by guests of the upstart Welly Brys in an easily forgettable scene (I, 12) in *The House of Mirth.* The wording of Densher's appalled realization of Kate Croy's extraordinary plan, at that same party—"It was before him enough now, and he had nothing more to ask"—passes through Lawrence Selden's mind (II, 3) as he contemplates Lily Bart on the French Riviera: "It was before him again in its completeness, the choice in which she was content to rest."

Similarly, in the final sentence of *The House of Mirth,* the verbal description of Selden, kneeling beside Lily Bart's dead body and "draining their last moment to its lees," derives most probably from the language of the terrible denouement of James's "The Beast in the Jungle" (1901), when John Marcher, standing beside the grave that contains the corpse of May Bartram, "emptied the cup to the lees." The derivation of the one commonplace phrase from the other is confirmed when the famous remainder of James's sentence—"he had been the man of his time, *the* man, to whom nothing on earth was to have happened"— turns up in pale but recognizable shape in *The Age of Innocence* at the moment when Newland Archer sees himself as "a man to whom nothing was ever to happen." Wisps of substance no doubt stick to these verbal borrowings and get carried over from James into Mrs. Wharton; but they remain primarily verbal borrowings. What we eventually make of these similarities, in short, is simply this—that Mrs. Wharton took from James something of his verse, but little of his poetry.

James's poetry resided to a considerable extent *in* his words, often in his much-meditated proper names. The juxtaposition of May Bartram and John Marcher in "The Beast in the Jungle" is patently intended at once to enlarge and to focus the import of the tale by implicating the individual characters in a perennial contrast of seasons (May and March) which is at the same time the fundamental contrast of life and death. The name of Christopher Newman in *The American* is almost too bluntly suggestive; more engaging implications flow from the name of Isabel Archer. But the names Edith Wharton seems to have evolved from those just cited—names like Lily Bart and Newland Archer—are, by comparison, no more than satisfactory sounds. The manuscript of *The House of Mirth* shows that, while Mrs. Wharton fiddled endlessly with the names of her characters, the changes she made do not bring with them any sizable amount of new meaning. Selden, Lily Bart, Judy Trenor, and Gerty Farish appear originally in Mrs. Wharton's longhand as Hensley, Juliet Hurst, Georgie Druce, and Nelly Varick, respectively; and Miss Juliet Hurst was modified briefly into Miss Lily Hurst before becoming once and for all Miss Lily Bart. But what the novel is trying to say is scarcely affected by those changes—the impotence of the relation between Selden and Lily Bart would be no less poignant if the persons concerned were called Hensley and Juliet Hurst. What has been achieved by the substitutions is a faint but definite gain of tonal propriety, of auditory relevance. The combination in Mrs. Wharton's heroine of gentleness and toughness is better conveyed by joining Lily to Bart than by joining Juliet to Hurst; and the sporadic vitality and congenital slackness of her lover is better suggested by Selden—probably because it sounds like "seldom" —than by Hensley. Further than this it would be difficult to go. For, again to cite the manuscript, Mrs. Wharton's countless emendations of words and phrases rarely aim at broadening the range of implication or at packing the expression symbolically, in the manner of James. They serve rather for rhetorical and dramatic tightening, for an increase in visual clarity, for pushing ever closer to accuracy of psychological and historical detail, and sometimes for a more ladylike decorum.

If Mrs. Wharton borrowed little of James's poetry, it was because her own poetry rarely got into her language. It resided elsewhere. For one thing, it was (especially in *The House of Mirth* and *The Age of Innocence*) the poetry of the hidden life, the poetry of silence and the unspoken word. "And in the silence there passed between them the word which made all clear." That final clause in *The House of Mirth* fittingly and ironically concludes a tale in which the necessary word is habitually withheld until it is too late. It is a tale, moreover, in which the heroine, Lily Bart, often withholds the necessary word from her own consciousness. "Her mind shrank from the glare of thought as instinctively as eyes contract in a blaze of light" (II, 13). The poetry of such a tale must attempt, paradoxically, to suggest the dramatically unrealized, must seek the effect of psychological reticence and encourage the reader to supply the sense of panic or illusory hope or sheer protracted suffering that Lily Bart will not give voice to, either to others or to herself. (In this respect, Lily Bart's fit of the horrors in chapters 13 and 14 of Book I, when she feels pursued by some Furies out of Euripides, is a rhetorical flaw, the less persuasive the more it is outspoken.) But, in addition to vibrating thus faintly beneath unexpressed or only partly expressed emotional reactions, the poetry of *The House of Mirth* resides also and no less obliquely in the description of a house, a hillside, a teashop, a waterfront. The drama that is artfully unrealized in the human encounters can be detected working itself out in the intricate play of "contexts." This brings us back to Mrs. Wharton's grasp of what I have called the drama of houses, or more simply the drama of place. It brings us back, in fact, to the implications of the title of *The House of Mirth.*

III

That title is only the most conspicuous example in the novel of Mrs. Wharton's method of identifying persons—individuals, family clans, entire social groups—in terms of place. Two other examples may stand for many. The Gryce clan (into which Lily Bart schemes for a while to marry) is summed up at a stroke in the image of their home on Madison Avenue (I, 2)—"an appalling house, all brown stone without and black walnut within, with the Gryce library in a fire-proof annex that looked like a mausoleum." Subtler and more precise is the description of Lily's aunt, Mrs. Peniston: first by reference to the "glacial neatness" of her drawing room, which is evidently a correlative of the meticulous but frosty-hearted nature of the lady in question; and then in the comparison between Mrs. Peniston's secretively vigilant mind to "one of those little mirrors which her Dutch ancestors were accustomed to affix to their upper windows, so that from the depths of an impenetrable domesticity they might see what was happening in the street." Figures of that sort—though there are not many so brilliantly effective—build into a pattern which gives the book its structure and reveals the action that the structure is devised to carry.

As the examples just quoted may suggest, the action involves a portion of social history—of Mrs. Wharton's personal notion about the history of American society in the late nineteenth and early twentieth centuries. Social history of this kind provides the largest though the least clearly visible of the contexts from which characters and events draw their meaning; and we should consider it before closing in at last on the particular fortunes of Miss Lily Bart. In *The Custom of the Country,* Edith Wharton gives us her own explicit and eloquent summary of the matter. The passage is worth quoting, since it is Mrs. Wharton's most expert use of houses as representative of persons. It is an extended architectural image of an entire society in transition, in a sort of quiet convulsion, one segment disappearing and another emerging into prominence—and in a way that, in *The House of Mirth,* remains half-concealed from the book's view, though it is already happening and deeply affects the lives of Lily Bart and the others.

In the passage that follows, Ralph Marvell, the gentle and cultivated young man who is to be the second husband of Undine Spragg and who will destroy himself because of what she does to his life, is returning one evening to the Marvell home on Washington Square (I, v). He

> looked up at the symmetrical old red house-front, with its frugal marble ornament, as he might have looked into a familiar human face.
>
> "They're right,—after all, in some ways they're right," he murmured, slipping his key into the door.
>
> "They" were his mother and old Mr. Urban Dagonet, both, from Ralph's earliest memories, so closely identified with the old house in Washington Square that they might have passed for its inner consciousness as it might have stood for their outward form; and the question as to which the house now seemed to affirm their intrinsic rightness was that of the social disintegration expressed by widely-different architectural physiognomies at the other end of Fifth Avenue.
>
> As Ralph pushed the bolts behind him, and passed into the hall, with its dark mahogany doors and the quiet "Dutch interior" effect of its black and white marble paving, he said to himself that what Popple [a fashion-loving portrait-painter] called society was just like the houses it lived in: a muddle of misapplied ornament over a thin steel shell of utility. The steel shell was built up in Wall Street, the social trimmings were hastily added in Fifth Avenue; and the union between them was as monstrous and factitious, as unlike the gradual homogeneous growth which flowers into what other countries know as society, as that between the Blois gargoyles on Peter Van Degen's roof and the skeleton walls supporting them. . . .
>
> Ralph sometimes called his mother and grandfather the Aborigines, and likened them to those vanishing denizens of the American continent doomed to rapid extinction with the advance of the invading race. He was fond of describing Washington Square as the "Reservation," and of prophesying that before long its inhabitants would be exhibited at ethnological shows, pathetically engaged in the exercise of their primitive industries.
>
> Small, cautious, middle-class, had been the ideals of aboriginal New York; but it suddenly struck the young man that

they were singularly coherent and respectable as contrasted with the chaos of indiscriminate appetites which made up the modern tendencies.[5]

The whole of the above repays the closest scrutiny. There is nothing so good in *The House of Mirth,* no moment in that novel (or any other) where Mrs. Wharton's imaginative view of social and moral history is so firmly controlled and so justly balanced, no image in which the history is so richly bodied forth in an organic interplay of buildings and psyches. Nor could there be. By 1913, when Mrs. Wharton was writing *The Custom of the Country,* the process whereby "the chaos of indiscriminate appetites" was overwhelming the "coherent and respectable" ideals of old New York had become unmistakable. By 1920 and *The Age of Innocence* (and more skimpily in the four novellas of 1924, *Old New York*), Mrs. Wharton could portray those small and cautious virtues at the time of their flowering, with a sure sense both of their coherence and their perilous limitations, and with a settled conviction as to how and when the "chaos" set in and of the destructive course it had run. But in 1905, the issues were not so clear, the elements not yet sorted out; the moral and social landscape was heaving confusedly, but the source of the disturbance was not yet altogether evident. For Edith Wharton, this situation posed a challenge, and she triumphed over it. For Lily Bart, it posed a dilemma, and she succumbed.

The triumph is reflected in a novelistic structure which at first glance seems to have been badly fumbled. Between Books I and II of *The House of Mirth* there is what looks like an awkward imbalance, a yoking of two parts that are nearly incompatible in focus and narrative method. Book I adheres to a relatively "closed" situation; in a more or less traditional manner, it explores the interlocking intrigues of a single social set (the Trenor set at Bellomont and in New York City); it covers a short space of time (early September to the following January); and it is shaped distinctly enough by the rhythm, the faint flaring and uncertain flickering, of the love relation between Selden and Lily Bart. Book II is much more open, meandering, and episodic. It covers a long and unhappily drawn-out year (from April to April). It moves without any obvious design from one house or place to

5. Edith Wharton, *The Custom of the Country* (New York, 1913), pp. 72–74. Copyright, 1913, by Charles Scribner's Sons.

another—from the Dorsets' yacht on the Riviera to Mattie Gomer's estate on Long Island and then west to Alaska; to Carry Fisher's little house in Tuxedo; to the Emporium Hotel and the swank overheated suite of Mrs. Norma Hatch; to the depressing workshop of Mme. Regina's millinery establishment; to a narrow room with "blotched wall-paper and shabby paint" in a New York boardinghouse; to the bed where Lily Bart quietly dies of an overdose of sleeping medicine. Book I has its affinities with the fictional genre of which Henry James was the master; and in its compressed and circumscribed locale, "themes"—especially the theme of freedom and imprisonment—are made to palpitate in a notably Jamesian manner. Book II has affinities rather with the wandering, groping, uncentered, and downward-spiraling novels characteristic of American writing in the past decade; and amid all that loose and blurry movement, we do not easily find any mode of continuity, thematic or otherwise. Between them, however, the two parts form a curious but successful unit; they comprise the genre which, I have suggested, Mrs. Wharton virtually invented—to convey her sense of what was happening, historically, to the conditions of the only life that interested her.

What was happening was that the house of mirth—here represented by the Trenors and their playfellows—was *giving way* to those other "houses," those other and still more appetitive and treacherous social clusters represented, in Book II, by the Dorsets, the Gomers, the Hatches, and so on. The whole moral history of modern New York (to adopt a phrase of Henry James) is in the progression or descent from Bellomont to the Emporium Hotel. The selfish and mirthful world of the Trenors, having no moral coherence, cannot help dissolving into the meretricious jumble we encounter in Book II, when the chaos that was half-hidden beneath the spurious modishness of Bellomont becomes fully experienced. Examining Bellomont, we can see why. It is made up of people like the thoughtless if not ill-intentioned Judy Trenor, the perennial hostess who "knew no more personal emotion than that of hatred for the woman who presumed to give bigger dinners . . . than herself"; her husband Gus Trenor, red and massive, with his heavy eyes, his rumbles of coarse emotion, his perfect blend of financial and erotic acquisitiveness; Percy Gryce, the millionaire collector of Americana, whose arrested development is marked by the "settled look of dulness" that regularly creeps over his blankly candid features; Bertha

Dorset, petite, malicious, morally irresponsible; and others—
Kate Corby, Ned Silverton, Lady Cressida Raith, and the like
—dimmer in outline and no more discriminating in ethical awareness. This is the "crowded world of pleasure" that passes for
society in New York, 1905; and it has quite elbowed aside what
Mrs. Wharton would call the cautious and middle-class ideals
of the older New York. Of the latter, indeed, there is hardly any
sign whatever in *The House of Mirth,* except in the frozen forms
of the Peniston household, and, in a way to be examined, in the
bafflingly exhausted form of Lawrence Selden. The absence of
that old order is a main cause of Lily Bart's dilemma, though
she never quite realizes the fact.

Strictly speaking, of course, we encounter the deteriorating
jumble in Book II only as Lily Bart, victimized by and expelled
from the Trenor society (after Gus Trenor's attempted rape and
gross falsifications), forms her brief and increasingly tenuous
associations with the Dorsets and Gomers and Hatches. The
Trenor group may be imagined as continuing its round of pointless pleasure, and Bertha Dorset her lies and infidelities; but
what Mrs. Wharton has done is to compress her chapter of social
history into a period of nineteen months by passing her heroine
through a succession of "houses," each one a sort of degradation
of the one before. At the same time, however, *The House of
Mirth* does belong to Lily Bart; it is her story that engages us,
her history that we want to follow. The deterioration sketched
for us, and reflected in the novel's structure, is primarily a decline
in Lily Bart's "position," in fact in her very hold on life. Mme.
Regina's hat shop (in II, 10) is no doubt an ultimate and naked
instance of the dehumanized commercialism that is the root of
the social disintegration writ large in the novel. Walking back
to her rooming house (II, 10), Lily Bart seems to herself to be
walking "through the degradation of a New York street in the
last stages of decline from fashion to commerce." There is the
whole social history in a nutshell. But it is also a last stage in
the declining career of a particular young woman. What gives
artistic coherence to Mrs. Wharton's narrative image of spreading
moral incoherence—what protects the novel against what literary
critics call "the fallacy of imitative form" (whereby a disorderly
society is described by a disorderly book)—is the fictional logic
in the account of Lily's last year on earth. Within the general
disarray, there is a clearly traced process of narrowing, as Lily's

destiny almost literally closes in on he_; as she moves from the spacious grounds at Rhinebeck to the more restricted domain at Roslyn to the oppressive suite in the hotel to a single room in a boardinghouse to the narrow bed in which she dies.

IV

Lily Bart is one of the authentic creations of American fiction. She is by turns admirable, touching, exasperating, forlorn, sturdy, woefully self-deceptive, imprudent, finely proud, intuitive—and, for one reader at least, not much less than humanly adorable. She is not a tragic heroine. She does not have a truly fatal flaw, only a dangerous weakness: an inability to resist a certain kind of temptation. The temptation is not erotic; Lily Bart is not vulnerable (as are some of her associates) on the sexual side. She can imply a promise of exquisite intimacy; the gesture by which she leans forward to light her cigarette from the tip of Selden's has more real suggestiveness (and I do not mean symbolism) than a dozen pages of anatomical espionage from popular fiction. But Lily Bart is a creature, not of sexual passion but of a physical passion of a different order. She is, let us say, a nymphomaniac of material comfort; *that* is what she is helpless to resist. Her entire being in this respect is characterized by her attitude toward the notion of marrying Rosedale—that "plump rosy man of the blond Jewish type," whose "smart London clothes fit[ted] him like upholstery," and who somewhat surprisingly is permitted by Edith Wharton to manifest qualities ("a certain gross kindliness," "a rather helpless fidelity of sentiment") that distinguish him favorably from his gentile social superiors. Lily cannot quite bring herself to like him, or anyhow to like him enough; and as she contemplates married life with him (II, 6), "she did not indeed let her imagination range beyond the day of plighting; after that everything faded into a haze of material well-being, in which the personality of her benefactor remained mercifully vague." Into that same haze of material well-being, Lily's sexual reactions regularly tend to fade.

The career of Lily Bart (the action of *The House of Mirth*) is, as I have said, determined by the interplay of the character outlined above and the social scene in which she is required to make her moves. But the game is really lost in advance. For the only society in which Lily might have found the combination she sought—the older New York society, where decency did blend with an adequate material ease—was not observable on her horizon. It had been superseded by the house of mirth; and what was left of it had retreated into "the republic of the spirit." Entrance into the house of mirth had to be paid for by marriage to someone like the intolerable Percy Gryce; and, although Lily attributes her failure to establish a footing there to her own "unsteadiness of purpose" (II, 7), it was due in fact to a habit of discrimination that all her self-delusion cannot overcome. Edith Wharton's private feeling of belonging and not belonging to the social order that flourished in the 1870s and '80s was greatly exacerbated in Lily Bart's contradictory attitude—her urge toward and repugnance to—the Trenor society of a generation later. At every turn she undercut or slid away from her material opportunities, always regarding her refusal to make the final compromise as a failure of nerve. But the only alternative she is ever made conscious of (apart from the curiously compassionate proposals of Rosedale) is Lawrence Selden and his spiritual republic.

Lily Bart's journey is punctuated by the shifts in her relation to Selden. Each of the two books begins as Selden and Miss Bart are drawing toward one another, and each ends in separation. Through the house party at Bellomont and the New Year's gathering at the Brys in Book I, their intimacy and understanding grow to the point where Selden is about to ask Lily to marry him. Lily, while assuring herself that she will not of course accept him, is half-ready to hear him out—until the affair is blasted by the dreadful contretemps with Gus Trenor. In Book II, Selden is again caught up in Lily Bart's troubles and again rises to that point of animation where he is determined to propose to her. But while he is on his way to her shabby room, Lily takes an excessive dose of sleeping drops, and just before he arrives, she sinks through unconsciousness to death—a manipulation of timing and incident by Mrs. Wharton that would seem tediously contrived and melodramatic were not the mode of Lily's death the almost inevitable culmination of her sagging career.[6] The relation between Selden and Lily Bart thus gives the novel that "he loves me, he loves me not" pattern in terms of which *The Age*

6. A careful look at the final pages of II, 13 will convince the reader that Lily Bart's death was not an act of deliberate suicide. As to the danger of an overdose, against which she had been warned, "She did not, in truth, consider the question very closely," Mrs. Wharton writes; "the phys-

of Innocence is so much more smoothly constructed, and which, in the latter novel, is announced in the very opening scene by the song from *Faust ("M'ama, non mi ama")* the main characters gather to hear in the old Opera House.

What Lawrence Selden has to offer but never quite nerves himself to offer is companionship in "the republic of the spirit." Here, as against the house of mirth, the keynote is freedom: "freedom from everything," as Selden explains in the book's most moving, indeed its most passionate encounter (I, 6); "from money, from poverty, from ease and anxiety, from all the material accidents." It is a freedom, in short, from all the *external* pressures that limit or deflect the exercise of moral choice. The notion of so exclusive, so sparsely inhabited, and so morally elevated a society has provided one of the great and recurring themes in American fiction; and its appearance in *The House of Mirth* links Edith Wharton unexpectedly with Cooper, Hawthorne, Melville, and Mark Twain—each of whom dramatized his own ideal community, conceived in opposition to actual society and to which never more than two or three were eligible to belong.[7] But Lawrence Selden, as Mrs. Wharton's most illuminating critic has remarked, "is the least attractive ambassador of his 'republic of the spirit,' and Mrs. Wharton knows this as well as her readers."[8] If this is so—and the description may be a bit exaggerated—it is not only because Mrs. Wharton's view of the male sex, and her usual narrative strategy as well, led her time and again to depict her masculine figures as all too unmasculine, as intelligent but ineffectual (Selden, George Darrow in *The Reef,* Ralph Marvell, Newland Archer). It is also, and I think more importantly though relatedly, because Mrs. Wharton knew something else, an insight she shared with Henry James (who dramatized it, for example in *The Spoils of Ponyton*), but one that readers of both novelists have often failed to understand.

---

ical craving for sleep was her only sustained sensation." There was, of course, an element of the self-defeating in her nature, and by this time she was psychologically worn out. The reader may, if he wishes, impute to her a fatigued but quite buried desire for death.

7. This theme is the subject of a recent book by Mr. A. N. Kaul, *The American Vision: Actual and Ideal Society in Nineteenth Century Fiction* (New Haven, 1963).

8. Nevius, p. 59.

Edith Wharton knew that in the fatal modern dislocation between manners and morals, between actual conduct and ethical
principle, as the former become crude, the latter become blood-
less. This is not a matter of allegory; it is a matter of fact. Selden
is dimmer, dryer, harder to discern than, say, Rosedale, with
his vigorous vulgarity, because that kind of psychological fade-out
is (Mrs. Wharton saw) what is likely to happen to a man who
achieves the freedom arrived at by Selden—freedom not only
from material anxiety, but almost freedom from the material
world itself, from the flesh and blood of the actual. In *The Age
of Innocence,* the unfortunate split in question would be explicitly
named, as a division between "the actual" and "the real." But
while we have long been accustomed to accounts of the terrible
effect upon the actual of its divorce from the real (or ideal), we
hear less often about the opposite—how the real goes dry and
sterile when dissociated from the actual. There is a portion of
anxiety, or shall we say of moral alertness, that goes with the
condition of being human; and to break free of that is to break
away from humanity itself. The point about the republic of the
spirit is not (or not only) that Lily Bart is too impurely devoted to
material things to get into it, but that it is too airless for anyone
with blood in his veins to survive in it.

This great divorce is the "malice of fortune" which Lily Bart
vaguely invokes, along with her own infirmity of purpose, as the
cause of her failures. It is a historical malice, a calamity brought
about by historical developments within the social and moral
order; and Lily's infirmity is in good part due to her bemused
awareness that neither alternative that the times can offer will
satisfy. She wilfully spoils her chances for marrying into the
house of mirth; but she distrusts the republic of the spirit. She
has no place to go.

1962

THE CURRENT OF
CONRAD'S *VICTORY*

The opening sentences of *Victory* introduce us half-playfully to a number of "close relations," the surprising similarities between seeming contrasts—coal and diamonds, the practical and the mystical, the diffused and the concentrated, an island and a mountain. All of them have their literal and thematic importance in the story, which describes a profound conflict rooted in opposition and likeness, and which has to do with coal, diamonds, and an island; but the first effect of such dialectical teasing is the imparted sense of enlargement and creativity, of some idea or insight being made to grow. The last sentences of *Victory,* and especially its last word, are something else again:

> "And then, your Excellency [says good Captain Davidson], I went away. There was nothing to be done there."
> "Clearly," assented the Excellency.
> Davidson, thoughtful, seemed to weigh the matter in his mind, and then murmured with placid sadness:
> "Nothing!"

Between that initial sense of conceptual growth, with its cautious jocularity, and the thoughtful sadness of the closing negation there lies the truth of *Victory,* and its reality.

Victory is, in fact, a novel intimately concerned with questions of truth and reality, as it is with lies and illusion. Those big considerations force themselves on the imagination of the characters, and hence upon that of the reader; for it is that kind of novel, the kind Conrad normally attempted to write. In his preface to *The Nigger of the Narcissus,* Conrad defined art as the effort to render the highest justice "to the visible universe, by bringing to light the truth, manifold and one, underlying its every aspect." That creative ambition found an exact analogue in the experience narrated in *The Nigger of the Narcissus* itself, in the story's movement from the emphasized darkness of the ship's nighttime departure to the sunlit morning that greets its arrival in the English channel—after a voyage featured by the crew's effort to bring to light the truth and reality incarnate in the dying dark man, James Wait. And measured by Conrad's own standard, *Victory* achieves the conditions of art; for the manifold *and* unitary truth of things is just what Conrad succeeds in making real and visible, and what the persons of his island drama are most vitally concerned with. How the process is managed in this particular instance is the subject of present examination. But we have first to take a hard pull on our intellectual reins.

I

Revisiting *Victory* today, one cannot help being struck by its "existentialist" qualities—by how much it shares the intellectual preoccupations and postures notable in continental literature during recent decades. Here, for instance, is an elaborated image of human isolation: the isolation not only of man from man, but even more of man from his metaphysical environment—Axel Heyst, the rootless drifter, who has settled alone upon a singularly remote little island, near an abandoned coal mine, there to meditate in silence his late father's reflections upon "the universal nothingness" and "the unknown force of negation." Here, too, is the familiar counterattack upon metaphysical isolation, the unsteady impulse toward human fellowship—those compassionate gestures toward Morrison and the girl called Lena which belie Heyst's habitual detachment and are the source of his misfortunes and maybe of his redemption. Here is the articulated obsession with the feeling of existence and of nonexistence, as clues both to character and action. "If you were to stop thinking of me, I shouldn't be in the world at all," Lena says to Heyst; and, "I am he who is——" announces plain Mr. Jones, in a breath-taking moment which, in context, has an overpowering propriety. Here are modes of nihilism yielding to modes of self-annihilation, in the oddly similar catastrophes of both hero and villain. Here, in short, is a tale of violence that oscillates richly between the fundamental mysteries of being and nothing. Conrad, we are inclined to say, is the still insufficiently acknowledged grandfather of the most recent literary generation.

To say so is not necessarily to praise Conrad; and it is more likely, indeed, to impose upon him a false identity. *Victory* is not—and it cannot be discussed as—a novel of ideas, for example, in the manner of Malraux's *The Walnut Trees of the Altenburg.* Nor is it a calculated work of metaphysical revolt, like Camus' *The Plague.* Conrad did of course display attitudes, and he had a stiff little set of convictions. But E. M. Forster has rightly, if unsympathetically, made the point that Conrad had no "creed" —no coherent order of intellectual principles—and no more than other novelists writing on English soil did Conrad possess that occasional French and German talent for making the war of thought itself exciting. He wanted to exploit the power of words, as he said, in order "to make you hear, to make you feel—before all to make you *see*"; and the end of each of his best novels was simply its own composition. He did not believe with Malraux that art is "a rectification of the universe, a way of escaping from the human condition"; and he would scarcely have understood Camus' parallel and derivative contention that "the novel is born simultaneously with the spirit of rebellion and expresses, on the aesthetic plane, the same ambition." *Victory* dramatizes basic aspects of truth and being; but as regards the human condition, its main aim is only to observe it in the way of art—with that idle but no less intense and sustained attention for which Conrad accurately thought he had a natural ability, and with which he recalled observing the living model for *Victory's* heroine.

The novel's final word—"Nothing!"—is, accordingly, less a cry of appalled metaphysical recognition than the quiet acknowledgment that the adventure is over and the art that described it has peacefully exhausted itself. It is in the mood less of Camus' Caligula than of Shakespeare's Hamlet: "The rest is silence." The drama is done, and everybody who had a significant part in it is dead. Lena is dead, accidentally shot by Mr. Jones. Heyst has died by fire; Jones has died by water; and both deliberately, as it seems. Ricardo has been killed by Jones's second try at him; and Pedro has been dispatched by Wang, the houseboy. "There are more dead in this affair," Davidson remarks to the Excellency, "than have been killed in many of the battles of the last Achin war." The bungalow and the other two houses are burned to ashes; the boat has drifted out to sea; a corpse lies rotting on the scorched earth. To close the account, only the word "nothing" needs to be uttered.

And yet. If there is no metaphysical vision or purpose at work in the novel, there can nevertheless be felt running through it something like a metaphysical tide. Or better, perhaps, one senses the active presence, the dangerous undertow, of a metaphysical current giving the story its energy and its direction. In the same way, if the tale is not plainly intended as an allegory, one feels in it nevertheless something like an allegorical swelling, as though everything were about to become bigger than itself. That very impression affects the nerves of the persons in the book. "I have a peculiar feeling about this," says Mr. Jones. "It's a different thing. It's a sort of test." In the long list of Conrad's writings, *Victory* also comes to us as a different thing and a sort of test. It is Conrad's test of the nature of fiction: in general, of the ability of drama to move toward allegory while retaining intact its dramatic form and essence; and in particular, of the ability of fiction to move toward drama while retaining its identity as fictional narrative. It is a test of the way truth and reality can become the subject matter of a novel which hangs on to its novelistic nature. And the result, in my judgment, is indicated by the last word Conrad actually did write in this book, as he tells us: the single word of the title.

Victory (1915) is itself the last of those works both Conrad and his critics have agreed to call major; and it ranked with *Nostromo* (1904) as Conrad's personal favorite. Conrad's appraisal of his writings was, I think, both sound and suggestive. He always had a special fondness for *The Nigger of the Narcissus* (1897), recognizing it for what it was, his first genuine artistic accomplishment; and his satisfaction with *The Secret Agent* (1907) was grounded correctly in his belief that he had succeeded, in that novel, in treating "a melodramatic subject ironically," as he wrote in the copy he gave his friend Richard Curle. But he disagreed with readers and critics who thought that *Lord Jim* (1900) was his best book; he felt the tale did not justify the great length of the novel, and suspected that he should have stuck to his original idea, which was to restrict the narrative to the pilgrim ship episode. The most he could say for *Under Western Eyes* (1910) was "rather good." We should probably speak more warmly, but the pain of composition clings to the pages of *Under Western Eyes;*

and the congealing of the action (for example, in Part III) is for long stretches greater than all the interpolated reflections on the art of fiction can overcome. About *Chance* (1913), in a manner not uncommon with authors, he began to talk deprecatingly the moment it became so huge a success. But he remained steadfast in his conviction that his two supreme efforts were the vast tale of the South American seaboard and the tight little story of Axel Heyst.

Surely he was right. *Nostromo* was, as Conrad knew, his largest canvas and his "most anxiously meditated work." It is also one of the greatest novels in English, with a greatness so complex and extensive that only belatedly and partially has it become appreciated. *Victory* is a triumph of a different kind, of a nearly opposite kind. Here Conrad has presented almost all the themes that interested him, but he has refracted those themes through the closely observed conduct of a tiny group of people in a tiny and absolutely isolated setting. *Nostromo* and *Victory* thus stand in a relation similar to the relation between *King Lear* and *Othello* (or perhaps like that between *The Possessed* and *Crime and Punishment*). Both *Nostromo* and *King Lear* comprehend more of the world and of human experience than the mind can comfortably contemplate; both are made up of a variety of parallel plots and involve several different groups of persons; in each we discover what Francis Fergusson calls "action by analogy," and the action so richly exposed in its multiplicity of modes reveals something not only about the individuals concerned but about the hidden drift of history, the secret and tragic movement of the universe. Both works engage the artist's most disturbing power —the prophetic power—which is of course not the ability to read the particular and immediate future, but the ability to read the future implicit in every grave and serious time, the future man is perennially prone to. In *Victory,* on the other hand, as in *Othello,* the action emerges directly from the peculiar temperaments of a few eccentric individuals. What happens, both artistically and psychologically, happens as a result of the impact of one unique personality upon another. This is not to deny any largeness to *Victory;* it is only to identify the source of the special largeness it does reveal. It is to say that the novel shows an allegorical swelling rather than an allegory, and that the creative force is less a pre-existent design the characters are re-enacting (for example, the myth of Eden, of the man and the woman in the garden and the invasion by the serpent) than the jarring effect of the human encounters.

The germ of *Nostromo* was an anecdote, the theft of a lighter-full of silver. But the germ of *Victory* seems to have been the remembered look of several unrelated persons glimpsed at sundry times and in sundry places. *Nostromo* houses characters enough for half a dozen novels; but it says something about Conrad's attitude toward them that he took most of their names from an old book of memoirs (G. F. Masterman's *Seven Eventful Years in Paraguay,* published in 1869) which gossiped about people called Carlos Gould, Monygham, Decoud, Fidanza, Barrios, and Mitchell (*sic*). Conrad's inventive power in *Nostromo,* I am suggesting, was mainly or at least primarily directed to the exposure of action through plot. In *Victory,* however, we remark a thinness, almost a casualness, of plot invention; for Conrad's attention here was directed initially toward people—toward the exposure of action through character. The distinction is exaggerated, and with luck we can make it collapse; but for the moment it can be helpful. It is intended, in any case, as a slight revision of the wonderfully fertile distinction offered by Jacques Maritain in *Creative Intuition in Art and Poetry*—the distinction between "the poetry of the novel" and "the poetry of the theater." The latter, Maritain argues, is essentially the poetry of the action; action comes first in the dramatic composition, and other elements —character, especially—are subordinated to and controlled by the shape of the action, which it is their chief function to illuminate. The poetry of the novel, Maritain continues, is the poetry of the agent, for the aim of fiction is not so much to present an action as to shed light upon the human heart. The incidents in a novel are accordingly selected in order to illuminate the peculiar and representative nature of individual human beings. M. Maritain's remarks and my respectful revision of them help explain the sense in which *Victory* is a test of the nature of fiction. For the "agents" of the book did come first in Conrad's planning and in his writing. But by his manipulation of his characters, Conrad brought into being an action virtually invulnerable in its design.

II

"Conrad was fond of discussing characters in *Victory,*" Curle reports; and in his author's note, Conrad discusses little else. He shares with us the memories that went into the making of the novel: a professional cardsharper he had seen once in the West Indies in 1875; the silent wide-eyed girl in a café orchestra in the South of France; the wandering Swedish gentleman who became "the physical and moral foundation of my Heyst." "It seems to me but natural," Conrad says, "that those three buried in the corner of my memory should suddenly get out into the light of the world." The reference was actually to the three bad men, Mr. Jones and Martin Ricardo and Pedro; but it applies equally to the three key figures in the story. They gathered together irresistibly in Conrad's imagination, just as they gather together for the culminating experience of each of their lives on Heyst's island. They are made known to us exactly through the process of gathering. And indeed the first and most obvious way to chart the unfolding scheme of the book is to point to the important moments in that process.

We meet Axel Heyst on the first page. We hear of Lena thirty-six pages later in Mrs. Schomberg's reluctant mutter to Davidson: "There was even one English girl." Mr. Jones makes his appearance fifty-five pages later yet: "a guest who arrived one fine morning by mail-boat . . . a wanderer, clearly, even as Heyst was." Conrad then devotes nearly seventy pages to acquainting us with the three desperadoes, and with the critical differences between them. But even before he begins that section, the gathering process has been at work in the meeting and the drawing together of Heyst and Lena, and their flight to the island refuge. The entire group of major characters (the Schombergs, of course, excluded) is not assembled in a single place until a little more than halfway through the book: when Wang interrupts the moment of deepest intimacy between Heyst and Lena to announce that a boat (containing, as we learn, Mr. Jones and his henchmen) is approaching the jetty. From that instant, the whole of the novel is caught up in the collision of personalities—in what Henry James (speaking about one of Ibsen's plays) called the lunging of ego against ego, the passionate rocking of soul against soul; every ego against every ego, in Conrad's masterful treatment of it, and every soul against every soul. From the instant the boat is sighted—or, more accurately, from the instant Heyst goes down to the jetty to stare in amazement at the spectacle of the three white men drifting in from nowhere, seemingly more dead than alive—Conrad's complex artistic purpose becomes clear and begins to fulfill itself. The individual characters, explored individually or in small combinations, now meet and join in an adventure which becomes an action larger and more significant than any of them. The novel, that is, begins to assume the defining quality of drama.

Throughout the course of it, however, Conrad continues to exploit the peculiar resources of the novel, for the traditional aims of the novelist; but he does so, at the same time, as a way of heightening and solidifying the dramatic design. In elaborating the distinction I have mentioned, Jacques Maritain observes that since the shape of the action is determining in a drama, contingencies and coincidences and simple accidents have no place there; but that these devices are proper to fiction, since they can be exactly the occasion for some special insight into character. During the latter half of *Victory,* the plot is heavily dependent upon a series of "evitable" incidents, of which two may be cited as typical: the theft of Heyst's gun by Wang and the shooting of Lena by Mr. Jones. The latter is pure accident: Jones had intended to kill Martin Ricardo. The former is a contingency: Wang might have had a gun of his own, or Heyst another revolver hidden away somewhere. Each incident is important to the plot as plotted, but alternatives can easily be imagined, and neither incident seems indispensable to the larger purpose. Yet both incidents serve to shed light on the characters involved and are insofar novelistically justified; and in the light they shed, a truth and a reality begin to appear, as elements toward which an action is steadily in motion.

These incidents, in short, are literally accidental, but they are symbolically inevitable and dramatically appropriate. The theft of the gun tells us a good deal about the curiously hidden nature of the houseboy, his swift and agile selfishness with its portion of quiet cruelty; and it reinforces the sense pervading the world of the book, that in it the distance between men is nearly absolute. At the same time, by rendering Heyst physically defenseless, it provides an "objective correlative" for his more fundamental defenselessness, that of a man of thought like himself in the hour of necessary action. The time spent in puzzling and worrying over the absence of the gun is time artistically well spent. The death of Lena has a still higher degree of propriety. Mr. Jones's bullet, though aimed at Ricardo, only grazed Ricardo's temple before burying itself in Lena's heart, just "under the swelling breast of dazzling and sacred whiteness"—the accident is compounded by the terrible chance that the bullet should strike her exactly there. Yet we need little instruction from the Freudians to perceive that the accident probably masked an act of deepest deliberation. Toward Ricardo, Mr. Jones felt only fury mixed with a lively sense of danger; but toward Lena, toward any woman, he felt the much more destructive emotion of radical disgust. The shooting of Lena is one of the last and most meaningful of the gestures by which we take the full measure of plain Mr. Jones—the evil ascetic, the satanic figure whose satanism springs from a loathing of woman and a horror of sex. (Graham Greene, who has written a short essay called "Plain Mr. Jones," and who is indebted to Conrad on many counts, has provided a comparable image in Pinkie Brown, the inflamed ascetic of *Brighton Rock*.) And in the mode of her death, we have the final revelation and indeed the vindication of Lena's character. Hers is the touching figure of the young woman of smudged virtue who prays she may lose everything for the sake of the man she loves (again, a figure we encounter in Graham Greene). She has drawn upon herself the death that threatened Axel Heyst. To do so is not only a part of her character; it is a part of her plan.

Each of the main figures in *Victory* has his or her private plan; and in this respect, *Victory* too, like *Nostromo,* has a number of plots—as many as the number of central characters; the plot in each case being what happens at last to the individual plan. As each plan is lit up for us, so much more of the action comes into view. In human terms, the separate plans are catastrophically irreconcilable, and in their difference they provide the "manifold" truth—to use Conrad's word—that the novel brings to light. But artistically, they form a living pattern of parallels and contrasts, and so provide the unitary truth Conrad equally envisaged.

Each of these secret programs of conduct is rooted in the mystery of one or two absolute characteristics. Schomberg's malice, for example, is an absolute trait of character, as unmotivated as the malice of Iago. Like Iago's hatred of Othello, Schomberg's hatred of Axel Heyst can pretend to a specific reason: Heyst's snatching away of the girl, which led to the funny Faulknerian madhouse involving Schomberg and the orchestra leader Zangiacomo, over which Conrad used to laugh reminiscently. But the hatred existed already, existed even before the episode, which Schomberg so evilly misrepresented, of Heyst and poor

Morrison. Schomberg's private plot, rooted in his malice, is the business of his so-called revenge upon Heyst, along with the business of diverting the outlaws from his own hotel to the safe distance of Heyst's island. In its vicious way, it is successful, but not because it has anything to do with the facts about Heyst and Lena. Schomberg's plot is strictly his own creation; it is not nourished to any real extent by external circumstances. The same is true of his malignancy. It is a key factor in releasing the terrible events of the book; but it is not developed by outside pressures, it is *revealed* by them. Thus it is with the determining features of the other people in *Victory*. For here, as is customary in Conrad's work, the characters do not grow; they only grow more visible. That is the precise effect of their mutual impact.

Mr. Jones is perhaps the most fascinating instance in the novel of the motion toward visibility, if only because it is the most paradoxical. What becomes fully and finally visible about him is a kind of absence, a nothingness. His plan is the least reconcilable of all the plans, and hence the most irreducible symptom of the "manifold" aspect of *Victory:* because Mr. Jones's plan opposes not only the substance of all the others but the very terms of their existence. Ricardo, we remember, has his own particular reasons—reasons he cannot disclose to Mr. Jones—for urging the invasion of Heyst's island; and no doubt some dumb dream of conquest occupies the primitive skull of Pedro. But the mission of Mr. Jones undercuts all that. It has to do with the condition of his being, which is, as it were, a mockery of being itself. Heyst reports to Lena on his conversation with Jones:

> " 'I suppose you would like to know who I am?' " he asked me.
>
> "I told him I would leave it to him, in a tone which, between gentlemen, could have left no doubt in his mind. He raised himself on his elbow—he was lying down on the campbed—and said:
>
> " 'I am he who is——.' "

"No use asking me what he meant, Lena," Heyst adds. "I don't know." What Jones meant was probably a theatrical blasphemy. In very similar words, according to the Old Testament, God announced his name and his nature to his chosen people: "I am," or "I am that I am." Jones, of course, is not god-like, and especially not god-like in the sense of representing the source of being itself. He is devil-like—his character bulges in the direction of the devil (he is not *the* devil, any more than *Victory* is an allegory); and exactly because he represents the source of non-being.

The association with Satan gratifies Mr. Jones immensely. He describes, in an echo from the Book of Job, his habit of "coming and going up and down the earth"; and Heyst replies that he has "heard that sort of story about someone else before." Jones at once gives Heyst a ghastly grin, claiming that "I have neither more nor less determination" than "the gentleman you are thinking of." But the nature and end of his determination emerge from a later allusion to the devil. Jones speculates for Heyst's benefit that a man living alone, as Heyst had been living, would "take care to conceal [his] property so well that the devil himself——." Heyst interrupts with a murmured "Certainly."

> Again, with his left hand, Mr. Jones mopped his frontal bone, his stalk-like neck, his razor jaws, his fleshless chin. Again, his voice faltered and his aspect became still more gruesomely malevolent, as of a wicked and pitiless corpse.

Those last four words summarize the character of Mr. Jones and point to his unswerving purpose: he is not only deathly, he is the cause that death is in others. To Schomberg, too, Jones had seemed "to imply some sort of menace from beyond the grave"; and in Heyst's first view of him, Jones is "sitting up [in the boat], silent, rigid and very much like a corpse." At the outset of their duel, Jones seems to exert a greater force of sheer existence than Heyst; for Heyst, as he confesses mournfully in language highly reminiscent of one of Hawthorne's isolated men, has lived too long among shadows. But Heyst's determining quality has only been lying dormant; he is like the indolent volcano, to which he is lightly compared on the second page of the book; he is moving—though moving too late and too slowly—toward existence and reality. Jones's characteristic movement is all in the other direction.

The force in Jones is all negative, though not the less emphatic for being so. That is why he hates and fears women, for they are fertility incarnate and the literal source of life. Jones's particular and personal plot is not really to seize Heyst's alleged treasures, but to inflict his deathiness upon others. He comes as an envoy of death, disguised as an envoy of the living: of death not in the sense of murder, but in the sense of a fundamental hostility to existence. He is the champion of the anti-real, and he arrives at just the moment when Heyst, because of the presence and love of Lena, is feeling "a greater sense of reality than he had ever known in his life." Jones's plan, too, is superficially successful: everyone he has brushed against on the island is dead. Jones is dead also; but he has not been killed, he has simply shrunk, collapsed, disintegrated. He has reached the limit of his true condition. And what is visible of him at the end is exactly the outward sign of that condition. "The water's very clear there," Davidson tells the Excellency; "and I could see him huddled up on the bottom between two piles, like a heap of bones in a blue silk bag, with only the head and feet sticking out."

Mr. Jones's most astute enemy in the book is not Heyst but the girl Lena, though Jones and Lena never in fact confront one another. But Lena is the one person able to understand not only the threat represented by the invaders, but the very threat of the threat; and she understands it so well that, as things develop, she can formulate her own plot and purpose to herself with exactness —to "capture death—savage, sudden, irresponsible death, prowling round the man who possessed her." Lena stands for a possibility of life. Yet, curiously enough, her role as the actual source of Heyst's sense of being is rendered less visible—rendered, that is, with less apparent success—than are the deadly negations of Mr. Jones. Lena is the one member of the cast who remains in partial darkness. Many critics have remarked upon this, and some have gone on to say that Conrad rarely had much luck with his women. But his achievement elsewhere is not always unimpressive: Winnie Verloc, in *The Secret Agent,* seems to me one of the most compelling females in modern literature; and one has little difficulty making out the attractive features of Emily Gould and Flora de Barral, in *Nostromo* and *Chance* respectively. It may even be that a kind of haziness, a fragility of substance was intended in the portrayal of Lena. She *is* like that, and the frailty of her being determines the nature of her plot. For her aim is precisely to win for herself a greater measure of reality by forcing upon the man she loves a greater recognition of her. She lives in his acknowledgment of her: "If you were to stop thinking about me I shouldn't be in the world at all. . . . I can only be what you think I am." This is a trifle unfortunate, since Heyst, the only human being who could have seen Lena, can never manage to see quite enough. Richard Curle observes nicely about Lena that she is "the supreme example of a 'one-man' woman, so supreme that even the reader is kept out of the secret." Heyst peers at her in the half-light, and we peer over his shoulder, dimly discerning a creature of considerable but only guessed-at bodily appeal and intense but only partially communicated spiritual desire.

Her desire is stated plainly enough for us, as it takes form after Ricardo's attempt to rape her. From that moment onward, "all her energy was concentrated on the struggle she wanted to take upon herself, in a great exaltation of love and self-sacrifice." And we know enough about her history to find that exaltation plausible. We have heard of her mother's desertion of her father, of her father's career as a small-time musician and of his removal to a home for incurables; we have heard of her bleak childhood and adolescence, her blurred unhappy life with a traveling orchestra; we can easily imagine what Heyst's compassion must have meant to her. "I am not what they call a good girl," she has said; and through Heyst's impression of her, we are struck by her mixture of misery and audacity. She alone fully understands that it is Schomberg who has put the outlaws on Heyst's trail, and she can comprehend the hotel keeper's motiveless motive. Lena's plot, accordingly, is the most coherent of all the plots, and the most important. It is also the most private, since it requires of her that she lie both to the man she hates and the man she loves. She is altogether successful, at least as successful as Schomberg or Mr. Jones. She does disarm Ricardo, literally and psychologically; the dagger she takes from him is indeed "the spoil of vanquished death" and "the symbol of her victory." By dividing Ricardo from Jones, she creates a situation in which, as the demonically brilliant Jones instantly realizes, Ricardo must be killed; and through a chain reaction, she is responsible also for the death of Pedro and Jones himself. All this we know, understand, and can rehearse. But Conrad has nonetheless not finally managed to fulfill his ambition with respect to Lena. He has not made us see Lena completely. Between her and ourselves, there falls a shadow. It is, of course, the shadow of Axel Heyst.

III

If the victory is Lena's—if her end, as Conrad insisted, is triumphant—the major defeat recorded in the novel is that of Heyst. His is the ultimate failure, and for the reason he gives in almost the last words we hear him speak: "Ah, Davidson, woe to the man whose heart has not learned while young to hope, to love—and to put its trust in life." But that very statement demonstrates that Heyst, by acknowledging his failure and perceiving its cause, has in the literary manner of speaking been saved. He is, at the last, completely in touch with truth. And, similarly, if Heyst's personal plan—which is not only to rid the island of its invaders and to protect Lena, but also to join with Lena in an experience of full reality—if that plan is the least successful plan in the book, Heyst is nonetheless the true and steady center of the novel from its beginning to its end. So central is Heyst within the rich composition of *Victory* that neither his character nor his conduct may be clearly seen apart from that composition. They are identified only through a series of analogies and contrasts, and as the vital center of the book's design.

As analysis moves to the figure of Axel Heyst, it moves of necessity from the Many to the One—from the many separated individuals with their irreconcilable differences of purpose to a pattern of action in which they seem to echo and reflect and repeat one another. It is the felt flow of the Many into the One that accounts for the feeling one has of a strong metaphysical current running deep through the novel, of very real human beings and events gathering together in a way that suggests an allegory of universal proportions. Let it be emphasized again that we have to do with a process, not with an imposition. And as it develops, we begin to detect parallels between contrasting and inimical elements, continuities between divisions—and by the power of the book's current, more radical contrasts between newly observed parallels. At the center is Axel Heyst, whose entire being—*artistically,* within the actual pages of the book—is created by the play of likeness and difference.

We must, accordingly, approach Heyst by way of those relationships—which is to reconsider some of the persons already inspected, but to consider them now not in their enormous differences, but in their unexpected similarities: an undertaking the first page of *Victory* (with its references to the similarities between coal and diamonds, an island and a mountain) has warned us would be the key to the novel's meaning. Between Lena and Ricardo, for example, between the mystically devoted young woman and the thickheaded roughneck who plunges headlong through the blue serge curtain to assault her, an unexpected likeness is uncovered. It is a fatality in Ricardo's crude imagination that he should exaggerate it. "You and I are made to understand each other," he mumbles, after a stupor of surprise and admiration at the vigor of Lena's resistance. "Born alike, bred alike, I guess. You are not tame. Same here! You have been chucked out into this rotten world of 'ypocrites. Same here!" Because of his conviction of their likeness, Ricardo trusts Lena more simply and unquestioningly than Heyst trusts her; Ricardo trusts what there is in Lena of his own animal and prehensile nature, and he dies of that trust, as Heyst dies of mistrust. But within disastrous limits, Ricardo is right—he and Lena do have a good deal in common. "Perhaps because of the similarity of their miserable origin in the dregs of mankind," Lena realizes, "she had understood Ricardo perfectly." Even her physical strength and tenacity match his: "You have fingers like steel! Jiminy! You have muscles like a giant." That is scarcely the pathetic child seen through Heyst's impression of her, the child suffering helplessly the venomous pinchings of Mrs. Zangiacomo; and the ferocity of her response to Ricardo's attempted rape correctly suggests a ready perception, based on experience, of that kind of jungle behavior. It also suggests the strength in Lena which has been brought to the surface since the Zangiacomo days: brought to the surface and focused as a powerful instrument, through the effect upon her of Heyst.

An important ingredient in her strength is a talent for lying, exercised for the sake of truth. Ricardo is quite justified in attributing to Lena a duplicity equal to his own; he knows that both of them have had to become skilled in duplicity as the one indispensable resource in the world's hypocritical "game of grab." "Give the chuck to all this blamed 'ypocrisy," urges Ricardo. Lena seems to agree, and she embarks deceptively upon a plot to deceive Heyst—"her gentleman," as Ricardo calls him—which notably parallels Ricardo's systematic deception of *his* gentleman, Mr. Jones. It seems to Ricardo natural that Lena should lie to the man who has befriended her; such is the norm of behavior in the world he inhabits—that is, the world of *Victory*. It is what people do to each other in that world: witness Mrs. Schomberg's trickery of her own gentleman, her fat braggart of a husband. The cluster of duplicities has, up to a point, a common element, for each aims initially at the salvation of the man deceived. Mrs. Schomberg, when she helps frustrate her husband's plans (his "insane and odious passion") by helping Lena to escape, imagines she is keeping Schomberg out of serious trouble and preserving their wretched marriage. Ricardo's organization of the invasion of Heyst's island is a contrivance to rescue his chief from the habitual state of sloth into which Jones had fallen. To do so, Ricardo must cunningly keep silent about the presence on the island of a young woman; since, were Jones to hear about it, he would instantly abandon the adventure. Only later does Ricardo's helpful deceit deepen into betrayal. And as to Lena, "she was not ashamed of her duplicity," because "nothing stood between the enchanted dream of her existence and a cruel catastrophe but her duplicity." She will deceive every one, and she will especially deceive Heyst; she will wear the mask of infidelity to save the life of the man toward whom her fidelity is the very assurance of her existence.

The relationship between Lena and Ricardo thus illuminates one of the major themes of the novel—the theme of truth-telling, and the significance of truth-telling, as a value, in the scheme of human behavior. By the same token, Lena and Ricardo illuminate the character of Axel Heyst; for it is almost a weakness in Heyst that—at the opposite extreme from Mr. Jones and his self-association with the Father of Lies—he has an absolute regard for truth. He is so obsessed with truth that he becomes literally disempowered when confronted with lies; and he is so inflexible toward truth that only lies can save him. Even more than the theft of his gun, as it seems, it is the lies Schomberg has spread about Heyst's treatment of Morrison that, when they belatedly reach Heyst's ears, succeed finally in rendering him defenseless by provoking in him the emotion of paralyzing disgust. His only defense thereafter is the multiple duplicity of Lena.

It is not inappropriate that such should be the case, for between Morrison and Lena, too, there is a revealing similarity. Lena shares with Ricardo a certain seamy background and a certain practical toughness; but with Morrison, the unfortunate master of the trading brig *Capricorn,* she has shared the magnanimity of Axel Heyst. The story of Morrison is a sort of rehearsal for the story of Lena; for, like Lena, Morrison is not only the object, he is in a sense the victim of Heyst's compassion. Morrison is miraculously rescued by Heyst in a way that, as events work out, both leads to and makes plausible the rescue, not long after, of Lena; and the consequence in both cases is a fresh involvement, a chance for life, that results in fact in their death. Both look upon Heyst as a kind of god, especially because to both of them Heyst's conduct appears purely gratuitous, like the undeserved and disinterested mercy of God. It is not merely pity; Heyst's father had advised him to "cultivate that form of contempt which is called pity," but the salvaging of Morrison and the benevolent theft of Lena are due to no such calculated attitude. They reflect rather a temperament which, as we are told, was incapable of scorning any decent emotion—a temperament so fine and rare as to seem literally godlike to the bedeviled of the book's world. When Heyst offers Morrison the money to save the latter's boat, Morrison gazes at him as though "he expected Heyst's usual white suit of the tropics to change into a shining garment down to his toes . . . and didn't want to miss a single detail of the transformation." In the procedure typical of *Victory,* a reaction which will later become serious, complex, and tragic is presented in the early pages in simple and partly comic tonalities. Lena's reaction to Heyst's rescue of her is less extravagant and open-mouthed; but it partakes of a still deeper awe and of a genuinely self-sacrificial reverence.

In the same way, it is Morrison who first strikes the note, in his droll and touching way, which will develop into a theme close to the tragic heart of the book. Morrison wonders in panic if Heyst is joking about the money. Heyst asks austerely what he means, and Morrison is abashed.

"Forgive me, Heyst. You must have been sent by God in answer to my prayer. But I have been nearly off my chump for three days with worry; and it suddenly struck me: 'What if it's the Devil who has sent him?' "

"I have no connection with the supernatural," said Heyst graciously, moving on. "Nobody sent me. I just happened along."

"I know better," contradicted Morrison.

That moment has its louder and more serious echo a couple of hundred pages later, when Heyst catches sight of Jones and his henchmen approaching the jetty. He stares at them in disbelief: "[He] had never been so much astonished in his life."

The civilisation of the tropics could have nothing to do with it. It was more like those myths, current in Polynesia, of amazing strangers, who arrive at an island, gods or demons, bringing good or evil to the innocence of the inhabitants—gifts of unknown things, words never heard before.

"Gods or demons, bringing good or evil"—those ambiguous phrases greet the first glimpse Heyst and Jones have of each other; and they frame and give shape to the most telling of the patterns of similarity and contrast that *Victory* has to offer—the one that says most about Heyst himself, and the one that best reveals the drama of which he is the protagonist. Between Heyst and Jones, the differences are of radical dimensions. Heyst is a bringer of good (though the recipients of his gifts suffer evil by consequence). Jones is a bringer of evil (though his gift is the occasion of greatest good for Lena, and her victory). Heyst has some godlike element in his nature; but the insinuation makes him highly uncomfortable. Jones has a kind of private understanding with the Devil, and that insinuation never fails to excite him. But between Axel Heyst and plain Mr. Jones, there is a vibrant flow of analogies, a movement back and forth like electrical currents.

A likeness is registered at the instant Jones first turns up in the novel; a guest at Schomberg's hotel arriving from Celebes, "but generally, Schomberg understood, from up China Sea way; a wanderer clearly, even as Heyst was." Both men are drifters by profession ("I'll drift," Heyst had decided as a young man); both have occupied themselves for many years by "coming and going up and down the earth." Both men are gentlemen, in the conventional meaning of the word and within the book's definition as pronounced by Martin Ricardo: "That's another thing you can tell a gentleman by, his freakishness. A gentleman ain't accountable to nobody, any more than a tramp on the roads." Heyst invokes a comparable notion: "I, Axel Heyst, the most detached of creatures in this earthly captivity, the veriest tramp on this earth." As gentlemen and as tramps, both Jones and Heyst are products of highly civilized society who have chosen the career of the rootless outsider. Both are wellborn, perhaps aristocratic; they are elegant, sophisticated, mannerly; both have an excessive vein of fastidiousness, a too easily outraged austerity. And both are outcasts who in different ways are outside the law: Heyst by being in some manner beyond and above it, Jones by being several degrees beneath it. With one of his ghastly grins, during their first interview, Mr. Jones confesses to Heyst that the latter was not the man he had expected to meet. For he sees or thinks he sees, startlingly, *son semblable, son frère.*

Jones misjudges Heyst just as Ricardo misjudges Lena, and with the same limited warrant. "We pursue the same ends," Jones remarks; and he argues that his presence on the island is neither more nor less "morally reprehensible" than Heyst's. Jones assumes that, like himself, Heyst is simply a gentlemanly scoundrel, sharing with him the impulse common to gifted men—the criminal impulse. About this mistake there is something as ridiculous as it is fatal; but Jones has intuited a fragment of the truth. Heyst does share with Jones a basic indifference to the habitual practices of society and to its moral verdicts. He appraises the world in terms nearly identical to those of Jones: "The world's a mad dog," Heyst tells Davidson. "It will bite you if you give it a chance." These two lean and handsome gentlemen, these radical drifters, have an extraordinary amount in common, and Jones's contention is justified—"Ah, Mr. Heyst . . . you and I have much more in common than you think." Jones and Heyst reflect each other with a sort of perfection, the way an object is reflected in a mirror. Each is the other seen wrong way round.

That is why they are dramatically indispensable one to the other—the visibility of each is dependent upon the presence of the other. They come from opposite ends of the universe, and they meet where opposites are made to meet: in a work of art. The strength of each often appears as an extension of the other's weakness and vice versa; which is one reason why the conflict between them, as it assumes its form, seems to extend endlessly, to enlarge almost beyond the reach of human reckoning. It brushes the edge of allegory and touches briefly on the outskirts of myth— one of "those myths, current in Polynesia, of amazing strangers . . . gods or demons." But the drama hangs on to its human vitality and its immediacy and continues to draw its force from the peculiar nature of the two men involved—the man of intellectual sensibility with an inadequate but incipient trust in life and the man of occasional action with a strenuous but insufficiently examined faith in the power of death. Mr. Jones's tendency to sloth, which leaves him spread motionless over three chairs for hours at a time, is reflected in Heyst's long periods of meditation on the hostility of thought to action, while he lounges on the verandah and smokes his cheroot. But Jones's condition has the terrible and explosive power of an ancient sin; and Heyst's skepticism is marred by a vein of tenderness. If Heyst had mistrusted life more completely, he would perhaps have been a better match for Jones from the outset. As it is, the novel catches him at the moment when mistrust is giving way to an urge toward reality and communion.

He had long since, so he tells Jones during their last conversation, divorced himself from the love of life; but then he adds, with painful accuracy, "not sufficiently perhaps." So he acts and reacts without "distinctness." His conception of the world, taken from his father, had for too many years been of something "not worth touching, and perhaps not substantial enough to grasp." The experience of Lena was beginning to put substance into the world; but Heyst can neither participate fully in that experience nor resist it, for he has absorbed either too much or too little of his father's doctrine that "the consolation of love" is the cruelest of all the stratagems of life. He can still insist that "he who forms a tie is lost," but his actual feeling is that he is about to find himself, that Lena is giving him "a greater sense of his own reality than he had ever known in his life."

Greater: but still inadequate to fit him for the challenge that arises. For that challenge is exactly the embodiment of the challenge his father had honorably faced. "With what strange serenity, mingled with terrors," Heyst thinks about his father, "had that man considered the universal nothingness! He had plunged into it headlong, perhaps to render death, the answer that faced one at every inquiry, more supportable." It is only four pages later that Wang arrives to announce the approach of a strange boat. And Mr. Jones, the corpse-like figure at the tiller of the boat, is himself the harbinger and representative of that "universal nothingness." He is the body of that death "that faced one at every inquiry." Trapped between a waning skepticism and an undernourished sense of reality, Heyst cannot emulate his father; cannot make the plunge or launch the assault. All he can do, at the end, is to take death upon himself, purgatorially, by fire.

But if Heyst is unable to plunge, Jones (like Ricardo on his lower level) plunges too incautiously. The sinister mission he engages on is unsupported by the necessary amount of cold intelligence—of just that kind of intelligence that Heyst possesses supremely. Heyst begins finally to exercise it at Jones's expense during their climactic interview, after Heyst has learned the reason for the invasion of the island—Schomberg's preposterous falsehood about treasures hidden on it. At this instant, a reversal is effected, and Heyst takes command of their relationship; it is his strength now which becomes visible because of the revelation of Jones's weakness. "You seem a morbid, senseless sort of bandit," Heyst says with weary contempt. "There were never in the world two more deluded bandits—never! . . . Fooled by a silly rascally innkeeper," he goes on remorselessly. "Talked over like a pair of children with a promise of sweets." It is the logical weakness of Jones's asserted belief in universal fraudulence that it must contain in itself an element of the fraudulent. If he had been wholly convinced of the depravity of all the inhabitants of a wholly vicious world, Jones would have trusted less in the strength of his authority—his graveyard power—over Martin Ricardo; and he would not have overlooked the possibility of mere vulgar vindictiveness in Schomberg. He leapt too swiftly from sloth into action, in a way that, in retrospect, invests one of Heyst's casual pronouncements, made early in the book, with prophetic implications: "Action is the devil."

Heyst and Jones need each other for artistic visibility; but both of them need Lena, as she needs them, to make clear the full shape of the drama they have begotten between them, when the current of the novel carries them (this is one's impression) into a dimension beyond the dimension occupied by all the other persons in the book. The action disclosed by the effect of those three upon each other is the gradual location of that dimension, of the very domain of reality and truth. The domain lies somewhere between the dialectical stirrings of the book's first page and the observation of nothingness on its last—somewhere, as it turns out, between the intellectualism of Heyst and the deathiness of Jones. Between the two kinds of failure, Lena's victory is squeezed out in a way that is a victory both for her and for the novel in which she has her being. As against Jones, Lena has dedicated herself to the actual cause of living; and as against Heyst, she has seized with fingers of steel upon the immediate and necessary facts of behavior. Her practicality (again the book's first page is recalled) derives from a mystical exaltation that transcends the particular situation and attains to universal value while remaining sharply and intently focused upon the single figure of Axel Heyst. Lena's accomplishment reflects the accomplishment of the novel. *Victory* is, in a sense, a reproach to the fascination with death of so much modern fiction. But even more, perhaps, it is an admonition about the tendency of both fiction and criticism to intellectualize the art—to lose the drama in the allegory—or to deform the art—to lose the novel in the drama. The form of *Victory* grows dramatic, and it gives forth intimations of allegory. But it remains faithful to its own nature, for it never makes the mistake of Mr. Jones—it never fails to take account of the variable and highly unpredictable character of individual human beings.

1959

MALRAUX AND HIS CRITICS

"Malraux is interested in painting," Maurice Blanchot remarked in 1950, "but we know that he is also interested in man." What is beguiling about the remark is not only its deceptive simplicity—in an essay not otherwise notable for simplicity—but the ordering of its key terms. Blanchot to be sure, was engaged at the moment in appraising Malraux's interest in painting as reflected by *The Psychology of Art;* even so, his formulation was, and I think, remains essentially correct, especially when he continued: "To save one through the other—[Malraux] was unable to resist this great temptation."

Not many readers were as quick to grasp the point: the intimate relation between Malraux's supposedly new concern with the total world of art forms and his abiding concern with the condition and the destiny of man. Writing in 1957, Armand Hoog remembered "the outburst of surprise . . . and bafflement that accompanied the publication, in 1948, of the *Musée Imaginaire,"* the first part of *The Psychology of Art.* "More than one critic," Hoog said, "marveled, however admiringly, that such an excellent novelist should turn into an art historian." No novelist of his generation had been more closely associated, in the vague consciousness of the reading public, with the raw violence of contemporary events. Malraux had dramatized the 1926 uprising in Canton (*The Conquerors,* 1928[1]), his own penetration of the Siamese jungle with something of the tribal warfare going on there (*The Royal Way,* 1930), another and larger phase of the Chinese revolution (*Man's Fate,* 1933), aspects of brutality and enslavement in Nazi Germany (*Days of Wrath,* 1935), the Spanish Civil War (*Man's Hope,*

1. Dates are those of the first French edition.

1937), and most recently a poison-gas attack on the German-Russian front in World War I, preceded by a glance at the Young Turk revolutionary movement before that war and framed by memoirs of World War II (*The Walnut Trees of the Altenburg,* 1943). No writer, not even Hemingway, could seem less likely to the unknowing to devote himself to researches into Sumerian or Gothic art.

But the surprise occasioned by Malraux's art studies was due of course, as Hoog says, to an inattentive reading of the novels just mentioned, and to popular ignorance of Malraux's several interrelated careers. It is now clear that there is an astonishing unity to everything Malraux has written; one is inclined to add "everything he has done," since his first significant book, a sort of epistolary novel bearing the Spengler-echoing title *The Temptation of the West* in 1926. A main element of that unity has been a persistent preoccupation with art: with works of art and the cultures they comprise and express; and with the role of art in a generally "absurd" universe. It was Malraux who, in *The Temptation of the West,* introduced the word "absurd" into the modern philosophical vocabulary: in a contention that to the eye of modern man the universe appeared fatally bereft of meaning because of the loss of compelling and explanatory religious belief and, with it, the collapse of any direction-giving concept of man; because of the successive "deaths" of the idea of God and the idea of man. Most of Malraux's novels have been symbolic assaults upon history, in an endeavor to wrest from history a persuasive definition of human nature and a dependable guide and measure of human conduct; while in his life, Malraux has been committed to intensive action and to what Picon calls "the myth of the great individual" as sources, perhaps of insight but certainly of compensation. But he has also and ever more strenuously been committed to the great art-work as performing, more satisfactorily yet, these same functions. If Malraux evidently still believes in the efficacy of the master, he believes even more in the saving power of the masterpiece.

The play of these terms—man, the absurd, action, history, and art—has been constant in Malraux's writing from the beginning. But before criticism could arrive at them, it had to get beyond a prior misapprehension—namely, that Malraux was primarily a chronicler of contemporary revolutions, a skillful journalist of the political and economic upheavals peculiar to his age.

I

Leon Trotsky posed the issue in 1931 when he said about *The Conquerors:* "The book is called a novel. What in fact we have before us is a fictionalized chronicle of the Chinese revolution during its first period, the Canton period."[2] Trotsky, as we know, had an uncommonly quick perception of literature; he was among the first, a couple of years later, to detect the achievement of Ignazio Silone's *Fontamara*—in which, he said, revolutionary passion was raised to the level of art. He felt that *The Conquerors* was itself a work of considerable art and made some acute and generous observations about its beauty of narrative. But he felt that the author's revolutionary passion was flawed; that Malraux's effort to give a faithful portrait of insurrectionist China had been (in Trotsky's word) corrupted, both by an "excess of individualism" and by "aesthetic caprice." Even in retrospect, the charge (which Trotsky supported with considerable and pressing detail) is not without substance and pertains to a wider problem: for there has always been a sort of murky imbalance between Malraux's political affinities (the presumptive ones in his novels and the actual ones—communist and then Gaullist—in his life) and his stated or implied beliefs about literature. Nonetheless, Malraux had reason to say, in answer, that his book was not intended and should not be judged as a fictionalized chronicle, and that, in effect, it was just the individualism and the aesthetics that made it a novel.[3] As to the former, the book's stress was placed "on the relationship between individual and collective action, not on collective action alone." As to the latter, Malraux made the crucial remark that the novel was dominated not by considerations of doctrinal loyalty and historical inclusiveness, but by the vision, the way of looking at things—in Malraux's French, by *"l'optique"* —proper to the novel as an art-form. The entire critical "problem" of Malraux—the "Malraux case," as some French commentators have called it—lies, implicit but bristling, in this early exchange.

2. "La Révolution Etranglée," *Nouvelle Revue Française, 211* (1931). Most of the critical essays discussed here can be found in the paperbound volume of Twentieth Century Views *Malraux*, ed. R. W. B. Lewis (Englewood Cliffs, N.J., 1964).
    3. "Réponse à Trotsky," *Nouvelle Revue Française, 211* (1931).

Still, when *The Conquerors* was followed by a more full-scale narrative of the Chinese revolution, the betrayal and defeat of the communist effort to seize Shanghai in *Man's Fate,* and that by an account (manifestly first-hand in part) of the Spanish Loyalist rebellion in *Man's Hope,* it became generally agreed that Malraux, even more than Silone or Koestler, was *the* novelistic historian of the great social agitations of the century. However original he might be as a craftsman, his subject, it was agreed, was the specific contemporary battle between socialism and capitalism —"the central struggle of modern times," according to Haakon Chevalier in his introduction to his own English translation of *Man's Fate,* "the struggle of a dying order with the forces within it that are molding a new world." That opinion, too, now strikes us as limited rather than misguided: and limited exactly in its failure to see Malraux's passionate hostility to limitations. For Malraux's heroes, as Joseph Frank has observed, "were never simply engaged in a battle against a particular social or economic injustice; they were always somehow struggling against the limitations of life itself and the humiliation of destiny."[4] The socialist revolts loomed, in Malraux's view, as instances, urgently important in themselves, of a much grander revolt; and he took them as occasions for depicting in fiction the revolt of man against his spiritually and intellectually hemmed-in condition. This was why Malraux's writing had so immense an impact during the thirties upon the rebellious spirits of so many different countries with their so different modes and objects and strategies of revolt, and why he was able to enlist a far-flung loyalty that has persisted with a sometimes unsubdued fierceness.

Malraux's main characters really are protagonists: that is, etymologically, primary combatants. What they do about the human condition is to take arms against its historical embodiments; and they will go to the ends of the earth to seek them out. The point has been noticed more than once: Garine, son of a Swiss father and a Russian mother, comes in *The Conquerors* to southern China; Perken, in *The Royal Way,* literally as well as psychologically *heimatlos* (his native state, Schleswig-Holstein, has been annexed by Denmark), probes uncharted areas of Siam on a crusade against death; in *Man's Fate* and *Man's Hope,* persons from many nations foregather in Shanghai and Madrid, as they

4. *The Widening Gyre* (New Brunswick, N.J., 1963), p. 106.

did in actual fact, at the moment of supreme historical crisis; the Alsatian Vincent Berger, in *The Walnut Trees of the Altenburg,* pursues a mirage of Ottoman nationalism through central Asia. Berger's mission is a failure: the holy war he believes in is not to be kindled; but the others find and take part in the (losing) battle of their deepest desire. In short—and the commonplace is worth repeating, since it applies more unequivocally to Malraux than to any other modern novelist—Malraux's heroes make their test of life in those places and times where human experience is most intensified, where indeed it has become most decisively embattled. It is on a succession of darkling plains, where ignorant armies clash by night, that Malraux's characters attempt to find an explanation of man's essential nature, a justification of his condition, a glimpse of his destiny, a reason for his being.

But as they do so, we move with Malraux into perplexities which, if not wholly philosophical in nature, are at least sources of logical anxiety. Time and again, Malraux has implied that it is in *action* that the strong-willed individual may hope to find not only assuagement but revelation. Victor Brombert reminds us that many of Malraux's key personages are intellectuals— former university professors and the like—but intellectuals who for the most part have lost faith in the values of ideas as such and who have come to distrust the pure exercise of mind.[5] They have therefore abandoned the contemplative or the teaching life and have turned to some arena of explicit action—usually by attaching themselves to a revolutionary cause where the cause is undergoing trial by warfare—in search of some truth more vital than the truth of ideas. It is a belligerent version of the perennial pragmatic strategy. Chiaramonte remarks that Malraux "pushed to its extreme consequences the modern pragmatic impulse which tends to see in the world of action the only reality, and, what is more, to reject any proposition which cannot be directly translated into a force, an act, or series of acts." The word "modern" in that admirable sentence might well be replaced by the phrase "ancient and traditional," for it has always been the hallmark of the pragmatist that he sees "in the world of action the only reality." Customarily, moreover, the pragmatic temper not only rejects propositions that cannot be translated into actions; it also

5. "Malraux: Passion and Intellect," in *The Intellectual Hero* (Philadelphia, 1961), pp. 165 ff.

dispenses with any branch of thought and despises any activity of mind that is not involved with—cannot be tested by—human experience. So it is that *history*—that is, precisely, "the world of action"—history in both its first and second intentions, as a series of actual events and as the record of events: history, in the usual pragmatic scheme, takes the place of metaphysics and of any independent theory of knowledge. The tumult of history becomes the one accessible context of truth and value; and inspecting it, the pragmatist has often been able to disclose some developing and meaningful shape, some gratifying or alarming design of things past and passing and to come. His chart of that design is the pragmatist's account of reality. The very troubling question about Malraux and for Malraux is whether he has ever managed to suggest in his fiction any such disclosure.

But Malraux is or has been a novelist, a person dedicated (as he told Trotsky) to *l'optique* of fiction rather than that of history or philosophy. The literary issue here is at least as complex as the philosophical one, and goes far beyond the confines of this essay. It has to do with that level of a work of literature—that is, of any work that aspires to such a level—on which the literal incidents and characters, the actual clashes and conversations, can be seen enacting an allegory of some large and generalized historical process: a process in which an entire social order may be caught up, or even a whole world; and a process which may or may not be "true" in the perspective of a scientific historian as it fixes on the historical period where the process is allegedly unfolding. Conrad's *Nostromo*—to stay simply with the modern novel (and apart, that is, from the tradition of epic poetry) —is a splendid example; and so of course is Dostoevsky's *The Possessed.*

In *Nostromo,* the various convulsions that rend and then reshape the little South American republic of Costaguana, the assortment of plots and purposes, the interaction of a host of ambitions and devotions: all this secretes an appalling myth of modern economic, political, moral, and even religious history. It is the history, most generally, of the devious and yet absolute conquest by "material interests" of the spirit and energy of modern man; more particularly, of the process by which material interests, trusted and supported as a source of order and justice in a repressive and unstable backward society, bring in their own brand of intolerable injustice and repression and thus assure further upheavals in the future.[6] One looks in vain for anything like so powerful if so grim a pattern in *The Conquerors* or *Man's Fate* or *Man's Hope,* or in the three taken together. Nor can one make out in those novels the tremendous and still more emphatic kind of historical pattern (the inevitable spawning of nihilism by liberalism in mid-nineteenth-century Russia) set forth in *The Possessed.* Nor, at an opposite extreme of fictional stress, do we find the sort of far-away but sizable implications about social and moral history that exist somewhere in the depths of James's *The Golden Bowl.*

Malraux's dilemma, if dilemma it be, is caused in part by the very subject—contemporary historical violence—which he has been brave enough to deal with. When, as in *Man's Fate,* he remains faithful to the historical outcome of the struggle, he concludes with a disaster which is not, *within the novel,* invested with any particular significance. But when, as in *Man's Hope,* he shapes historical fact to his fictional purposes (by concluding with the Loyalist victory at Guadalajara), he suggests an outcome and a meaning other than those history was already bleakly providing. Chiaramonte, who makes this latter point, relates it to what he describes as Malraux's evasion of "the implications of tragedy";[7] but I am not so sure. The case of *Man's Hope* is problematic; but it may well be that in most of his novels, Malraux, far from evading the implications of tragedy, was resolutely facing up to something more terrible yet—to the absence of tragedy as a discernible and determining form at work in modern historical experience. Needless to say, one great way to find and to make evident an illuminating design within the confusions of history is to subject the course of the events in question to the organizing power of the tragic imagination. Herman Melville did exactly that when he confronted the turbulence of the American Civil War in his loosely epic volume of war poems, *Battle-Pieces.* Most of those poems were written while the war was still in progress; but looking back both at the war and the poems after the pacifica-

6. In *Politics and the Novel* (New York, 1957), Irving Howe credits *Nostromo* not only with dramatic significance but with historical accuracy and even prescience. It verifies, says Mr. Howe—"in the limited way a novel can verify anything"—"Leon Trotsky's theory of the 'permanent revolution' "; and, on the level of actual history, it describes in advance what would be "a basic pattern of Latin American politics."

7. "Malraux and the Demons of Action," *Partisan Review* (1948).

tion, Melville (in a prose supplement) could draw upon Aristotle's definition of tragedy in the *Poetics* to define the war as a "great historic tragedy" which he prayed had not "been enacted without instructing our whole beloved country through terror and pity." But Malraux has not felt or envisaged the civil wars he has participated in as genuine tragic actions: not, at least, on any scale beyond that of a few driven and defeated individuals.

The importance, indeed the artistic and spiritual "value," of those individual destinies should not be minimized. It is true, as several critics have noticed, that there are no truly evil figures in Malraux's novels: no persons who either are evil through some private wayward impulse or who represent the force of some evil principle in the universe. But it is not true, as Claude-Edmonde Magny would have us believe, that Malraux has never created a character who "changes and really grows."[8] Malraux does not concentrate his narrative on the change and growth of an individual psyche with the patience, say, of a Flaubert or a Proust. Change, in Malraux's fiction, is a regular phenomenon, but it occurs spasmodically, with earthquake speed and shock, and almost always during moments of greatest intensity. Ch'en in *Man's Fate* has grown into an altogether different phase of being before the novel is ten pages old; Vincent Berger's very soul turns over in the midst of the apocalypse on the plains of Russia. And, in fact, all those persons whom Frohock has called "Neophytes"[9] (the narrator of *The Conquerors,* Claude Vannec in *The Royal Way,* Kassner in *Days of Wrath,* and so on) change and grow to a greater or lesser degree, and in fits and lurches; and the mark of their development is the acquisition of insight. It is an insight, customarily, into the solitary, mortal, spiritually blinded and fundamentally helpless condition of individual man; and with it, a conviction about the supreme value of human companionship, "virile fraternity." This is one of the great themes of contemporary fiction, and no writer has handled it more efficiently (and influentially) than Malraux. But these insights do not arise, so to speak, as the lesson of history: for example, as its tragic import. They are much rather the individual human response to history's failure to deliver any lesson at all.

That failure is acknowledged with devastating rhetoric in the

8. "Malraux le fascinateur," *Esprit, 149* (1948).

9. *André Malraux and the Tragic Imagination* (Stanford, 1952), pp. 142 ff.

extraordinary debate that occupies the center of Malraux's last novel, *The Walnut Trees of the Altenburg*. Here Malraux's entire personal and fictional endeavor, the whole "action" of his life and his novels over two decades, is recapitulated in terms of intellectual discourse: when the question of the definable nature of man is posed as a question about the continuity and coherence of the *history* of man. The debate seems at least, via the somber climactic speech of the anthropologist Möllberg, to set the seal on incoherence as the only fact, as it were the truthless truth, discoverable in history. One might still turn to human fraternity as a form of consolation, on the edge of this abyss of meaning. But had no other truth been seized from the plunge into action, the long encounter with history?

II

In one perspective, the answer has to be in the negative. Insofar as it aimed at anything more than sheer nervy excitement, the pragmatic impulse had been defeated along with the revolutionary causes in which it had variously exerted itself. Contemporary history had proven to be as shapeless and discordant as the vast history of human cultures so bleakly examined by Möllberg; from neither could those passionately sought-after explanations be extracted. But if Malraux's pragmatic strategy had failed, what we might call his Romantic strategy had been faring a good deal better; and in another perspective, the perspective of art, a very different and decidedly affirmative answer had long since begun to issue. Malraux had learned—the hard way, as the saying goes —and had shown his characters learning that, in E. M. Forster's phrase, human history "is really a series of *dis*orders"; but he had also learned with Forster that "[Art] is the one orderly product which our muddling race has produced." Perhaps he had always known this. It is implicit in a part of his reply to Trotsky; and it is even more implicit in his developing style. For, as Geoffrey Hartman remarks, from *Man's Fate* onward "the style itself intimates the author's freedom from the law to which his world remains subject, so that if the idea of Man remains inseparable from the idea of tragedy"—or, as I would prefer to say, of incoherence and absurdity, seen perhaps as tragic fatalities—"the idea of the artist pairs with the idea of freedom."[10]

10. *Malraux* (New York, 1960), p. 55.

About this contention, however, there has been a significant disagreement: significant because it bears upon the nature and degree of Malraux's own artistic achievement, and on the relation between it and the absurdities he has confronted in his subject matter. Mme. Magny, for example, before registering her deep disapproval of what she takes to be Malraux's message, warmly and brilliantly praises Malraux's style, and exactly on the grounds that (far from being "free" of the world it treats) it is a splendidly contrived equivalent of its own setting—that the syntactical disjointedness, the jerky cadences, the rapid transitions, and the startling juxtapositions in Malraux's novels serve as a precise enactment of the discordant realities they describe. Malraux's best novels, this critic says without any detectable trace of irony, are "beautiful, disconnected and truly *decomposed.*" Mme. Magny, in short, endorses Malraux's effort to commit what American criticism sometimes calls the fallacy of imitative form: the fallacy of trying to render a decomposed world by a decomposed book.[11] Gaetan Picon appears to agree with Mme. Magny; he tells us that "Of all the novels, *Man's Hope* is the one that vibrates most with discordant voices (and perhaps for that reason it is the greatest)." But Picon is satisfied that one can locate the source of harmony in Malraux's novels—in a virile fraternity, as we might say, of ideas and attitudes. Although Malraux "never stops dramatizing inimical truths," and though his is unmistakably "a universe of debate," nonetheless "all those enemies are brothers," because all of them "unite in the one who animates their dialogues," in the creative consciousness and the narrative voice of André Malraux.[12]

In this view (which approximates Hartman's), what provides wholeness and harmony in Malraux's writings is not so much the arrangement of the incidents or the patterns of characters and relations between characters, and even less the control and shaping power of some dominant idea.[13] It is rather a style, a presence,

---

11. "The fallacy of imitative form"—a critical concept to which I referred in the essay on Edith Wharton—was best and perhaps first formulated by Yvor Winters in *Primitivism and Decadence* (Denver, 1937), mainly in the essay called "The Morality of Poetry."

12. *Malraux par lui-même* (Paris, 1953), p. 38.

13. "Malraux has little esteem for ideas. He would tend to say that they serve to obstruct or to betray the moment of decision, and to be mere adornments to those sham dialogues between beings or groups who have nothing to say to each other"—Emmanuel Mounier, *L'Espoir des Déses-*

what Henry James would call a tone: some quality of artistic expression, however we name it, that works against and away from the images of chaos and defeat that the novels otherwise contain. Such, certainly, has been Malraux's increasingly dedicated purpose. "The way to express the unusual, the terrible, the inhuman," he has said, talking about Goya, "is not to represent carefully an actual or imaginary spectacle but to invent a script capable of representing these things without being forced to submit to their elements." Nor was this any casual matter. For Malraux, everything—his own literary achievement, his view of the human condition and of the possibility of human freedom—hang on the capacity of inventing that "script." This is, finally, the grand "truth" that emerges from the debate at Altenburg.

The Walnut Trees of the Altenburg is probably the best place to test any claim one would wish to make about Malraux as a novelist. For my part, I can only hope that Malraux's reputation will not stand or fall on *Man's Hope,* which, despite some uncommonly fine individual episodes, strikes me as a showy and ultimately a rather tiresome performance, and one in which the style is held captive by the subject; though the reader (who will have his own opinion anyway) is invited to consider the high estimates cogently argued elsewhere. *Man's Fate* has, of course, been Malraux's most widely admired novel, and it is no doubt his major contribution to the history of literature in his generation; beyond that, and beginning with its original title (*La Condition Humaine*), it is so impressive and enduring a challenge to its own content that it is likely to endure long after that revolutionary content has ceased to agitate the mind of readers. But the work of Malraux's which best fulfills the requirements of art—in Malraux's terms or anyone else's—seems to me to be *The Walnut Trees.*

The accomplishment of *The Walnut Trees* is the more astonishing, since it consists of only the first third of a novel called *La Lutte avec L'Ange,* the remainder (which Malraux may yet rewrite) being destroyed by the German Gestapo during the war. (Another mystery, as Frank says, is that the book "should still

---

pérés (Paris, 1953). It is a challenging statement, partly true and partly defensible, but eventually misleading. Victor Brombert, who quotes the first of the two sentences, offers a subtle and necessary corrective of the argument.

not have appeared in this country seventeen"—now twenty—
"years after it came out in French.")[14] I have elsewhere suggested
certain reasons, in part extra-literary, for the special significance
of *The Walnut Trees:* mainly, the handsome way it crystallizes
and gives final shape to themes and human figures that between
them define the age of fiction represented by Silone, Camus, and
others. The themes include those of isolation and alienation, and
of companionship as expressed most decisively in an act of unmistakable charity; and the chief figure is the one I have described as a sort of saintly picaro—a human being who is at once
all too human, corrupted and corruptible, but who also possesses
the modern humanistic form of sainthood which is, precisely,
charity in action.[15] In *The Walnut Trees,* this vitally contradictory character appears as a "shaman"—a type which, as a Russian
soldier explains to the hero's son, is represented not less by men
of action (like Trotsky) than by artists (like Hölderlin and Poe),
not less by persons who effect national or world history than by
pure visionaries; not less in idiots than in geniuses.

Action and art, history and vision, involvement and transcendence: we are back where we started, even to the citation of Leon
Trotsky. Or, rather, *The Walnut Trees* throws light backward on
Malraux's career, illuminating that early exchange with Trotsky
and clarifying the precarious and continuing combination in Malraux of the adventurer and the artist, the minister of state and
the art historian. It does so because it is constructed in such a way
as to throw light forward and backward on itself. We should not
forget that Vincent Berger and the poison-gas attack, as well as
the discussion of shamanism, are *elements in a novel:* that is, in
a work of art, and in one which has at its center Malraux's most
forthright statement about the nature and function of art as the
means of escaping the human condition, as man's greatest resource for achieving freedom from history.[16] It is presumably

14. A translation was published in England in 1952. This is not quite as
shocking a job as Frank indicates; it is not even as bad as the American
version of *Man's Fate* which at times makes you rub your eyes; but it is
anything but satisfactory. It occurs to me that what may really be needed
here is not so much further essays on Malraux as a fresh translation into
English of all his novels.
15. *The Picaresque Saint* (Philadelphia, 1959).
16. Malraux, by implication, stressed the *novelistic* quality in the account of Vincent's Russian experience, when he said in a prefatory note

no longer possible for anyone to suppose, as some of the novel's first readers did, that when Möllberg asserts the utter discontinuity between human cultures he speaks for Malraux: or, anyhow, that he is the whole voice of Malraux; for, like the other characters, Möllberg is a part of Malraux and one way of looking at the history Malraux had lived through. But a much larger part of Malraux is bespoken in the midst of the Altenburg debate in the quiet voice of Vincent Berger, saying what Malraux had tried to say to Trotsky before he had himself quite grasped the principle:

> To me, our art seems to be a rectification of the world, a means of escaping from man's estate. The chief confusion, I think, is due to our belief—and in the theories propounded of Greek tragedy, it's strikingly clear—that representing fatality is the same as submitting to it. But it's not, it's almost to dominate it. The mere fact of being able to represent it, conceive it, release it from real fate, from the merciless divine scale, reduces it to the human scale. Fundamentally, our art is a humanization of the world.

What Berger says (and what, later, Malraux would say in reference to Goya) is precisely what the novel illustrates and enacts. The real answer to the despair of Möllberg lies in the novel he inhabits: in the movement and texture, the composition and tone of *The Walnut Trees* itself. The novel is the final confirmation of its own stated conviction.

III

In the light of that conviction, Malraux's subsequent and voluminous art studies are so little surprising as to be altogether inevitable. *The Psychology of Art* and *The Voices of Silence* are vast discursive demonstrations of the theory about the relation between art and man's estate of which *The Walnut Trees* was the great fictional presentation. This is what, for us, lends a strangely moving accent to Maurice Blanchot's discussion of Malraux's

---

to the 1948 Gallimard edition that Berger's "appeal to happiness is here simply a psychological reaction"; as it were, a phase in Malraux's fictional characterization of the man.

"museum" as standing for "the end of history."[17] The American reader will notice in Blanchot's expert account certain parallels between Malraux's views and those espoused in Anglo-American critical theory, parallels that help clarify the idea of art as escaping from history. There is, for example, something like T. S. Eliot's notion about the literary tradition, and the way every new masterpiece subtly reorders the body of past literature. More striking yet is the parallel with Northrop Frye's *Anatomy of Criticism* and its concept (spelled out more emphatically than it had been by Eliot) of the self-contained nature of literature, the sense in which the *literary*—or, more broadly in Malraux, the artistic—element of the art-work exists outside of time, and belongs to the timeless trans-historical order of art itself. But it is not easy to find any sort of parallel to the sheer passion (reflected in Blanchot) with which Malraux has proclaimed and elaborated these principles. It is the passion born from the encounters with history—those of Malraux's life and those of his fiction—and its form is the passionate conviction that, while history has to be reckoned with, has to be entered and participated in and investigated, it also has to be transcended; for when all is said and done, the truth is not in it. The knowledge provided by the "museum," says Blanchot, "is historical, it is the knowledge of histories, and of a series of histories that we accept"; but "at the same time, it is not historical, it does not concern itself with the objective truth of history . . . and this is the knowledge we accept and even prefer." We prefer it, according to Malraux, because the knowledge discoverable in the timeless, trans-historical world of art forms (the museum without walls) is a definition of man as free, heroic, creative, and purposeful. Art restores the definition that had been questioned and shattered by history: restores it and gives it an unassailable permanence. "To save one through the other—[Malraux] was unable to resist this great temptation."

1964

17. "La Músée, l'Art, et le Temps," *Critique, 43* (1950) and *44* (1951).

DAYS OF WRATH AND LAUGHTER

And I am a red arrow on this graph
Of Revelations.
ROBERT LOWELL, "WHERE THE RAINBOW ENDS"

"What's that about the Apocalypse?"
UNIDENTIFIED VOICE IN HERMAN MELVILLE'S
The Confidence-Man

"Our American literature and spiritual history," Emerson observed something over a century ago, "are, we must confess, in
the optative mood." Today, in the 1950s and '60s, we have
equally to confess that those elements—especially in fiction—
have entered much rather into a resoundingly apocalyptic mood.
Several traditions converge here, and we shall need to make a
good many distinctions as we go along; but we can begin with
the narrowest and gloomiest meaning of apocalypse—namely,
the foreboding of some total catastrophe or cosmic wreckage. In
part, this has been a natural response to the second World War
and the invention of the atomic bomb, to the quite literal threat
of planetary destruction. But only in part. For the bomb, when
it has been mentioned at all in our imaginative literature, has
usually been taken as a symptom and an instrument: the inevitable
product of the diseased energies of mankind, and the physical
force that can bring about that grand conflagration which, morally
speaking, mankind has long been striving to deserve. (So it has
been at comparable earlier moments of world history: the Reformation doomsters, for example, once regarded the menacing
Turkish hordes, the atom-bomb incarnate of that age, with the
same mixture of horror and satisfaction.) The current imagery of
disaster, moreover, carries forward directly from the apocalyptic
peerings of the earlier or prewar and prebomb generation, not to
mention that of several still earlier generations. What has been
added in recent years, and again especially in fiction, is a pervasive sense of the preposterous: of the end of the world not only
as imminent and titanic, but also as absurd.

The addition may be all important. It testifies, anyhow, to the healthful influence of Nathanael West; for it was West, following hard on Melville and Mark Twain, who established for contemporary American writing the vision of the ludicrous catastrophe, and who searched out and bodied forth some of its human sources. A complex apocalyptic vision ran through all of West's short novels; but it reached its climax, of course, in the last book he lived to write. *The Day of the Locust* (1939) borrowed its title and much of its conviction about the course of human events from the seminal Book of Apocalypse, or Revelations, in the New Testament: "And the fifth angel sounded . . . . And there came out of the smoke locusts upon the earth: and unto them was given power . . . . and their faces were as the faces of men." But West's hate-filled and mindless locusts appear finally, to the creative eye of their observer, as a mob of "screwballs," carrying baseball bats and torches through the streets of California, dancing amid the fires they have lit to burn down Los Angeles and implicitly the whole of America, chanting their allegiance to an unnamed "super-promiser," their maniacal leader. It has been by exploiting a perspective of just that kind that novelists as variously gifted as Ralph Ellison and John Barth and Joseph Heller and Thomas Pynchon have made the day of doom the great saturnalia of our time—a *dies irae* converted into a *dies irae risusque*. For our literature and our spiritual history are in fact caught between the wrath and the laughter; and our survival, in many meanings of the word, may hang upon the outcome.

I

The apocalyptic mood, in this or any other generation, has by no means been limited to fiction; though fiction seems at present its most appropriate habitat, and though elsewhere the tone has been less regularly relieved by the partially healing sense of the comic. Forty years ago Hart Crane (himself, as I shall say, the possessor of a very different mode of apocalyptic imagination) could contend in an excellent formula that the fashionable poetry of the day was the poetry of "humor and the Dance of Death." But by "humor" Crane meant chiefly the ironic Laforguian wit that T. S. Eliot had been making available for English poetry. It was this that permeated Eliot's death-dancing in *The Waste*

Land, and that would color Eliot's more purely apocalyptic pronouncement of a couple of years later that

> *This is the way the world ends*
> *Not with a bang but a whimper.*

Crane might also have meant the steely amusement with which Robert Frost (in 1924) had meditated two further alternative theories about the world's end:

> *Some say the world will end in fire,*
> *Some say in ice.*
> *From what I've tasted of desire*
> *I hold with those who favor fire,*

and so on. Eliot foresaw the human spirit fading out in mere animal mouthings; Frost looked instead for a final choice between lethal lust and lethal malice. But let me pause to suggest that Frost's little poem is a sort of poker-faced gloss on traditional apocalyptic theorizing—as set forth with grave precision, for example, by R. H. Charles in his definitive study of the matter, *Eschatology:*[1]

> According to science, there are two possible endings of the earth. Either it will perish slowly through cold . . . or the earth will suddenly be destroyed catastrophically, by the impact of some other heavenly body, or by the outburst of its own internal fires. While science of necessity can only predict two possible endings of the world, apocalyptic declared that the end of the present order of things will be catastrophic.

Apocalyptic writing, like Frost, has always held with those who favor the quick holocaust rather than the gradual freeze.

Even the wry detachment of "Fire and Ice," however, is missing from Frost's later piece of eschatology, "Once by the Pacific," where the catastrophe occurs in a new way—or, rather, in the oldest way, by a flood like the flood with which God destroyed the wicked according to the Book of Genesis. The voice in this poem is conversational, but the wrath is uncontaminated by laughter; the waves crashing in upon the Pacific coast seem to

---

1. (London, 1899; paperback New York, 1963.)

the onlooking poet to presage the extinction of a humanity whose own bestial rages will bring down the annihilating anger of God and the reversal of his world-creating *fiat lux:*

> *It looked as if a night of dark intent*
> *Was coming, and not only a night, an age.*
> *Someone had better be prepared for rage.*
> *There would be more than ocean-water broken*
> *Before God's last* Put out the Light *was spoken.*

And in the characteristic early poetry of Robert Lowell, the most eminent American poet in the generation after Eliot and Frost, both irony and wryness get swallowed up in sheer apocalyptic fury —a fury that takes charge of the rhetoric to the point of becoming not only emotional substance but a sometimes exceedingly effective poetic strategy.

Recently, though still watchful of the cruelties and folly of society at large, Lowell's poetry has centered upon the personal fatality: the "skunk hour" of the private self ("I myself am hell;/ nobody's here— / only skunks . . . ."). But his first volume, though in its turn kindled by autobiographical passion, envisaged the entire human landscape as spiritually blasted and desiccated—

> *Is there no way to cast my hook*
> *Out of this dynamited brook?*

It was, in the medieval formula Lowell adapted for his title, a "land of unlikeness"; and the poems explored the skunk hour of a world in which the human soul, having forfeited the god-resembling image in which it was formed, had for that reason also lost its likeness to itself, to its specifically human essence. Lowell was dealing with something like a theory of history, and looking at what seemed to him the present consequences of an American and especially a New England culture that had combined a driving piety with a ruthless acquisitiveness. The most hideous of these consequences, in Lowell's view, was the second World War (or anyhow, America's conduct of that war); and his apocalyptic vigor reached its own peak of grandeur in the poems that were wrenched out of him in the mid-1940s, and published in *Lord Weary's Castle,* when his ferocious pacifism was challenged past endurance by the greedy belligerence of the time. Poem after poem expressed a highly intensified vision of finality—

> *This is the end of the whaleroad and the whale*
> *Who spewed Nantucket bones on the thrashed swell*
> *And stirred the troubled waters to whirlpools*
> *To send the Pequod packing off to hell:*
> *This is the end of them, three-quarters fools . . .*

The vortex of death thus realized in the heaving rhythms and flailing language of "The Quaker Graveyard at Nantucket" is the ultimate consequences of the warlike, indeed the murderous, materialism of modern man; and Lowell, drawing upon Melville's *Moby-Dick,* finds his most terrible representation of modern man in the old Quaker whale hunters—those allegedly peaceable, loving, and God-serving people who were nonetheless, as Melville had put it, "the most sanguinary of all sailors and whale-hunters . . . fighting Quakers . . . Quakers with a vengeance." Out of its own bloodthirsty folly, the Pequod (the modern world, or at least modern America) launches its assault upon what turns out to be the godhead itself, and is smashed and utterly destroyed and packed off to hell.

These poems of the mid-1940s echo with the continuing dry thunder of a Last Judgment. In both "Where the Rainbow Ends" and "As a Plane Tree by the Water," Lowell contemplates his representative city of Boston on the fateful day amid echoes of the Book of Revelations, the fiery indicator of which Lowell (in the first of the two poems) declares himself to be:

> *the scythers, Time and Death,*
> *Helmed locusts, move upon the tree of breath;*
>
> > *. . .*
>
> *I saw my city in the Scales, the pans*
> *Of judgment rising and descending. Piles*
> *Of dead leaves char the air—*
> *And I am a red arrow on this graph*
> *Of Revelations.*

The day of wrath—or the hour or season, according to the figure —is everywhere visible and audible; and even a private domestic drama like Lowell's "Between the Porch and the Altar" reaches its self-lacerating climax when

> *the Day*
> *Breaks with lightning on the man of clay,*
> Dies amara valde.

The famous Latin hymn there quoted (*"Dies Irae"*) continues, one may remember, *"dum veneris judicare saeculum per ignem"*: "that day, great and bitter above all, when Thou shalt come to judge the world by fire."

American writers in the modern epoch can almost be distinguished by their individual notions, or imagery, first of the causes and then of the nature of the catastrophe that many of them have agreed is very nearly upon us. In "The Fire Next Time" (1963), the essay by which James Baldwin—as accomplished an essayist as Lowell is a poet—summoned expository prose onto the field of apocalyptic vision, it is American inhumanity rooted in racial terror and racial hatred that will bestir the ultimate wrath. As to the form of the latter, Baldwin also holds with those who favor fire; his epigraph, from a Negro slave hymn, is emphatic on the choice:

> *God gave Noah the rainbow sign,*
> *No more water, the fire next time!*

Upon this thoroughly traditional view of the last things, a commentary has been supplied far in advance by Jonathan Edwards in *A History of the Work of Redemption* (lectures written in 1739):

> And if the wickedness of the old world, when men began to multiply on the earth, called for the destruction of the world by a deluge of waters, this wickedness will as much call for its destruction by a deluge of fire.

"No more water, the fire next time!" Like Edwards, the anonymous Negro hymn-writer (who probably got the idea from touring evangelists) was speaking about the actual and physical obliteration of this world because of human sinfulness, while he will hide himself for his salvation in the Rock of Ages. But in the context of Baldwin's essay and of current events, the marvelously resonant, even springy little couplet announces a secular and symbolic though not less dreadful development. Against a technological background that poses, as Baldwin puts it, "the threat of universal extinction" and so "changes totally and forever the nature of reality and brings into devastating question the true meaning of man's history," Baldwin sees in the hate-ridden American foreground the quickening possibility that Negroes can "precipitate chaos and ring down the curtain on the American dream."

If they do so, Baldwin believes, there will occur a tremendous act of vengeance for the white man's suicidal refusal to transcend his whiteness and achieve his manhood—a manhood he shares with the black man, whose transcendence of his own color the white man must not arrogantly allow or condescendingly encourage, but must wholesouledly acknowledge here and now. But the act of vengeance will not at all be a purely Negro adventure. It will be an act of and by history; it will express as it were the wrath of history itself, a terrible secular equivalent to the wrath of God. It will be "a vengeance that does not really depend upon, and cannot really be executed by, any person or organization, and that cannot be prevented by any police force or army." This is why, in closing, Baldwin calls it "cosmic vengeance," something forced into being by uncontrollable disturbances within the human cosmos, an "outburst [to quote R. H. Charles again] of its own internal fires." Baldwin's apocalyptic diagnosis is selective; but the continuing facts of life in America have not yet done very much to belie it.

The difference between Baldwin's most aggressive essayistic predecessors—H. L. Mencken, for example—and Baldwin himself is parallel to the difference between the Eliot of *The Waste Land* and the Lowell of *Lord Weary's Castle*. It is akin to the difference—the distinction is an ancient one and hard to hang on to—between the prophetic and the apocalyptic; between the demand for moral rehabilitation, accompanied by warnings and animated by the belief that they can be listened to in time, and the expressed feeling that it is very likely too late to prevent the coming holocaust (that is, total destruction by fire; from the Greek words for "whole"—*holos*—and "burnt"—*kauston*). The rhetorical postures have much in common, but the difference should be suggested; in part because it is also the difference between the mood of the 1920s and the much darker mood of the period beginning in the 1940s. It is made palpable in the very cadences of poem and essay. Like Lowell's, Baldwin's argument is exalted by a rhetorical fervor that sweeps through and beyond the actualities that have aroused it. Irony and humor would be mainly out of key here. Only occasionally, indeed, and much less often than in his earlier volumes of essays, is *The Fire Next Time* lit up by that extraordinary change of expression, that sudden and electrifying smile of utter and yet oddly delighted incredulity, that have characterized Baldwin's writings and his public *persona* in the past. The result, it seems to me, is a foreshortening of reality. "Reality" is more and more a major term for Baldwin, and one which he uses both to threaten and persuade. But a true view of reality in our time depends, I think, not only upon an unflinching confrontation of horror, but also upon the measuring and accommodating power of laughter—that is, of what Hawthorne called "the tragic power of laughter." That power, anyhow, has been affectively absent from Baldwin's recent declarations, as well as from his fiction and his dramatic work.

Even literary criticism has of late proved vulnerable to the apocalyptic impulse, no doubt infected by constant exposure to the same in poetry, fiction, and the essay. The very titles of some recent books of criticism by some of our most notable and "younger" critics indicate the shared concern. Irving Howe, invoking a phrase from Leon Trotsky—*A World More Attractive* (1963)—reminds us of another of the basic distinctions to be elaborated upon later: the secular apocalyptic tradition which, descending through the imaginative responses to the American and French Revolutions and catching fire again with the Russian upheaval, has focused less upon the grand conflict than upon the millennium it will usher in; with only the bad old world coming to its predestined end, and the incomparably more attractive new society being realized once and for all. The theme is in fact muted in Mr. Howe's luminous and muscular essays, but it lies just beneath his conviction about the crucial "relationship between politics and literature, action and reflection." Stanley Edgar Hyman, for his own collection of essays over the years, borrows a portion of the most famous apocalyptic passage in English literature, the exchange between Kent and Edgar gazing at the dead body of Cordelia and at her grief-stunned father in the final moments of *King Lear:*

> *Is this the promis'd end?*
> *Or image of that horror?*

But to judge from the emphases in *The Promised End* (1964), Mr. Hyman has in mind, as he quotes the phrase, not so much the age-old notion of the ultimate earthly catastrophe to which it overtly refers as the tragic vision of human life which that dramatic moment is bringing to full and final disclosure, and upon which Mr. Hyman discourses with much learned vivacity.[2] Leslie Fiedler is closer to the queer temper of postwar writing, which indeed he examines in some detail, in the title and content of his book-length essay *Waiting for the End* (1964).

Mr. Fiedler's title comes neither from the Book of Revelations nor a Negro hymn, neither from Trotsky nor Shakespeare, but from a rambunctious ballad by William Empson:

> *Shall we go all wild, boys, waste and make them lend,*
> *Playing at the child, boys, waiting for the end?*
> *It has all been filed, boys, history has a trend,*
> *Each of us enisled, boys, waiting for the end.*

The end Mr. Fiedler is awaiting and describing is the end of civilization, at least as he has known it: the end of the modern novel and the modern poem; the end of those ("three-quarters fools," one can almost hear Mr. Fiedler saying), the novelists and the poets, who have occupied the literary scene since the age of Faulkner and Stevens. Mr. Fiedler sees modern culture ending as the creative imagination is defeated at every turn: by a failure of nerve and a decline of sheer talent; by the rise to literary authority of minority spokesmen who promptly lose or shed or are robbed of the minority characteristics (Jewish and Negro, mainly) that had empowered them; by a situation in which the entire reading public, perhaps the entire middle class, has become avant-garde or anyhow so welcomes the avant-garde as to smother it to death; by a moral and philosophical anarchy which deprives the writer not only of a subject but even of an enemy. *Waiting for the End,* in its racier and cheerfully irresponsible way, is composed in the spirit of Pope's *Dunciad;* and, like Pope in the closing lines of that matchless apocalyptic satire, Mr. Fiedler traces the process whereby

> Art *after* Art *goes out, and all is Night.*

Mr. Fiedler, too, arrives at his American version of Pope's conclusion:

> *Lo! thy dread Empire, CHAOS! is restored;*
> *Light dies before thy uncreating word.*

2. Mr. Hyman has since intimated that his title has a much more private and personal, and half-humorous, connotation.

But this is to say that Mr. Fiedler does not fully believe his own message of disaster; and in fact the poem by Empson from which he takes his title (it is called "Just a Smack at Auden") is a parody of the apocalyptic imagination rather than a statement of it. Like some of his novelistic contemporaries, Mr. Fiedler aspires, by mingling the catastrophic with the comic, to help avert the worst possibilities of the former.

We return to the narrative arts. The movies made a start at providing a visual image of apocalypse in such vaguely science-fiction films and solemn artifices as *On the Beach*.[3] But with *Dr. Strangelove* (1963), the medium came at one stride into the area not only of the truly catastrophic imagination—the planet earth really is being blown to smithereens at the fadeout—but also of the comical catastrophe. The end of the world in *Dr. Strangelove*—as envisaged by Terry Southern and his collaborators on the film-script—is due to bumbling inefficiency, antic mischance, and a sort of hearty and yet total inhumanity,

---

3. The huge contribution of science fiction to modern apocalyptic literature would be very much worth investigating, but it is beyond the scope of this essay and the competence of this writer. I suspect, though, that such an investigation would show that science fiction has often worked very squarely within the long apocalyptic tradition and has manipulated the great apocalyptic archetypes.

Let me name a few personal favorites which can also stand as superior examples of countless similar treatments of the great theme. In *When Worlds Collide* (1929), not only is the end of this world accomplished in one of the familiar ways—"the earth" (to quote again from R. H. Charles) is "destroyed catastrophically by the impact of some other heavenly body." The saving human remnant, more importantly, is transferred (by spaceship) to another planet, in an engagingly literalistic version of the Old Testament notion—which I discuss in the next section—of the righteous being carried off from the annihilated earth to the heavenly kingdom of God. In Sax Rohmer's *The Day the World Ended* (1929), a story fairly teeming with recognizable apocalyptic imagery, the world is in fact saved at the last instant; but before that happens, the would-be agent of destruction, a Satanic dwarf named Anubis, offers a rousing indictment of mankind as fatally corrupted and unsalvageable, even as the pornographic quality of his dominion (a castle in the Black Forest) suggests that *his* is in fact the final apostasy. In A. Conan Doyle's recently republished *The Poison Belt* (1913), the emphasis is upon the actual catastrophic process; and we can identify the latter as one of those enormous periodic disasters envisioned in Revelations as a portent of the final horror—perhaps, for Doyle in retrospect, as a symbolic portent of the World War which erupted a year after the original publication.

plus of course the instrument of annihilation, the super-bomb it-self. There is a rough political allegory in the film; but as more than one reviewer has observed (Miss Midge Decter in *Commentary,* especially), the allegory is thin and lopsided. The villains are exclusively of the fascist variety; and the depth and breadth and complexity of the destructive mentality in America today are scarcely hinted at. Both the humor and the human nature in the film are, as a result, markedly narrowed in range. But *Dr. Strangelove* is an adventurous piece of work, and one full of well-compounded fright and fun. It is also a film that comes closer than any yet made to the fictional achievement of Nathanael West, and Terry Southern's glimpse of an America conniving with mindless intensity at its own annihilation at least approximates West's vision of the absurd debacle toward which the country is hurrying.

But much of the superior power of West's diagnosis and of the shape he gave it came from his sense—in part his knowledge, in much larger part his creative intuition—of the long and contra-dictory Judaeo-Christian apocalyptic tradition. We need to re-hearse that tradition at this stage, at whatever risk of gross over-simplification. For the accomplishments both of West and of those contemporary novelists who follow him can best be measured in terms of it; and those terms, however much in fashion, need to be a little straightened out.

II

The concept of apocalypse—a word which basically means no more than a revelation or uncovering from the Greek word for such an act[4]—may be thought of as a branch of eschatology: a word which, in turn, means the knowledge or doctrine of the last things, of what is ultimately in store for man, nature, the world, the universe (from the Greek *eschatos,* furthest or uttermost). At some time in the later but still pre-Christian period of Judaism, the dominant theory of the last things turned from what is called the prophetic to what would eventually be known as the apocalyp-tic. It began, that is, to point forward to cataclysms so enormous that they would utterly destroy the earthly world and lead to the

---

4. *Apokalupsis.* The root, verb, *kalupto,* means to cover or conceal; and the dictionary reminds us that it was the function of the nymph Calypso (in the English spelling) to conceal Odysseus on his way home from Troy.

Day of Judgment for all mankind, and to the establishment of a Kingdom of Heaven inhabited purely by the saints and the angels. In the earlier or prophetic period, the eschatological imagination had concerned itself with the earthly destinies of men and nations, and upon the morality or immorality that would determine them; even at its most somber, it had remained convinced that men could return to righteous ways and could thus in part control their earthly fate; and at its most hopeful, it had anticipated a permanent Messianic Kingdom on this earth. But around 100 B.C., according to R. H. Charles, "the earth had come to be regarded as wholly unfit for this kingdom," and it then began to be taught "that the Messianic Kingdom was to be merely of temporary duration, and that the goal of the righteous was to be—not this temporary kingdom or millennium—but heaven itself." Along with this radically pessimistic view of the moral salvageability of the earth, there arose the necessary and corollary notion of the catastrophe—usually a cosmic conflagration—which would put an end to the world, while the saintly remnant was transferred to the eternal kingdom above.[5]

"It was," Charles argues, "from the apocalyptic side of Judaism that Christianity was born." The statement is probably true, but it is misleading. The Christian vision of history is undoubtedly apocalyptic: if we can grant that latter term a high degree of dialectical flexibility. But Charles tended to identify apocalypse with catastrophe, and hence with an uncompromisingly glum view of the moral and spiritual potentialities of mankind. Given that identification, I should prefer to say that a certain great phase of Christianity was born out of Judaean apocalyptics—and I am tempted to call it "the Lutheran phase," as against the Thomistic

5. Among the studies which have been particularly indispensable for the summary report in this section, and which I do not always cite even while drawing from them are: R. H. Charles, *Eschatalogy* (London, 1899; paperback New York, 1963); Martin Buber, "Prophecy, Apocalyptic, and the Historical Hour," in *Pointing the Way* (New York, 1957; paperback New York, 1963); Austin Farrer, *A Rebirth of Images* (London, 1949; paperback New York, 1964); Ernest Tuveson, *Millennium and Utopia* (Berkeley, 1949; paperback New York, 1964); M. H. Abrams, "English Romanticism: the Spirit of the Age," in *Romanticism Reconsidered,* edited by Northrop Frye (English Institute Essays, New York, 1963); Perry Miller, title essay and the essay called "The End of the World" in *Errand into the Wilderness* (Cambridge, 1956); James P. Martin, *The Last Judgment* (i.e. in Protestant theology; Grand Rapids, 1963).

phase, for example, or even the Augustinian; using quotation marks to indicate a strain as old as Christianity and one which seems to be in the ascendancy today, and on not unreasonable grounds. The apocalyptic side of Judaism, at any rate, was what found expression in the Old Testament books of Ezekiel, Daniel, and Zechariah. And the earliest of the Christian writings in which (to borrow a phrase from Austin Farrer) those older apocalyptic images were given "rebirth" include the Gospel of Saint Mark, the Second Epistle of Saint Peter, and supremely of course the Book of Revelations by St. John the Divine of Patmos. The latter is the enduring treasury of apocalyptic elements, allusions, archetypes. It is here that we encounter the seven blasting trumpets, the seven seals, the seven vials of wrath; here are the seven candlesticks and the figure whose hair is "white like wool"; here are the four horsemen of the apocalypse and the locusts with faces like men and the beast that rises out of the sea; here is the symbolic number 666, here the battle of Armageddon; here are the Whore of Babylon and Gog and Magog; and here the vision of "a new heaven and a new earth" and of "the holy city, the new Jersusalem, coming down from God out of heaven, prepared as a bride adorned for her husband."

It is in Revelations, too, that we make out—dimly, as through an enchanted glass—the most crowded and extensive of the Christian visionary accounts of history. Such is the complexity of St. John's imagination, however, that "history" is an imprecise word: better, perhaps, a revelation of spiritual reality which sometimes takes the form of an actual historical process, of future events narrated in sequence, and sometimes invokes events to come as pure metaphor; the constant subject being the universe as designed by God. The account touches more or less seriatim upon a succession of "moments," some of which we may select and number for our present purposes: (1) periodic natural disturbances, earthquakes and the like; (2) the advent and the turbulent reign of the Antichrist or the false Christ or false prophet (sometimes called the period of the Great Tribulation); (3) the second coming of Christ and (4) the resultant cosmic warfare (Armageddon) that brings in (5) the millennium—that is, from the Latin, the period of one thousand years, the epoch of the Messianic Kingdom upon earth; thereafter, (6) the gradual degeneration of human and physical nature, the last and worst apostasy (or falling away from God), featured by (7) the second and briefer "loosening of Satan"; (8) an ultimate catastrophe, the end of the world by fire; (9) the Last Judgment; and (10) the appearance of the new heaven and earth.

These have always been among the major ingredients of apocalyptics in all ages, but only in Revelations, if there, do all the elements appear; and only there, if ever, do they appear in the order just indicated. There has been as much controversial wrestling with the meanings of Revelations over the centuries as there have been shifts and rearrangements of the elements by other and later apocalyptic writers. On the one hand, for example, it seems now generally believed that phrases like "a new heaven and a new earth" and "coming down" are primarily spatial metaphors; that "a new heaven" is not God's heaven, but the visible heavens—taken metaphorically, however, as part of a radically transformed spiritual condition; while God's heaven, the divine kingdom, continues as traditionally to be the eventual domain of the blessed —but, again, as the name of a spiritual estate, wherever the blessed might be simplemindedly thought to reside in physical fact. On the other hand, both before and after Revelations, from version to version of the apocalyptic "story," this or that element is omitted; or two elements are fused into one—especially the Great Tribulation and the second visitation of Satan; the moment or moments, the figure or figures, given stress differ crucially.

The author of the Book of Revelations, for example, saw the earthly millennium in the far future, and was not, one gathers, very much interested in it; though the sense of the universal triumph on the far side of the millennium, and after the worst apostasy, pervades his verses. The prophecy of Christ, as recorded in the thirteenth chapter of Saint Mark, concerned itself mainly with the long period of persecution, and with the activities of "false Christs and false prophets" who "shall rise, and shall show signs and wonders, to seduce, if it were possible, the elect"; and only in four short verses does this voice foretell the time of total darkness over the earth, the second coming of Christ, and (skipping the millennium altogether and all subsequent plot complexities) his drawing together all the elect "from the uttermost part of the earth to the uttermost part of heaven." The African-born convert Lactantius, writing in the latter part of the third Christian century, was eloquent about the massive variety of evil in the age about to come, but he was no less eloquent about the earthly paradise which would succeed it—when "the rocky mountains shall drop with honey . . . [and] those things shall come to pass which the poets spoke of as being done in the reign of Saturn." (The poet whom Lactantius must have had chiefly in mind was Virgil, with his description—in *Aeneid* VIII.319 ff.—of the descent of Saturn from heavenly Olympus, and his union of the belligerent Italian tribes into a single nation: "the period called in legend the Golden Age." Throughout Western literature, it has often been rather the *Aeneid* than the Bible, or sometimes the *Aeneid* combined with the Bible, which has supplied the poetic imagination with its apocalyptic patterns and tropes.)

Lactantius marks the end of the first great wave of apocalyptic writing. The second wave coincided with the Protestant Reformation; and here the emphasis is almost entirely upon the irreversible dark finality. It is indeed from sixteenth-century apocalyptics that the modern connotation of the word "apocalypse" as the revelation of imminent catastrophic horror most obviously derives; and when Martin Buber in an indispensable essay says that "the mature apocalyptic . . . no longer knows an historical future in the real sense," and that in its view "the end of all history is near," his words apply less to St. John of Patmos than, say, to Martin Luther. It was Luther, in a preface to Revelations in 1545 and out of his profound and infectious mistrust of mankind's capacity to do anything whatever in the way of self-regeneration, laid it down that the millennium foreseen in Revelations was by his (Luther's) epoch already far in the past. It had simply been the first thousand years of Christianity. The real reign of Antichrist, which for Luther followed rather than preceded the millennium, began with the rise to power of the Papacy at Rome in the eleventh century; and now, five centuries later, the world trembled on the brink of the all-engulfing catastrophe. John Foxe, whose apocalyptic scheme in *Actes and Monuments* (1596) is probably the closest among Reformation writings to that of Revelations, calculated all these matters with hardheaded arithmetical precision. The first age of Satan, Foxe argued, had run to the end of the third century; the Christian millennium that followed that time of tribulation (and which apparently did not need a second coming of Christ to initiate it) lasted until about 1300 A.D. The world thereupon entered, as Revelations had said it would, into a second and more frightful reign of Antichrist, and this, as of the moment of writing, was nearing its climax: holocaust and the last judgment were in the offing. For though the author of Revelations, according to Foxe's arguable interpretation, had predicted a series of Antichrists, he had made it clear that "the head and principall Antichrist" would not appear until "the later end of the world, at what time there shall be such tribulation, as neuer was seene before: whereby," Foxe concluded with gloomy satisfaction, "is meant (no doubt) the Turke"—the Turk, that is, as the scourge or, perhaps even more dreadfully, as the secret agent of the Papal Antichrist. And so it went, with each writer eager to claim the worst of visits by the worst of Satans for his own particular generation.

What is common to all these visions is a fundamental rhythmic alternation of tribulation and triumph, of disaster and felicity: whether the rhythm occurs once, as in St. Mark, or whether it is a sort of habitual universal sistole and diastole, as in Revelations and perhaps John Foxe. But on the whole, and not surprisingly, the apocalyptic writers of the Bible and the early Christian centuries saw just about everything happening in the future—or they were more disposed to employ a futuristic metaphor—and they tended to hang on more hopefully to a conviction about a season of earthly happiness as well as an unending heavenly glory in the far distance. The Reformation commentators saw just about everything happening in the past or in the present time; they were fascinated by inventories of the symptoms of worldwide apostasy and less committed imaginatively to the possibilities of the heavenly world to be. This is a main part of what I mean by "the Lutheran phase" of Christianity as it has regularly announced itself apocalyptically. And it is just this sense of the historical moment and this emphasis that some of the contemporary novelists I shall belatedly get round to share with the Reformation writers: time present in the contemporary American novel is precisely the moment of the last loosening of Satan.

So convinced were speculators in the sixteenth and early seventeenth centuries about the very real approach of the day of doom that they rather enjoyed making estimates of its exact date. Henry Bullinger (a Swiss writer whose sermons were published in London in 1573) drew upon the numerology of Revelations, and by adding 666 to 1000 came up with the year 1666 as the time of the world's termination. But as these *anni horribiles* came and went, and the world wagged on, the apocalyptic emphasis gradually underwent another fundamental change. There is neither space nor occasion here to explore the effect upon apocalyptics of the developing theory of history as cyclical (whereby world history, instead of arriving at its explosive end, simply returns to the beginning of the cycle) or the theory of unbroken human progress (which eliminates catastrophe completely). I move on to the end of the eighteenth century, when, for large historical reasons, the apocalyptic stress rested (briefly) upon the element of millennial triumph—and led to the next-to-last important phase of the apocalyptic imagination for the purposes of this discussion.

The causes mentioned were primarily the successful outcome of the American Revolution and, much more importantly, what seemed at first to be the successful outcome of the French Revolution. For a range of English writers in the 1790s, those Revolutions *were* the titanic upheavals foretold in Scripture—the cosmic war announced in Revelations—and the new social orders begotten by them were the long anticipated millennium, at which point history—in the sense of further basic change—could have a stop. For the English imagination of the decade, in short, the word "apocalypse" meant not a vision of horror but of dazzling splendor, not of catastrophe but of the epochal and triumphant social transformation that catastrophe led to.

The English Romantic spirit, M. H. Abrams has recently and brilliantly argued, was essentially revolutionary; but its rhetorical expression was biblical—it "looked upon contemporary politics through the perspective of Biblical prophecy," and it tended to describe human progress in terms that were "Messianic, millennial, and apocalyptic." One notices the transforming effect upon the term "apocalyptic" there (as against, say, the Reformation usages of the concept) of the associated adjectives "Messianic" and "millennial." For with early English Romanticism, we arrive at what Martin Buber has aptly called an "inverted apocalyptic," "an optimistic modern apocalyptic" (of which, according to Buber, "the chief example . . . is Marx's view of the future"). It is this that Wordsworth announced, in a passage quoted by Mr. Abrams from *The Excursion,* a characteristic mingling of Virgilian and biblical millennialism:

> *I sang Saturnian rule*
> *Returned,—a progeny of golden years*
> *Permitted to descend and bless mankind.*
> *—With promises the Hebrew scriptures teem.*

And it is this that Blake enacted in *The Four Zoas* (1797), an epic fragment which, as Mr. Abrams remarks, "explodes into the most spectacular and sustained apocalyptic set-piece since the Book of Revelations."[6] But as it does so, what *The Four Zoas* celebrates is not the cosmic explosion itself but what had been exploded into being: the grand new world, the permanent good and just human society. Such was the apocalyptic idiom of the age: "Hey for the New Jerusalem! The Millennium!" This cry, of one Thomas Holcroft, was the age's echoing motto.

The Romantic apocalyptic was indeed optimistic, and—considering the apocalyptic tradition generally—it was "inverted." It was also altogether secular and humanistic; it manifested, in Buber's phrase, an "immanent dialectic"; it surveyed forces working entirely within human history, and the triumph it saluted was not that of saints and angels in the heavenly kingdom but of men and women in the earthly here-and-now. It is in part a tribute to the vigor of Romantic rhetoric that these happy connotations of "apocalypse" have survived long after the faith that begot them had died. For, in fact, the Romantic enthusiasm scarcely lasted through the decade of its origin. Historical developments in France proved all too rapidly to be a source of the bitterest disillusionment. What the Romantic imagination thereupon turned to was what Mr. Abrams (it is his most valuable insight) defines as "apocalypses of imagination." The expression of apocalyptic confidence, that is, while still conveyed in biblical and especially in Revelations imagery, tended to refer less and less to the current actualities of social change and more and more to an achievement of the poetic imagination—to events occurring not in France but in poetry. The millennial hope remained, Mr. Abrams says,

> but the hope has been shifted from the history of mankind to the mind of the single individual, from militant external action to the imaginative act; and the marriage between the Lamb and the New Jerusalem has been converted into a marriage between subject and object, mind and nature, which creates a new world out of the old world of sense.

6. In *Blake's Apocalypse* (New York, 1963), Harold Bloom has made this aspect of Blake's poetry the center of his massive and definitive study, concentrating attention where he believes it should at long last *be* concentrated—on those late epics which are sometimes called "prophetic books," but which Mr. Bloom contends are more accurately called apocalyptic.

The issue of that wedding (in the Romantic view) may some day and somehow and astonishingly enough *be* an actual and historical millennium, through the very force of the poetic vision upon history, through its capacity to alter the consciousness of mankind: whereby, in the extraordinary closing lines of *Prometheus Unbound,* "hope" is seen by Shelley as creating "from its own wreck the thing it contemplates." It is, we should observe in passing and further to clarify the point, from this second and major phase of Romantic apocalyptics that, in the American twentieth century, Hart Crane unmistakably emerges. *The Bridge* (1930) is the very type of the apocalypse of imagination: a poem written out of a deepening despair over the conditions of life in America, but a poem which, while in no way seeking to falsify or sentimentalize the grim observable facts, aims nonetheless at establishing a new relation between the human consciousness *and* that life; and by so doing, but only by so doing, to assist a little in the conversion of the age of iron into the age of gold.

III

Hart Crane, however, stands virtually alone among twentieth-century American poets in perpetuating the mood of apocalyptic *hope,* even though his hope rests, as I have just said, upon faith in the power of poetry rather than faith in the goodly impulses of men or the benevolent dispositions of history. Crane indeed had few companions in mood in the whole history of American literature; Poe, I will suggest, was the closest of his predecessors; for while the millennial temper has been notable and noisy in America, it has not often found expression in imaginative writing —and it is of course toward imaginative rather than discursive or speculative writing that I have been gradually shifting.

Before completing that shift, we may remember that the notion of New England as the scene of the New Jerusalem was widespread during the first years after the Massachusetts settlements. Such men as John Cotton and Thomas Goodwin, in commentaries on Revelations (both sets compiled in 1639), predicted the start of the millennium in the very near future: Cotton dating the grand event as early as 1655, Goodwin more cautiously putting it around 1700.[7] There was some dispute as to whether Christ would

7. For this and related information, I am grateful to *The Puritan Apocalypse,* an unpublished Yale doctoral dissertation (1964) by Joy Bourne

personally initiate the splendid age and inhabit the earth during it or whether he would appear only at the end. But there was considerable agreement in those hopeful decades with the quaintly worded announcement of John Eliot, the apostle to the Indians, that "In these times the Prophesies of *Antichrist* his downfall are accomplishing," and with the heady declaration of Richard Mather that the time was coming, and soon to be, "when all Kings shall fall down unto [Christ], and all Nations do him service . . . [as] plentifully foretold and promised in the Holy Scriptures." Such a sentiment could be voiced as late as 1697 by that most attractive of Puritans, Samuel Sewall in *Phaenomena Quaedam Apocalyptica,* or in its English title *The New Heaven upon the New Earth.*[8] Secular versions of the thesis continued to inform what might be called liberal American thought in the eighteenth and nineteenth centuries—for example, the histories of George Bancroft, with their (essentially Virgilian) image of America as the triumphant culmination of world history, and the proclamations of those settlers of frontier communities who attempted, as H. Richard Niebuhr has indicated in the title of his fine study, to establish *The Kingdom of God in America.*

Nonetheless, the major apocalyptic tradition in this country—and the one which has stimulated the literary imagination proper—dates rather from the later seventeenth century, when the felt failure of the New England mission produced a stream of "doomsday sermons," all of them envisioning the cosmic wrath by which God would punish an apostate people. It was then, in the second and third generations of Puritans, that, as Hawthorne would observe, the characteristic darkness of the Puritan visage set in, and the Puritan temper lost its capacity for laughter. It was then that the "Jeremiad"—a prophetic discourse, in the Old Testament sense of prophecy, combining lament and exhortation addressed to the backsliders—gave way to a more genuinely apocalyptic rhetoric, intoning the multiple agonies and the fractional beatitudes of the Day of Judgment.

"The Day of Trouble is Near," Increase Mather asserted dire-

Gilsdorf. Mrs. Gilsdorf underscores the effect upon early New England apocalyptic thinking of the guarded optimism of John Calvin about the spiritual progress of man in history, as against the severe Lutheran position.

8. Whittier included bits of Sewall's work, including the celebration of Plum Island, in his poem "The Prophecy of Samuel Sewall."

fully in the 1670s, quite reversing the cheerful claim of his father, Richard. A decade before, Michael Wigglesworth of Malden, had given an elaborate account of the awesome moment in *The Day of Doom* (1662), after mourning over New England's spiritual and moral decline in a poetic Jeremiad (published in the same year) called *God's Controversy with New England*. The former lengthy, oddly sweet-natured, and enormously popular piece of apocalyptic doggerel begins its disclosures on a serene and lovely night, when "wallowing in all kind of sin/ Vile wretches lay secure." At midnight precisely the catastrophe occurs. There "brake forth a light/ Which turn'd the night to day,/ And speedily an hideous cry/ Did all the world dismay." Violent upheavals follow, mountains catch fire, hills are set a-swaying, the earth is "rent and torn" by quakes, and the Son of God appears with his train to judge both the quick and the dead. The sheep, those invited to sit on Christ's right hand, are glanced at for a few stanzas; but the goats, those summoned to the left, take a good deal longer to sort out. Similarly with the act of judgment: the righteous are assigned their thrones with a certain briskness; but Christ cross-examines, crushes in argument, and sentences the multitude of sinners for something over one hundred and sixty stanzas. In the course of them, Wigglesworth provides an anatomy of impiety, a softly bouncing survey of humanity in its last and worst apostasy and of the infinite variety of the wickedness of the whole "sinful crew," as Christ calls them:

> *Adulterers and Whoremongers*
> *Were there, with all unchast:*
> *There Covetous, and Ravenous,*
> *That Riches get too fast:*
>
> *Who us'd vile ways themselves to raise*
> *t'Estates and worldly wealth,*
> *Oppression by, or Knavery,*
> *By force, or fraud, or stealth—*

and so on. After the immense task of unmasking, Christ commands the actual punishments to proceed, while Wigglesworth, shuddering delicately, averts his eyes—"Who can tell the plagues of Hell,/ And torments exquisite?" Only in a brief epilogue are the saints, those reborn into eternal life, again remembered: "O blessed state of the Renate!/ O wondrous happiness."

While Wigglesworth, in the guise of envisioning the post-catastrophic judgment, was thus exploring the worldly lapses that justify catastrophe, larger apocalyptic patterns still aroused interest elsewhere, mainly through the influence of speculative apocalyptic histories imported from abroad. We notice, among these latter, familiar and long-standing differences of opinion—as to whether, for example, there would or would not be a millennium or period of righteousness and earthly happiness between the present age and the ultimate apostasy which would lead to the ultimate disaster; and if so, whether those future good times should or should not be dwelt upon. It remained, as usual, for Jonathan Edwards to give the culture of the new world its major statement on the entire subject—in *A History of the Work of Redemption* (written in 1739, published in America in 1786).

The *History* is a sort of updated *City of God*—a long narrative of the Christian past from the Creation and the Fall through the career of Christ and on to the Protestant Reformation—combinded with the visionary pronouncements of Revelations. In the latter or eschatological portion of the work, Edwards argued that there would, at some moment in the future, begin a one-thousand-year period in which the world would be ruled by Christ and which, Edwards hints once or twice, might just possibly arrive sooner than one might think. But toward the close of it, the world would once more revolt or fall away from Christ; and this time to such a degree that Christ would declare the Day of Judgment and the planet would be destroyed by fire. (I have already quoted Edwards' conviction, recently seconded by James Baldwin, that next time the world would be annihilated not by flood waters but by fire.) This whole portion of Edwards' history has been described by Perry Miller, among others, as "simple, old-fashioned chiliasm": "chiliasm" being a word one uses when one is tired of the word "millennialism," of which, denotatively, it is an exact synonym (chiliasm coming from the Greek for one thousand—*kilias*—rather than from the Latin), though as used by historians the words have acquired somewhat different connotations. The word in any case is not quite accurate: for though Edwards' interest does divide between the rule of Christ and the catastrophe to follow, it is the disaster that rather engages his mind and imagination. In a sprightly essay of 1951, however, written in the wake of the atomic explosions and called "The End of the World," Miller suggested that Edwards' visual description of the cosmic explosion might after all be the most important part of his eschatology, and that it might indeed contain a large and un-settling amount of sheer realism—that Edwards had given a literal image of the way the world really would end, along with the sound of its bang.

To this, I think, we can add a quality of moral and meta-phorical realism. In our later generation, Edwards, as he draws upon the conventional machinery of the apocalyptic tradition, can perhaps be seen describing realistically enough the perennial degenerative tendencies of human nature, and providing meta-phors—in the form of world-consuming holocausts and the like —that can gauge their enormity. To some extent, this seems to be precisely what St. John the Divine had been doing—that is, com-posing a poem, not a tract, and poem crowded not with believed-in facts but with revelatory images and symbols. And this is just what Edwards' American successors have done, and it is why we find them not so much among the theologians but among the novelists and poets, among those who have recognized and real-ized the truth of the imaginative life. We find those novelists and poets deploying scattered remnants of the apocalyptic vocabulary for their own humanistic and creative purposes, and so recurrently as to encourage us to deal with them in the same vocabulary for our critical purposes (on the assumption that *for* those pur-poses the apocalyptic language may be as serviceable, say, as the Freudian or the existentialist or the sociological). What has happened on the creative side, I venture, and beginning in America with Edgar Allan Poe, is another "rebirth of images," another reanimating of those great and ancient archetypes by which Western man has periodically explained to himself the full range of his condition, and the most spectacular of his expecta-tions or terrors.

IV

Poe, perhaps surprisingly, seemed on one occasion to be the most thoroughly conventional of the apocalyptic visionaries among nineteenth-century American writers. In a curious little dialogue-in-heaven called "The Conversation of Eiros and Charmion" (December 1839), Poe gave an account of the end of the world not only charged with quotations from Revelations, but told from the vantage point of the superterrestrial realm to which the blessed have already been transferred. What happened back on earth, the shadowy male figure Eiros tells his shadowy female companion Charmion, was "the entire fulfillment, in all their minute and terrible details, of the fiery and horror-inspiring denunciations of the prophecies of the Holy Book." It was also, we might observe, in exact accord with the later theorizing statement of R. H. Charles: another planet approaches the earth and shuts off its supply of nitrogen, whereupon the earth is destroyed by an outburst of its own fires.

> Then, there came a shouting and pervading sound, as if from the mouth itself of HIM; while the whole incumbent mass of ether in which we existed, burst at once into a species of intense flame, for whose surpassing brilliancy and all-fervid heat even the angels in the high Heaven of pure knowledge have no name. Thus ended all.

The conversation occurs in the domain of Aidenn (as it is spelled), a place full of "joys and wonders" and pervaded by "the majesty of all things": Poe's aesthetic version of the biblical heavenly kingdom.

But Poe turns out, as always, to be a very special case. His imagination was persistently apocalyptical in both the terrible and the hopeful sense. It was drawn regularly to the imagery of utter catastrophe—to the wiping out of a whole community, as in "The Masque of the Red Death" ("and Darkness and Decay and the Red Death held illimitable dominion over all"), or of a family and its mansion and estate, as in "The Fall of the House of Usher." But both the frequent catastrophes and the occasional glimpse of post-catastrophic otherworldly bliss belong to what Richard Wilbur has eloquently identified as Poe's "myth of the poet."[9] In this highly original version of a most central Romantic theme, what is being symbolically destroyed in tale after tale is the power of earthly beauty and the grip of worldly life; and what is being sometimes realized is the recovered vision of perfect beauty once enjoyed in childhood but lost in maturity. "The Conversation of Eiros and Charmion" is in this perspective a beatific sequel to "The Fall of the House of Usher" (of which it was in literal fact a sequel, the two stories following one another

9. Wilbur's interpretation of Poe is available in his preface to the Dell Laurel volume of Poe's poetry (New York, 1959) and his introduction to the Poe section in *Major Writers of America* (New York, 1962).

in *Burton's Magazine* in September and December 1839). Poe's essential design—vision; the disappearance of vision; the struggle to recapture it—is the obvious American ancestor of Hart Crane's epical design in *The Bridge*. But it would take us much too far afield, however fascinating the detour, to pursue Poe's special contribution to American apocalyptics. In our own now narrowing context, the key American figure of the past century was Herman Melville, and the key book was *The Confidence-Man*.

Much of Melville's best writing is animated by a sort of apocalyptic intuition; and indeed "apocalyptic" is a more precise adjective for Melville's imagination than the more usual ones, "mythic" or "metaphysical." Like every other element in this highly dynamic vision, however, the apocalyptic element was constantly in motion, constantly modifying or reversing itself. In *Moby-Dick* (which cites the Book of Revelations on several occasions), the focus is on catastrophe: the catastrophic end of the *Pequod,* seen as a microcosm of America or even the modern world ("the world's a ship on its passage out"); the disastrous result of the human effort to transcend human limits and to penetrate and destroy the divine or at least nonhuman power secreted in the heart of reality. But this mad, majestic enterprise is set alongside quite different apocalyptic motifs: for example, the doomsday tract called "The Latter Day Coming; or No Time to Lose," which the hypocritical Captain Bildad presses on Queequeg, or the apocalyptic screechings of the self-styled prophet Gabriel, who, at secret meetings of the Neskyeuna Shakers, used to "descend from heaven by the way of a trap-door, announcing the speedy opening of the seventh vial" (the last of the vials of destruction) "which he carried in his vest-pocket." Gabriel is simply a humbug prophet; but Captain Ahab is that incomparably grander traditional figure, the False Prophet or False Christ: with something in him of Satan, especially Milton's Satan ("There was an infinity of firmest fortitude, a determinate, unsurrenderable wilfulness" in his glance), but also something of Christ the King ("moody stricken Ahab stood before them with a crucifixion in his face; in all the nameless regal overbearing dignity of some mighty woe"). In the apocalyptic pattern of *Moby-Dick,* Ahab is the Antichrist, misleading mankind to the point of bringing down upon it the annihilating wrath of God; but in the book's supple play of perspectives, he is also of course the Antichrist as a noble, heroic, and tragic figure.

ble. The cool indifference with which young Satan per-
s some miraculous atrocities of his own simply expresses a
nihilism which the villagers, including the adolescent nar-
nd his companions, hypocritically deny even while acting
ord with it. Mark Twain ends his parable with a peculiarly
ive sort of metaphysical or even ontological catastrophe:
e reported end of the world in ice or fire, but the revelation
he world, the very universe, does not even exist and never
'Nothing exists," Satan informs the narrator Theodor at the
ent of his disappearance; "all is a dream. God—man—the
d—the sun, the moon, the wilderness of stars—a dream, all
am; they have no existence. *Nothing exists save empty space*
you."

eyond that uncovering of absolute nothingness, the apocalyp-
magination can hardly venture. But Satan also knows what
k Twain knew, and what this devastating *Nunc Dimittis* has
n constantly exemplifying—the implicit first principle of mod-
American apocalyptics: namely, as Satan puts it, that our
man race has only

one really effective weapon—laughter. Power, money, persuasion, supplication, persecution—these can lift at a colossal
humbug—push it a little—weaken it a little, century by century.
But only laughter can blow it to rags and atoms at a blast.

atan's metaphor, as apt as it is unexpected, helps to identify
e imaginative aim of a series of novels which, over the past
vo and a half decades, have explored a thickening American
haos, an America hovering ever more perilously on the day of
oom. For while attempting to do full justice to the conditions
erceived, these novels have a further apocalyptic purpose—to
eveal the essential fraudulence within the horror, to uncover the
idiculous within the catastrophic; in the hope, at least, of letting
in a little light.

V

We might well begin with Faulkner's *The Hamlet* (1940), where
the unmistakable figure of Satan unloosed is named Flem Snopes,
where the victory of the Antichrist over the novel's world is
virtually complete, and where laughter is indeed a major instrument for coping with the awfulness. But this antipastoral master-

The characteristically radical ambiguity of Melville's apocalyptic outlook is perhaps even better displayed in "The Conflict
of Convictions," the main opening poem of *Battle-Pieces* (1866),
Melville's volume of poems about the Civil War. Here, with
somber allusions to Satan and Raphael and the eternal battle between good and evil, Melville posed the ultimate alternatives—the
fundamental dialectic, as it were, of the entire apocalyptic tradition. Out of the violent intranational upheaval, during which the
very "gulfs their slimed foundations bare," there might emerge
the millennium: "the final empire and the happier world." Or,
on the contrary, the nation might—spiritually speaking—be
catastrophically destroyed; become utterly dominated by power
without grace, whereat "the Founders' dream shall flee,"

> *And death be busy with all who strive—*
> *Death, with silent negative.*

As the war moved forward, Melville seems to have felt that the
iron age was a more probable outcome than the happier world;
and, like the English Romantics observing the defeat of their
millennial hopes in France, Melville concluded *Battle-Pieces* with
an "apocalypse of imagination": a poem called "America" which
provides a vision, true rather for the poem than in the fact, of an
America reborn out of the agony, possessed of a "hope grown
wise. . . . Law on her brow and empire *in her eyes*"[10] (italics
added).

But Melville's most searching statement about the fatal direction in which America was heading was contained in his pre-
Civil War novel, *The Confidence-Man* (1857), an extraordinary
work that ranks second only to *Moby-Dick* among his writings.
With it, I come at last to the peculiar modern American strain of
the savagely comical apocalypse; for if *Moby-Dick* is in a sense
the American culmination of the older apocalyptic tradition, *The
Confidence-Man* stands at the start of a distinctive new genre,
its first and still its most remarkable example.

The Confidence-Man is a narrative image of the American
world at the moment of its last apostasy. In the course of describ-

10. Melville himself felt the analogy between his own forebodings and
the English Romantic reaction to the developments of the French Revolution. In a footnote to *Battle-Pieces,* he compared the dismay aroused in
America by the events of 1860–61 to the impact upon "kindred natures"
of "the eclipse which came over the promise of the first French Revolution."

ing a day-long journey aboard a Mississippi river steamer wryly called the *Fidèle,* the novel gives a relentless series of examples, each more formidable than Wigglesworth's, of (to borrow some of Wigglesworth's categories) the covetous and the ravenous, of oppression and knavery, of force and fraud and stealth. At the outset, there appears briefly a seemingly Christ-like figure, a nameless and gentle person whose head and hair, in one of Melville's favorite quotations from Revelations, are "white like wool"; but, whoever he is, he is derided, reviled, and dismissed. Thereafter, under the auspices of the metaphoric Confidence Man himself, the narrative dramatizes and forces into prominence those qualities of greed, hypocrisy, ignorance, moral timidity, and ice-cold heartlessness through which the American society, a world that had once promised to become the millennial heaven-on-earth and still claimed to be just that was in fact steadily turning into a hell-on-earth, as though to fulfill the bleak prediction of Jonathan Edwards. These are the conditions which invite the catastrophe: an event, one is intended to suspect, which will take place only a second or two after the book's closing sentence. The final scene is awe-inspiring. In a darkening ship's cabin, a conversation between the title figure and a nearly senile old man is interrupted three times by shouted phrases from some person hidden in one of the bunks—three exclamations which, within the darkly ritualistic atmosphere of the scene, come like three blasts of the apocalyptic trumpets. First, when one speaker makes a reference to the Gospel, or "good news": "Too good to be true." Then, when Ecclesiasticus is quoted about the wiles of the devil: "Who's that describing the confidence-man?" And finally, after the word "apocrypha" has been invoked: "What's that about the Apocalypse?" Not long afterward, the Confidence Man extinguishes the cabin's last lamp (an object decorated with what appear to be symbols borrowed from Revelations) and leads his befuddled companion out into the total darkness. It is just on the stroke of midnight, and surely some revelation is at hand.

If this often disconcertingly realistic fable is, as I am contending, the pivotal text in the history of apocalyptic literature in America, it is because, while drawing heavily upon the familiar elements, it is also the first to exploit what would be the chief features of so much of the imaginative apocalyptic writing that followed. It is a conventional inspection of humanity during the last loosening of Satan: but its perspective is profoundly and al-

most shatteringly comic. The sin
lous as they are unredeemable; a
which is flawlessly executed throu
of the great rhetorical inventions
or meditation and by a slow grav
strip each of the *Fidèle's* passenge
layer, until each is revealed in all h
the novel explores "the later end o
phrase, and introduces what Foxe
principall Antichrist," the Antichr
course, the Confidence Man himsel
an expanding list of Satanic comedi
talent, geared to a world bereft of
moral stability, is a talent for metam
of change and the changing, a very
novel is through, he has appeared in
roles and personalities and garb. His ge
for satire, rooted in a profound unders
depravity of mankind; and in a world
(such as "confidence" and "man") have
posites or to mean nothing, he is a mas
and exposure. In nature he is a fabulous c
—a demonic angel and an angelic devil v
posterous contradictions of that humanit
escorting to its doom. His descendants ar

The first of them, perhaps, is the young
Mark Twain's *The Mysterious Stranger.* T
rifying character, who seems to be a nephew
is—like Melville's hero—an inveterate com
acteristically with Mark Twain, a comedian
and prankster type. With this story, which
posthumously in 1916, Twain carried into th
the American genre of the comical apocalypse
brought to their finality fictional themes and
the human race that had been growing stead
imagination from *Huckleberry Finn* through *Th*
Pudd'nhead Wilson to "The Man That Corrup
(1900). The mood of *The Mysterious Stranger* is
chill; during a long wintry season in the late sixtee
citizens of the Austrian village of Eseldorf (Donk
in incident after incident an icy inhumanity that

corrigi
petrate
moral
rator
in acc
inven
not th
that
has.
mom
worl
a dre
and
B
tic
Ma
bee
ern
hu

piece has such a variety of fictional tones and narrative modes that an effective analysis of it would pull us off course. We will do better to begin with Nathanael West's *The Day of the Locust,* and its hardminded comic portrait of the imminent destruction of America by a holocaust of hate. The Satanic character in West's novel, the harnesser of all that hatred, goes in fact unnamed; but we know that he will be an even greater scoundrel, making even wilder promises, than the lesser demagogues we have seen throughout the book serving the bitter frustrations of the aging California citizenry. He will be a successor as well to West's earlier Antichrists, the editor Shrike in *Miss Lonelyhearts* (1933) and Shagpoke Whipple in *A Cool Million* (1934). The realm of the California super-promiser, however, seems larger than that of Shrike and Shagpoke; for if there is not, unarguably, an increase in West's imaginative power from *Miss Lonelyhearts* to *The Day of the Locust,* there is an observable increase in the range of the horror always comically explored.

The world of *Miss Lonelyhearts* is an airlessly tight little island —Manhattan Island, in fact, plus a short stretch of countryside; a world so narrowed, in a novella so compressed, that its rhythms and tensions (which themselves are eschatological in nature and have to do with the last things) are well-nigh uncontainable. The novella moves unfalteringly between nightmare and actuality, its tone between horror and jesting; which is West's exemplary way of apprehending *our* world as under the dominion of a contemporary Antichrist. The human condition thus apprehended is characterized by a sort of absolute dis-order, by a dislocation observable pre-eminently in the relations of love, in almost every heterosexual and homosexual variety; but also a dislocation in man's other crucial relations—his relation to things, to words, to the rituals of life, to his own perennial aspirations. Human life, as depicted in *Miss Lonelyhearts,* has become a grotesque parody of itself; and the name of the book's Antichrist, Shrike, has the merit not only of meaning a toothbeaked bird of prey, but also of being as it were a parody of the name Christ, or Christ almost spelled backward. It is Shrike who rules over and preys upon an urban scene composed of the heartless, the violent, and the wretched. And it is Shrike who pits himself against the would-be imitator of Christ, the hapless columnist we know only by his pen name Miss Lonelyhearts, and whom Shrike torments in particular by spoken parodies of the Eucharist—that holy *communion* after which Miss Lonelyhearts so yearns. The central image of the novella, indeed, is a parody of the Gospel encounter between Christ and the Devil—in this case between a man, on the one hand, whose soul is sickened by a human misery he cannot assuage; and, on the other, the spokesman of an ice-cold and yet witty and intellectually brilliant inhumanity. In speech after speech, Shrike tempts and taunts Miss Lonelyhearts with vistas of grandeur, channels of escape, resources of compensation; until he drives the columnist to attempting the final absurd miracle. In a ludicrously ill-timed and feverish effort to embrace and hence to redeem by love at least one individual human victim— a crippled homosexual named Pete Doyle—Miss Lonelyhearts is accidentally shot and killed; and in the abrasively ironic escha- tology of this novella, the field is left to the further machinations of the Antichrist. But Shrike, consummate satirist though he be, is at the same time an object of satire—that is, of West's satire— and the field of his triumph is no more than a frozen chaos.

The enlargement of setting in *A Cool Million* is suggested by this: that Miss Lonelyhearts is shot (in an obscure rooming house) not even by a man but, as though in its supreme revolt, by a thing, by the freakish explosion of a gun wrapped in a newspaper; while Lemuel Pitkin, whose gradual "dismantling" is half of the theme of *A Cool Million,* is shot by a hired assassin, "Operative 6348XM," during a huge political rally staged in New York by the National Revolutionary Party. The satire in *A Cool Million* is cruder and broader than in *Miss Lonelyhearts;* and West is not himself implicated in that which he satirizes, as he had been earlier. Still, while *A Cool Million* plays comical havoc with the Horatio Alger tradition and the American daydream of the easy surge upward to fame and fortune, it is also this country's most vigorous narrative vision of the political apocalypse—far more penetrating, for example, than the rather hastily contrived image which appeared the following year in Sinclair Lewis' *It Can't Happen Here*. The devil as the editor Shrike is succeeded in *A Cool Million* by the devil as national political Fuehrer: by Shag- poke Whipple, a more ambitious and amiable and even more completely fraudulent figure than his predecessor. The "mantling" of Shagpoke, former President and future dictator of the United States, is the other half of the book's theme; his loudmouthed and evidently interminable reign is just beginning as the story ends. On the national holiday commemorating young Lemuel's assassination, Whipple spells out his triumphant program to shouting thousands at a Fifth Avenue parade:

The National Revolutionary Party [has] triumphed, and by that triumph this country was delivered from sophistication, Marxism and International Capitalism. Through the National Revolution its people were purged of alien diseases and America became again America.

This is a fine example of what Richard Hofstadter has defined as the paranoid style in American politics: a style historically based, as Mr. Hofstadter points out, on a most intensive apocalyptic outlook—a belief in some evil worldwide conspiracy, an identification of a wild conglomeration of elements as agencies of the Antichrist (communism, eastern capitalism, intellectual sophistication, and so on), a conviction of approaching disaster unless counteraction is swiftly taken.[11] West's complex achievement in *A Cool Million* is to satirize this apocalyptic temper in such a way as to show that it is itself the source of the potential catastrophe. But Mr. Hofstadter was talking primarily not about the political debaucheries of the 1930s, the actual scene of *A Cool Million,* but about the presidential campaign of 1964; and it is because that phenomenon is still so close to us that one finds it harder to laugh at Shagpoke's speech or at Shagpoke than it used to be. Yet, even as we are once again astonished at the capacity of life to follow slavishly in the wake of art, and as our admiration for West's prophetic power deepens into downright awe, we also become aware that the perspective in *A Cool Million* is exactly right. For in West's perspective of rough-hewn satire, the squalid reality of American fascism—the absurdities that pervade its spurious nostalgia and its venomous racism, its radical ignorance and contradictory assortment of fears—gets utterly exposed. What passes among the brutalized citizenry as the New Jerusalem is revealed to be a catastrophic vulgarity. And the very real menace, even as it is uncovered and defined, is in part overcome (insofar as a work of art can ever overcome anything) through the restoration of sanity by laughter.

But *The Day of the Locust,* as I have already said, is West's supreme Book of Revelations. This beautifully composed novel makes dreadfully and hilariously evident in the superb dance of

11. *Harper's Magazine,* November, 1964.

its elements a threat beyond that of *A Cool Million:* a threat to the very roots of life in America, a threat as it were to the human nature of American humanity. It is a threat incarnate in a certain mass of people—bored, frustrated, vindictive, and moribund—who have come to California impelled by a dream of their own obscene millennium, by a sterile lust for some experience of violence that might exhilarate and revivify. They are disappointed —"nothing [could] ever be violent enough to make taut their slack minds and bodies"—and with a devouring sense of having been betrayed, they await the summons to provide out of themselves the violence denied. The summons begins to be audible in the animal roaring of a mob rioting outside a Hollywood theater as the novel ends.

Against that tremendous force of hatred—and for West, since love is the sign of spiritual grace, hatred, its polar opposite, is the defining quality of apostasy and damnation—West poses the allied powers of art and comedy. His hero is a young painter named Tod Hackett, presently employed as a set designer in Hollywood; a tougher-spirited Miss Lonelyhearts and a more self-protective Lemuel Pitkin. It is Tod who takes to studying the dead ferocity of the invaders, seeking them out in odd nooks and corners of the city, driven by a profound fascination with their "awful anarchic power" and determined to represent them on canvas. He finds them gathered, more than anywhere else, in the temples and churches, the lunatic-fringe cults of California; for one of the most terrible of the truths and prophecies disclosed in *The Day of the Locust* is the organic connection in America between radical religiosity, an extreme Protestantism gone finally insane, and the organized impulse of hatred and destruction.

As [Tod] watched these people writhe on the hard seats of their churches, he thought of how well Alessandro Magnasco would dramatize the contrast between their drained-out feeble bodies and their wild disordered minds. He would not satirize them as Hogarth and Daumier might, nor would he pity them. He would paint their fury with respect, appreciating its awful, anarchic power, and aware that they had it in them to destroy civilization.

Nathanael West does not precisely satirize them either; despite its carefully wrought poetic intensity, *The Day of the Locust* stays closer to a palpable historical reality than his other fictions. The tone and movement of the novel are comic, nonetheless, and both are suited to a world in which, due to the utter instability of its outward forms, everything is on the verge of giving way.

The scene upon which the locusts descend is a scene made up of masqueraders and impostors; of movie actors dressed up as French and British generals and of ordinary citizens dressed up as Tyrolean hunters. Even plants and natural phenomena are fictitious: cactus plants are made of rubber and cork; a hill on a movie set, as it collapses, spills the nails and rips the canvas of which it is composed. A world so grotesquely insubstantial is ripe for conquest; and yet within its atmosphere, the wrath to come can be contemplated with just that drunken and hazily amused equanimity that Tod Hackett expresses when, lying on his back in a clump of wild mustard, he thinks about the invasion of California by "the cream of America's madmen" and feels certain that "the milk from which it had been skimmed was just as rich in violence. The Angelenos would be first, but their comrades all over the country would follow. There would be civil war." That antic Armageddon, however, takes place not quite in the actual rioting and lynching and sexual assaults of the final scene; but, rather, in an interpretive work of art, in the painting (and it is to be a great painting, West clearly wants us to believe) Tod Hackett is meticulously projecting on the last page, even as he is being mauled and half-crushed by the frenzied mob.

Thus superimposed in thought above the actual disorders, the painting—it will be called "The Burning of Los Angeles"—will eventually explain and comment upon the apocalypse it describes by the patterned juxtaposition of its elements. It will show a "mob carrying baseball bats and torches" down a long hill street, a mob that includes "the cultists of all sorts" whom Tod had been observing—"all those poor devils who can only be stirred by the promise of miracles, and then only to violence." Now, "no longer bored, they sang and danced joyously in the red light of the flames," following the leader who "had made the necessary promise"; "they were marching behind his banner in a great united front of screwballs and screwboxes to purify the land." Elsewhere on the canvas, various postures suggest various responses to that savage absurd Puritanism: a girl running naked in smiling mindless panic; a man named Claude turning to thumb his nose; Tod himself pausing to throw stones at the mob like a small boy. Nose thumbing and stone throwing are commendable

acts of derision; but Tod's major response is of course his painting, just as West's major response is the novel that contains it.
And both painting and novel fulfill their purpose by portraying
these maddened humans, whirling forward in their orgiastic dance,
as devils who are yet poor devils, seized by a fury of hatred which
is as silly as it is explosive.

Ralph Ellison's *Invisible Man* (1952) likewise ends with a riot,
the last and largest of several in the novel, and with a riot
similarly charged, in the account of it, with apocalyptic comedy;
though this time the scene is Harlem rather than Hollywood.
And the world as experienced in *Invisible Man* is again a world
spoiling for catastrophe: a world rank with duplicity and violence,
infested by cheats, liars, betrayers, and impostors, all caught up
in a continuing and somehow wonderfully exuberant masquerade.
In the novel's climactic stage, moreover, the world again reveals
itself as altogether bereft of stabilizing shape or form: a world
without boundaries, as the narrator dazedly realizes, "a vast
seething hot world of fluidity." Within such a world, the fluid man
is king; and his name here is Rinehart—Bliss Proteus Rinehart,
in fact. Rinehart is the very paradigm of Protean frauds, the
culmination of a long sequence of frauds of lesser or greater accomplishments strewn through the novel, from a Negro college
president in the south to a white political organizer in the north.
And with Rinehart, the "master of chaos" as the narrator calls
him and the man of "multiple personalities," we return—Ellison
has been the first to acknowledge it—to Melville's figure of the
metamorphic Confidence Man. After the narrator, groping his way
behind tinted glasses through the dim embattled streets of Harlem,
has been constantly accosted by mistake as Rinehart, he is able
to list some of the rascal's varied activities: "Rine the runner
and Rine the gambler and Rine the briber and Rine the lover and
Rinehart the Reverend." He is, in short, the Harlem Negro as
super-promiser; and a false priest and prophet in literal fact, a
"spiritual technologist" who holds forth at the Holy Way Station,
where he makes visible the invisible and unfolds the new apocalypse—"the NEW REVELATION of the OLD TIME RE-
LIGION." Nothing looser or more elusive can be imagined than
this slippery Satan, whom, indeed, we never actually encounter.
But his shadowy presence is the unmistakable sign of the traditional loosening of Satan, or, in the modern idiom, of all hell
breaking loose: it is almost immediately "after Rinehart appears

in my novel," Ellison has remarked, "that the riot breaks out in Harlem."[12]

It is the destiny of the book's nameless hero, as he wanders and stumbles and plunges across the scene, to discover chaos as the determining condition of life; and to become aware, belatedly, that the chaos is deliberate and planned. The rioting in Harlem has been carefully managed and directed by a political organization known as the Brotherhood; just as the battle royal the narrator had been forced to engage in as a schoolboy had been supervised by the leading white citizens of his home town; or as the free-for-all that erupts in a paint factory is artfully stimulated by unionists and management spies, and the sexual traps the unsuspecting young man falls into encouraged by complaisant husbands. The chaos is total and ubiquitous. It represents the considered program, as it were, of the agents of Antichrist for drawing the world onward to the great catastrophe—with the manifest intention of seizing power in the post-catastrophic wreckage. For Ellison has elevated his political theme, the familiar authoritarian strategy of making disaster serve the ends of conquest, into universal apocalyptic significance. In the same way, he has in the book's climax converted the original or "real-life" setting (the Harlem street wars of 1943, which Ellison covered for a metropolitan newspaper) into that nightmare country which Martin Buber finds the definitive scene of apocalyptic fiction, when "the actual historical-biographical situation of the speaker [or writer] is deliberately replaced by an alien scene taken over as analogous to his own."[13] And, finally, Ellison has heightened

---

12. *Shadow and Act* (New York, 1964), p. 181. Ellison has much to say in this volume about Rinehart and the tradition of the trickster-god, though he is skeptical about the critical category of the "archetype." So far as I can discover, Ellison added Rinehart's middle name, Proteus, retrospectively; in the novel, he is given only a middle initial P. Bliss is also the first name of the main character in Ellison's second novel, which at one time, I believe, was to be devoted to Rinehart or somebody resembling him. Ellison, by the way, seems not to have read *The Confidence-Man* before writing *Invisible Man;* the similarity he himself points out is due to an affinity of imagination with Melville.

13. One further result of Ellison's heightening and, as it were, ritualizing of the 1943 riot scenes is that his battle image has become prophetic of all later Harlem disorders: for example, the disorders that broke out in the summer of 1964, in which one could observe the same emotional sources, the same kind of triggering incident, and the same rhythm of events as those depicted in *Invisible Man.*

the racial theme into a representation of the condition of man as such; the plight of the Negro in the novel—his confused readiness to be recruited by all and sundry, his psychological invisibility—provides a perspective on the plight of every man under the modern circumstances.

Against all that, Ellison, like West, offers the counterforce of art, especially the power—the shaping power, the power to give form and hence explanatory meaning to experience—of comic narrative. The narrator fails to achieve visibility and vision through the normal channels of education or a job of work or sex or political action; and he fails in particular to achieve those things through his long and fiercely dedicated participation in what he took to be the struggle to make life more tolerable for his fellow Negroes. But his true resource, as it turns out, is story-telling. He becomes himself a master of chaos, of his own experienced chaos, by going underground and lingering there to draw his breath in pain and tell his story. But for all the very considerable pain, there is also the permeating comic awareness: which is to say that *Invisible Man* is in some sort an expanded narrative equivalent of that musical mode known as the blues, at least in Ellison's definition. "The Blues," he has written,

> is an impulse to keep the painful details and episodes of a brutal experience alive in one's aching consciousness, to finger its jagged grain, and to transcend it, not by the consolation of philosophy but by squeezing from it a near-tragic, near-comic lyricism. . . . [It is the] chronicle of personal catastrophe expressed lyrically.

Add the phrase "or even universal" to the word "personal," and we have a fairly exact summary account of this uncommonly distinguished novel, and a strong clue to its form.

In *The Sot-Weed Factor* (1960), John Barth's robustious novel about various fantastic forewarnings of the apocalypse in late seventeenth-century Maryland, the artistic dimension has become paramount, and in such a way as to offer an explanation, even a defense, of the prevalence of its genre—the genre of apocalyptic comedy—in our twentieth-century time. In essence, *The Sot-Weed Factor* (which is an archaic phrase meaning "Tobacco Merchant") is a portrait of the artist as an exacerbated and scandalously ill-treated young Colonial American. The portrait, it is important to know, is historically based, and *The Sot-Weed Factor* is among many other things a prodigiously learned historical novel. It gives us the life and times of a genuine historical figure, Ebenezer Cook or Cooke (1680 to 1730 or thereabouts), who was probably born in the New World, most likely spent some years in England and then (as he does in the novel) returned to America, where he really did write a satirical poem called *The Sot-Weed Factor,* which was published in London in 1708.[14] It is a rowdy poem of some seven hundred lines, emulating the manner and metrics of Butler's *Hudibras* and relating the astonishing (and, one assumes, imaginary) adventures of the author during a brief visit to Maryland, where he is persistently robbed and cheated, and alternately terrified and disgusted. Barth's Ebenezer Cooke suffers the same mishaps, along with a great many more of his own; he encounters the same people—white men and Indians, slatterns and doxies—and listens to the same reminiscences. Toward the end of the second part of the novel, we watch young Cooke convert these experiences into the same brisk, embittered satire.

Barth's modernistic device of multiple mirroring—a novel about a young man writing a poem about a young man and so on —goes even further than usual. For Barth himself is a Marylander to the core; all his fiction to date has been set in his own home county, almost his own backyard; and in his own *Sot-Weed Factor,* he enacts his major celebration of the region by supplying it with a hectic and racy myth of its seventeenth-century origins. The fictional myth is on an incomparably larger scale and more widely ranging and crowded than the original poem. It encompasses scores of events and persons, major and minor, historical and contrived; probably Barth alone knows how close is the resemblance between the "real-life" characters and his treatment of them, especially as they all tend to become participants in a farcical pornographic dance, which is the image of history that emerges in the novel. But it is Barth, anyhow, who has the more decisively earned the title "Poet and Laureate of Maryland" that

14. Cooke, in fact and in Barth's novel, was also the author of *Sotweed Redivivus* (1730), of a burlesque "History of Colonel Nathaniel Bacon's Rebellion" and of elegies on Nicholas Lowe (an important shadowy figure in the novel) and William Lock. The original *Sot-Weed Factor* is most easily available in the paperbound *Colonial American Writing,* edited by Roy Harvey Pearce (New York, 1950).

is granted his less talented predecessor. It is within this sometimes dizzyingly self-reflective context that we make out the great and thoroughly contemporary concern of *The Sot-Weed Factor:* which is a certain familiar kind of world, and the relation to it of the creative imagination.

On one level, it is the exhaustively evoked world of seventeenth-century England and America; but, on another, it is our immediate world as we have been taught by Barth and his peers to recognize it. The book's rhetoric is an echo and parody of the diction of Ebenezer Cooke's generation; Leslie Fiedler has remarked upon "the insouciance with which [the novel] moves in and out of its counterfeits of seventeenth century diction," and calls the book "a joyous series of raids on half-forgotten resources of the language, largely obscene."[15] But in content, in perspective, and in fictional method, *The Sot-Weed Factor* is as modern as can be; and if, as everyone who has mentioned it has inevitably and correctly said, it is Rabelaisian and Swiftian, it is also Melvillian, Joycian, Proustian, Faulknerian—and Westian. Barth can find the occasional apocalyptic cliché of the actual poem (where it is a device of comical exaggeration) handy to his purpose: for example, Cooke's statement that on the Maryland scene

> *all Things were in such Confusion,*
> *I thought the World at its Conclusion.*

But usually the condition of ultimate chaos is conveyed in the contemporary idiom, after it has been soaked in neoclassic cadences. There is no "pointed order to the world," Ebenezer's tutor, Burlingame, tells him; and continues in the curious blank verse he sometimes affects: "In fact you see a Heraclitean flux; whether 'tis we who shift and alter and dissolve; or you whose lens changes color, field and form; or both together. The upshot is the same." We are, in short, back in the "vast seething hot world of fluidity" that Ellison's narrator came to identify; and, like West's California, Barth's Maryland is, in Burlingame's phrase, "a happy climate for imposture." It is "a motley, mindless world," Burlingame adds; and Man is no more than "Chance's fool . . . a mayfly flitting down the winds of Chaos." The modes of chaos—the sources of the catastrophe apprehended—are

15. *On Contemporary Literature,* edited by Richard Kostalentz (New York, 1964), pp. 241–42.

erotic and political, usually both: in Maryland, the world seems transformed into one vast brothel and opium den, under the command of a "grand high whoremaster"; elsewhere it is rather a political stew, a "pot of faction and sedition" that boils and boils again, until, as someone exclaims, it must be "about to explode."

Barth's fictive seventeenth-century setting permits him to draw upon the traditional apocalyptic vocabulary more and with a greater propriety than most of his contemporaries. The word "apocalypse" is on everyone's lips, especially as the violently opposed political forces seem about to settle their struggle for power by meeting head-on in a Maryland Armageddon. Lord Baltimore identifies his arch-enemy John Coode as a "very Antichrist" and a "false priest," and portrays Maryland under Coode's control as a country dominated by Satan unbound. But we recognize again the modern imagination when Henry Burlingame, speaking of both Baltimore and John Coode, says to Ebenezer:

> It may be they are all that rumor swears: devils and demigods, whichever's which; or it may be they're simply clotpolls like ourselves, that have been legend'd out of reasonable dimension; or it may be they're naught but the rumors and tales themselves.

"Devils and demigods, whichever's which." The metaphysical and even theological doubt thus chattily and sardonically expressed is what the novel has been busy bringing all-powerfully into play. In no novel since *The Confidence-Man* has doubt of such universal proportions been disclosed as man's proper and necessary state of mind, the one intellectual fruit of his experience. Similarly and consequently, in no American novel since *The Confidence-Man*—not often in any work of literature since the *Odyssey*—has a supreme talent for metamorphosis been so much the distinguishing mark of a major character.

In *The Sot-Weed Factor,* it is Henry Burlingame who, as the man always ready at need, demonstrates his readiness by an ability to take on every variety of role and personality, according to the shifting dramatic situation. He exploits the special skill of Odysseus to the ends of Telemachus, for his private mission is to establish his identity by determining his true Burlingame ancestry —a search that leads him, among other things, to dig up and examine the lurid secret chronicles of Captain John Smith and his epochal defloration of the Indian Princess, Pocahantas. En route, Burlingame validates the theory spelled out in deeply serious mockery in Barth's superb earlier novel *End of the Road* (1958), which, with its apocalyptic title and closely woven content, relates to *The Sot-Weed Factor* as *Miss Lonelyhearts* does to *The Day of the Locust*. The theory voiced by a mountebank of genius in *End of the Road* is based on "good existentialist premises," and it holds not only that human existence precedes human essence and thus that man is free to choose his own essence, but that he is also free to change his essence at will. He can assign himself whatever role he pleases, depending upon the circumstances. "This kind of role-assigning," says the mountebank, "is myth-making, and when it's done consciously or unconsciously for the purpose of aggrandizing or protecting your ego . . . it becomes Mythotherapy." Burlingame, master mythotherapist in search of an ego, assigns himself the masks and personae of an engaging and learned young tutor to Ebenezer and his twin sister Anna; of a mysterious and influential old gentleman named Colonel Peter Sayer; of Tim Mitchell, the son of a plantation owner and a youth of singularly original and imaginative perversities; of Lord Baltimore in London and John Coode in the New World; of friend and foe, Catholic and Protestant, white man and Indian, sexual giant and sexual incompetent. In a world characterized and convulsed, like all great fictional worlds, by the two supreme forces of love and war, Burlingame's supreme mask is that of the erotic warrior. And his penultimate act—before he begets a child by Anna and disappears—is to deploy a monstrous erection to avert a battle that would have been a much bloodier and much more terrible version of the riots that suggested how the world might end in the novels of West and Ellison.

The metamorphoses of Burlingame are matched by the metamorphoses of the poem which Ebenezer Cooke comes to America to write; and it is in this dimension of the book that *The Sot-Weed Factor* contributes its exceedingly impressive statement about the creative or visionary possibilities in our time. As originally conceived, Cooke's poem was to have been an optimistic modern apocalypse, an epic celebration of the millennium arrived at in Maryland, modeled on the *Aeneid* and called the *Marylandiad*. But after attending to the shocking disclosures of Lord Baltimore (actually, as it develops, of Burlingame disguised as Lord Baltimore, uttering a farrago of truths and inventions) about the wild disorders and double-dealings in the new world, Ebenezer decides, gasping, that Maryland "were fitter for a Jeremiad! Ne'er have I encountered such a string of plots, cabals and machinations in life or literature." Baltimore-Burlingame, however, dissuades him from the prophetic mood, and urges him to "put [Maryland's] history out of mind," to look beyond the disgraceful actualities in order to sing a visionary Maryland of moral and natural perfection: to attempt, as we should say, something like an apocalypse of imagination. This indeed is what Ebenezer makes a start on during the first months of his journeys: for example, describing the *Poseidon,* the ship that brings him to America as

A noble Ship, from Deck to Peaks,
Akin to those that Homer's Greeks
Sail'd east to Troy in Days of Yore—

though in fact, as Burlingame points out sourly, "Thou'rt sailing west . . . and the *Poseidon* is a rat's nest." But an uninterrupted experience of indignity, humiliation, and colossal vice causes Ebenezer to abandon altogether even this reconceived *Marylandiad.* "Will I sing these lies? Here's naught but scoundrels and perverts, hovels and brothels, corruption and poltroonery." It is then that he settles upon what he knows to be the only appropriate literary mode for the world he lives in: the mode of apocalyptic satire. *The Sot-Weed Factor* that he eventually composes (and which includes and expands upon the historical original) begins with a ship "freighted with fools," and a voyage of "dreadful pain"; proceeds to a "shore where no good sense is found," and to the grotesque episodes and careening duplicity in which he had himself got involved; and ends with the poet's mighty curse summoning God to visit unredeemable Maryland with the final catastrophe; "May Wrath Divine then lay these Regions wast/ Where no Man's faithful, nor a Woman chast!"

Millennial epic, Jeremiad, visionary image, apocalyptic satire: the progression is clear, and it is exemplary. Ebenezer Cooke and his poem pass through the stages that any aspiring American writer might well pass through, in our appalling and preposterous times: to discover at the end that his available subject matter is "scoundrels and perverts . . . corruption and poltroonery"; his "world" unbounded and chaotic; and his creative weapon a laughter that both scorns and illumines. *The Sot-Weed Factor* is, after all, a portrait of the artist as a mid-century American.[16]

VI

The world-pervading warfare that is at least postponed in *The Sot-Weed Factor* has become the fixed condition of life in Joseph Heller's *Catch-22* (1961). Heller's novel is set in an American airforce base off the Italian coast during what is purported to be World War II. But in fact the novel carries us once again onto that "alien scene" identified by Buber as the locale of the fictional apocalypse: something dimly reminiscent of an historical locale by virtue of being a parodic distortion thereof. Heller's is a world of absolute entrapment, of permanent apocalypse and built-in catastrophe; a world in which the human situation is coextensive with total war. In it, the endlessly recurring representative act is the act of killing, and the defining emotion is the emotion of murderous hatred. "You haven't got a chance, kid," the book's hero, a navigator named Yossarian, tells his fellow airman Clevinger, "They hate Jews."

"But I'm not Jewish," answered Clevinger.

"It will make no difference," Yossarian promised, and Yossarian was right. "They're after everybody."

Clevinger recoiled from their hatred as though from a blinding light.

"They" are all those persons in the high commands of all the armed forces, most of them nameless and faceless, who have decreed for reasons unknown and unknowable that killing is the one and constant business of men. It is *they* who, from the standpoint of Yossarian's astounded and outraged egotism, have decided to kill *him*. And it is precisely as *they* that Satan makes his enigmatic appearance in this novel; for one of his masks, in the modern world and the contemporary American novel, is just that

---

16. In his admirable and insufficiently known study *Catastrophe and Imagination* (London, 1958), John McCormick argues that the reality confronted in both English and American fiction for most of this century has been catastrophic in nature; and that the major aim—in Mr. McCormick's view, the major accomplishment—of this fiction has been to find new narrative resources for taking hold of catastrophe. *The Sot-Weed Factor,* had it appeared in time, would have provided Mr. McCormick with a paradigm for his thesis.

of a faceless, impersonal, plural anonymity. The action of *Catch-22*, such as it is, consists in Yossarian's gradual discovery of the world's secret cabal, and his emphatic signing off, in flight at the book's end in the direction of Sweden, the only war-free (or, more simply, the only free) country that conceivably remains on the face of the earth.

In the perpetual and lunatic Armageddon of *Catch-22*, all values and standards are inverted, and opposites exchange place. Heller's main comic technique, which he tends to overwork, is similarly that of instantaneous reversal ("Appleby was a fair-haired boy from Iowa who believed in God, Motherhood and the American way of life . . . and everybody who knew him liked him. 'I hate that son of a bitch,' Yossarian growled."). The comedy in the novel contains, indeed, a good deal of unabsorbed zaniness, like the funny names (Scheisskopf, A. Fortiori, and so on) that abound like funny hats at some boring gala; but as the atmosphere tightens, even the horseplay is revealed as the symptom of a genuine desperation, a stay against hysteria. Survival, in a world that has gone coldly insane, is predicated upon a talent for clowning; *Catch-22* is also, in this regard, at once an addition to and an explanation of the genre to which it belongs. And as the clowning goes forward, one becomes conscious of a deeper comedy swelling into a deeper horror. Violence, as in *Miss Lonelyhearts*, is sudden and casual: an airman, capering naked on a beach, is literally cut in two when a plane piloted by a close friend swoops too low; in Rome, an ugly Italian chambermaid is raped by another airman and thrown out of the window and killed—when the police arrive, they (*they*) ignore the murderer and arrest Yossarian for being in Rome without a pass. It is during Yossarian's subsequent night-walk through Rome that the novel's apocalyptic vision, almost drained of its laughter, becomes the spectacle of greed, lust, and cynicism and of a human misery that, in his helplessness, simply infuriates Yossarian, as it had Miss Lonelyhearts. But at the heart of the horror there throbs the universe's enigmatic and immensely cruel joke: the cosmic catch, the given steel trap in human affairs—"Catch-22," or the principle, as an old Italian woman puts it, that *they* "have a right to do anything we can't stop them from doing." It is in defiance of the universe that Yossarian makes his hurried undignified farewell to arms and takes off for Sweden; but where madness rules, desertion is the act of honor.

Toward the end of Thomas Pynchon's *V.* (1963), the novel's semihero Stencil also departs in haste for Sweden. But Stencil wants desperately to believe that he is pursuing rather than running away; that he is simply continuing his life-long quest for a phantom female of many names and appearances, now rumored to be in Scandinavia. Stencil's decision betokens his refusal to accept the hideously circumstantial report of the death of the woman V., during an air raid on Malta during the second World War—if only because the manner and occasion of the death carry a symbolism too horrible for Stencil to accept. The symbolism has to do with nothing less than the settled meaning of modern history and the final end of Western man; and to accept it would be to acknowledge that the catastrophe had already happened. *V.* is a novel of enormous if unsteady imaginative power, and a work that often blazes with poetic and intellectual energy. More than any novel of its generation, *V.* faces up to the full political, technological, and war-making fury of the modern age; and in thus being a novel quite literally *about* history and possibly about the termination of human history, it also presents the purest, most savage, and at moments the funniest of the apocalyptic visions that pervade postwar writing.

Pynchon's historico-fictional onslaught takes two forms, and the relation between them is another illumination of the resources of the contemporary novel and the reason for their being invoked. On the one hand, there is the current human condition, represented by a bunch of New York misfits known as "the whole sick crew," a phrase Pynchon perhaps adapted and ironically modernized from Michael Wigglesworth's "You sinful crew," those Christ was dispatching to hell in the poem. The sickly New Yorkers are a conglomeration of drunks and renegade artists and sterile orgiasts and race-conscious nymphomaniacs and mindless do-nothings—components of a familiar but more than usually repellent world, a world on the far side of apostasy and already doomed and judged; though amid its vicious shadows the novel's other semihero, a "schlemihl" named Benny Profane (with one or two others), tries clumsily to keep alive some fragment of human decency. And, on the other hand, there is the figure and career of V. as Stencil and the reader reconstruct them: V., whom Stencil's father, formerly a member of the British Foreign Office, had known to his peril, and whose name across the decades and in many countries seems to be anything beginning with the letter

V—Victoria, Veronica, Vera, and whatever else. These two dimensions overlap: Stencil consorts with those crew members who can contribute biographical data on V., and Benny Profane accompanies Stencil to Malta on the last recorded stage of the quest-journey. But they are two distinct modes of narrative: the pictorial and the inquisitive; the representational and the dramatic. And they relate expertly as effect and cause, as present and past, as situation and diagnosis—as the given damned condition and its historic, even mythic, origins. The lady V. and her career enact in far-reaching historical terms the sickness with which the crew is afflicted; and while V.'s "awful anarchic power" (to borrow from *The Day of the Locust*) is treated with increasing respect and awe, the domain of the sickly is the object of a sort of nauseated laughter.

V. seems to have been born around 1880; but she enters the pages of history and the novel as Victoria Wren, late of Yorkshire, during the Fashoda crisis in Cairo in 1899—that is, as she approaches her majority, as the Middle East hovers on the brink of disaster, and as the twentieth century is about to begin. Cairo, where she seduces one Goodfellow of the Foreign Office, is the scene of the first of what young Herbert Stencil calls her "young, crude Mata Hari acts"; she goes on at once to perform a similar erotico-political role with the elder Stencil in Florence. More mature, refined, and dangerous intrigues follow in various places: "until 1913," Stencil reports, "when she knew she'd done all she could and so took out time for love." The amorous interlude, a peculiarly decadent Lesbian affair with a dancer named Melanie L'Heuremaudit, takes place in Paris; the next year, it is guessed, she went to Malta where she spent the years of the first World War; Herbert's father, Sidney, unluckily discovers her on the island just after the armistice. During the 1920s she showed up as an imperial agent named Vera Meroving in German South Africa; and it seems likely that she resided in Germany itself during the Hitler '30s (though there are also obscure reports of conspiratorial activities in Spain and Asia). In any event, she was back in Malta for the second World War—"Paris for love, Malta for war," observes young Stencil. And she was probably though not certainly killed in Malta in one of the worst of its almost daily air raids. Whether or no, war was her natural environment; and the "etiology of war" (the causal explanation) was, Stencil believes, the etiology of V., while "riot," he adds, "is her atmosphere." But what she represents is something even worse than war: it is "something monstrous" that "had been building" throughout her career.

Conspiracy, perversion, war, riot, and something more monstrous altogether: V. is of course the dark lady of the apocalypse, the Whore of Babylon. In the novel, she is associated with innumerable other V-formations (Venus, Venezuela, the Maltese town of Valletta, and a nightmare never-land named Vheissu; her name V. also seems to be an ideogram of female genitality). But we recognize her at once as the fateful female successor to Melville's Confidence Man and Mark Twain's Satan, to West's super-promiser, Ellison's Rinehart, and Barth's Burlingame; the promised end and climax of an extraordinary fictional species. She is Satan himself in the guise of the Whore of Babylon, let loose upon an apostate world to hurry, enlarge, and direct the great catastrophe; and to embody and symbolize it in her own being, her own very body. Young Stencil sees her as the contriver of "the ultimate plot that has no name." Wherever she walks, there are apocalyptic tremors; and even the name of the girl she takes as her mistress on the eve of the first war means, in English, the accursed hour. But it is the nature of the cosmic curse that for long escapes definition. The elder Stencil will not believe it to have been the horrors of World War I. "Ten million dead," he cries to a friend in Malta in 1919; "Gas. Passchendale. Let that now be a very large figure . . . but dear Lord, not the Nameless Horror, the sudden prodigy sprung on the world unaware." Soon thereafter, Stencil is destroyed by (apparently) the black arts of V., who is living on the island as Veronica Manganese, a friend of D'Annunzio and Mussolini; and the prodigy he apprehends is in fact already coming into view. For the real horror is neither war nor riot nor totalitarian terror. It is that something more monstrous—it is the progress, in young Stencil's formula, "towards inanimateness."

As she magnifies into the demonic spirit and presiding goddess of modern history—as the force which historical humanity has let loose upon itself—V. becomes equally the supreme mistress of metamorphosis, and assumes that multiplicity of roles which her great traditional function calls for. She seems at the end to be truly more than human; and, like her predecessors over the ages, her ultimate role is that of the False Prophet—on Malta in the second war and during her last days, she is known as "the

Bad Priest." But her major and continuing metamorphosis is something else again. It is the process whereby a human being slowly turns herself into an inanimate thing. Early on, out of some chilling caprice, she had acquired a foot of gold and an eye of glass, and had worn a watch imbedded in the flesh of her arm. The children who ransack her broken (but still breathing) body amid the rubble on Malta discover that both her feet are made of precious metal, and that, in addition to a wig and false teeth, she secretes a star sapphire in her navel. Young Stencil, day-dreaming in 1956 and persuading himself that V. is still alive, imagines the outcome of this grotesque process in a vision that is at once absurd (scientific double-talk) and unspeakable:

> Skin radiant with the bloom of some new plastic; both eyes glass but now containing photoelectric cells. . . . Solenoid relays would be her ganglia, servo-actuators move her flawless nylon limbs. . . . A complex system of pressure transducers located in a marvelous vagina of polyethylene; the variable arms of their Wheatstone bridges all leading to a single silver cable which fed pleasure-voltages direct to the correct register of the digital machine in her skull.

Such is the end of the human world, and the obliteration of whatever is animate in humanity. Pynchon's theme—that is, to put it oversimply, the mechanization of man—is of course a familiar one, and one that began to be formulated in the early nineteenth century with the first awareness of the effect of science and technology upon the human spirit. In English-language fiction, the great predecessor of *V.* in this regard is no less obviously Lawrence's *Women in Love,* which was written during the first World War but not published until 1920. And Gudrun Brangwen, the dark Satanic goddess of that novel and a young woman whom Lawrence describes as "a new Daphne, turning not into a tree but a machine," is the detectable predecessor of V. herself. Lawrence's apocalyptic vision in *Women in Love*—his vision of worldwide disaster—is close to absolute. It includes the passing fancy of a planet swept clean of humanity and given over to animal and plant life. England, where Lawrence introduces his own sick crew as the denizens of a London café, is compared to an aged parent suffering from an incurable disease; and indeed actual as well as spiritual death (and including the long-drawn-out

death of an incurably sick aged parent) invades almost every
nook and cranny of the novel. But, above all, Lawrence perceives
and expresses with a passion and eloquence a good deal more
powerful even than Pynchon's the dreadful paradoxical coupling
of mechanization and chaos—as in the famous account of the
"strict, terrible, inhuman" reorganization of the coal mines by
Gerald Crich, which is clearly the image of a universal development:

> It was the first step in undoing, the first great phase of chaos,
> the substitution of the mechanical principle for the organic . . . .
> It was pure organic distintegration and pure mechanical or-
> ganization. This is the first and finest state of chaos.

Lawrence understood, too, and strained to make palpable in
narrative a major symptom of the fatal modern illness, the
identical symptom observed by Pynchon: a limitless and immeasurably depraved and yet willed and intellectualized and so
hideously deflected eroticism; a "voluptuousness," as Lawrence
puts it, that "was like that of machinery, cold and iron." Again as
in *V.,* Lawrence's characters sometimes speculate about the apocalypse—they may even, like Gudrun and her new lover Loerke,
"laugh out some mocking dream of the destruction of the world
by a ridiculous catastrophe of man's own invention"—without
any consciousness that the catastrophe has already happened;
that disaster has already struck almost all of mankind. Only
Birkin and Ursula, those lonesome spokesmen for the inverted
or hopeful apocalypse, escape, fleeing together toward, as it were,
their own "Sweden"—fleeing into "nowhere," in Birkin's phrase;
for "nowhere" is the name and the location of heaven in the dying
world of *Women in Love.*

But Pynchon, though he is far less assured an artist (at this
stage anyhow) than Lawrence, has taken one or two steps beyond
Women in Love in his diagnosis and his narrative tone. On the
one hand, Pynchon's apocalyptic theme—and the comparisons
with Lawrence help finally to make this clear—is not exactly the
mechanization of man after all. It is rather the deliberate and
systematic *reicization* of mankind: the transformation of persons
not so much into machines as into sheer motionless *things.* That
process is somehow more blood-chilling yet; but Pynchon handles
it in the contemporary American manner with tigrish comedy. We
recognize once more the example of Nathanael West: not only

his image of the revolt of things in *Miss Lonelyhearts,* but also his sardonic narration of the dismantling of poor Lemuel Pitkin, who in the course of events had to replace various parts of himself—his teeth, an eye, a thumb, his scalp, and one leg—with artificial members, each of which was then knocked off or out each afternoon in a vaudeville act in which he was made to engage.[17] Pynchon goes beyond West too, in a vision not of the reicization by others of victimized innocence, but of all humanity by its own suicidal efforts—following the lead of its Satanic representative. The encroachment of the thing becomes, in this novel's world, the major historical motif: whether as a supplanting of the human, like the mechanical dancing figures introduced by the Germans into prewar Paris (in one of the book's moments of transparent political allegory); or as a process of conversion, like the "nose of ivory . . . check-bone of silver and . . . paraffin and celluloid chin" with which a wounded airman, V.'s sometime lover Evan Godolphin, seeks to repair his shattered visage. And it is of course in the postwar America (our America) of the whole sick crew that the act of de-animation is most evident.

The associates of Benny Profane show themselves willing if unconscious servants of the novel's Antichrist by their cheapened versions of V.'s characteristic indulgences—in their sordid malicious intriguing and their disconsolate alcoholic promiscuity. But with V. as paradigm, we can discern the more fundamental deterioration that is everywhere taking place: when, for example, a girl named Esther undergoes an operation to acquire an artificial gentile nose and, her mind caught in a confusion of surgery and sex, dreams of changing other parts of her anatomy; when a whole episode turns on the effort to steal a set of false teeth; and, most explicitly, during Benny's tour of duty as night watchman for Anthro-research Associates. His job is to guard two plastic mannikins named SHOCK and SHROUD, utterly synthetic and horribly lifelike creations of the researchers; and of an evening, he holds imaginary converse with one of them:

"What do you mean, we'll all be like you and SHOCK someday? You mean dead?"

17. Poe provided the earliest American version of this motif, in a joking anecdote called "The Man who was Used Up," wherein the elegant General Smith is found to be composed of a cork leg, false teeth and shoulders and chest, a wig, a glass eye, and a mechanical palate.

Am I dead? If I am then that's what I mean.
"If you aren't then what are you?"
Nearly what you are. None of you have very far to go.
"I don't understand."
So I see. But you're not alone. That's a comfort isn't it?

Months later, in Malta, it seems likely that Benny does at last understand: namely, that the human impulse to transmute live flesh into metal or plastic and the scientific urge to construct mechanical men are only the outward signs of the slow deliberate and perhaps inexorable petrefaction of the human spirit that is the ultimately discoverable fact of modern history. This is the unhappy crew's real sickness unto death; and it is no doubt with this ghastly revelation in his mind that Benny, in our last glimpse of him, dashes off into "the abruptly absolute night," toward the island's cliff edge and the Mediterranean beneath.

Contemporary American fiction, or the vein of it which I have been mining, seems determined to draw us on toward that cliff edge, or to watch with a sort of bitter contemptuous laugh as we draw ourselves on—only to leave us there, swaying ambiguously, just before the sound of midnight. *Is* this the promised end? It is not the end of American fictional apocalyptics, anyhow, or even of the comical apocalypse; fiction in this manner continues to outrun the critical absorption of it. James Purdy, who had offered intimations of the end of the world in the brilliant murk of "63: Dream Palace" and *Malcolm,* has now given us a full-toned apocalyptic blast in an uproarious if sometimes uncontrolled satire on American urban life in *Cabot Wright Begins.* And there are the much more exacerbated and compulsive visions, conveyed by a desperate harrying of the resources of fiction, of William Burroughs and Hubert Selby (especially in the section of Selby's *Last Exit to Brooklyn,* appropriately called "Land's End"), each of whom seems to represent in his own way a new and spreading mood of furious hopelessness. But, at the same time, one detects symptoms of an impatient counterimpulse, a restive disclaimer of the apocalyptic temper. "Safe, comfortable people playing at crisis, alienation, apocalypse and desperation, make me sick," says the letter-writing hero of Saul Bellow's *Herzog.* "We must get it out of our head that this is a doomed time, that we are waiting for the end, and the rest of it. . . . We love apocalypses too much, and crisis ethics and florid extremism with all its thrilling language. Excuse me, no," Herzog concludes. "I've had all the monstrosity I want."

Such remarks are refreshing; one does sometimes feel the way Satan himself was said to feel some years ago in the jauntily ironic ballad by John Crowe Ransom, "Armageddon": "The immortal Adversary shook his head: . . . . 'These Armageddons weary me much,' he said." But in a sense these are just the attitudes implicit in the fiction I have been primarily concerned with. West, Ellison, and the others have without a doubt kept us well informed about everything that is cruel, deadly, inhuman, hate-filled, disruptive, congealing, and in general chaotic and destructive on our modern American scene. The apprehension of immense catastrophe is close to the heart of their imagination. But at the heart itself is a humane perspective rooted not quite in hope but in a hope about hope. The sense of the comic is at once the symptom and the executive agency of that root sensibility. For if there is a large portion of bitterness in the laughter, and if laughter sometimes seems the only response still possible in a radically graceless world, it has served nonetheless to define, to measure and assess the horror, to reveal its sources and make visible its shape. To do this is to reassert the human. These apocalyptic visions indeed are offered as weapons for averting the catastrophe.

1964

INDEX